KU-490-216

SHAKESPEARE VERBATIM

Shakespeare Verbatim

The Reproduction of Authenticity
and the 1790 Apparatus

MARGRETA DE GRAZIA

CLARENDON PRESS · OXFORD
1991

Oxford University Press, Walton Street, Oxford OX2 6DP

Oxford New York Toronto
Delhi Bombay Calcutta Madras Karachi
Petaling Jaya Singapore Hong Kong Tokyo
Nairobi Dar es Salaam Cape Town
Melbourne Auckland
and associated companies in
Berlin Ibadan

Oxford is a trade mark of Oxford University Press

Published in the United States
by Oxford University Press, New York

British Library Cataloguing in Publication Data
De Grazia, Margreta
Shakespeare verbatim: the reproduction of authenticity
and the 1790 apparatus.
1. Great Britain. Established church. Dissent by
Roman Catholics & Puritans, history
I. Title 822.33
ISBN 0-19-811778-7

Library of Congress Cataloging in Publication Data
De Grazia, Margreta.
Shakespeare verbatim: the reproduction of authenticity and the
1790 apparatus / Margreta de Grazia.
Includes bibliographical references and index.
1. Shakespeare, William, 1564-1616—Editors.
2. Shakespeare, William, 1564-1616—Criticism, Textual.
3. Editing—History—18th century.
4. Malone, Edmond, 1741-1812. I. Title.
PR3071.D4 1991   822.3'3-dc20   90-48121
ISBN 0-19-811778-7

Typeset by Hope Services (Abingdon) Ltd
Printed and bound in
Great Britain by Biddles Ltd.
Guildford and King's Lynn

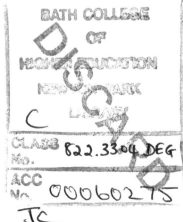

*For
my mother
and father*

ACKNOWLEDGEMENTS

ANY acknowledgements page supplements the title-page, extending its ascription to cover the non-authorial factors that went into the making of the book. This book is in large part about the need that this be done. The book began in solitude, but when roughly completed it received comments from more than its share of intelligent and sympathetic readers. Had I known how to call on them from the start, it would have been a better book.

For seeing in the manuscript more than I could and for helping others (myself included) to discern it, I will always be grateful to my colleagues Maureen Quilligan and Peter Stallybrass, as well as Catherine Belsey.

Howard Felperin, Timothy Murray, and Alexander Nehamas read the manuscript with both rigour and generosity. Albert Braunmuller, David Kastan, and Mark Rose patiently and politely noted errors. Jonathan Goldberg's more radical criticism should make the next book better. Stephen Booth deserves a monument for reading the manuscript as if it had been written in fourteen-line units. So does Marion Trousdale, for her laugh.

I wish to thank the National Humanities Center, North Carolina, for allowing me to begin this project when I proposed completing another, the University of Pennsylvania and the Folger Shakespeare Library for summer support while writing the book, Georgianna Ziegler of the Furness Library for her always alacritous help, and Peter Blayney, who is a research institution unto himself. Kim Scott Walwyn encouraged the project from an early stage, and the Press, Katie Ryde above all, followed through with exemplary tact; my anonymous copy-editor merits special recognition for her copious improvements, including the introduction of a first-person voice—a wonderful example of how even the most personalized touches are at heart corporative.

Three friends have watched over this book from start to finish: Peter Golfinopoulos who taught me how to work, Howard

Zeiderman who, prophet-like, foresaw and believed in the book, and my son Austin who is still trying to think of a better title.

CONTENTS

LIST OF ILLUSTRATIONS

LIST OF MAJOR EIGHTEENTH-CENTURY EDITIONS OF SHAKESPEARE

The Works of Mr. William Shakespear, 6 vols., 8vo, ed. Nicholas Rowe (J. Tonson, 1709). Cited as Rowe, *WWS*.

The Works of Shakespeare, 6 vols., fol., ed. Alexander Pope (J. Tonson, 1723–5). Cited as Pope, *WS*.

The Works of Shakespeare, 7 vols., 8vo, ed. Lewis Theobald (J. Tonson [etc.], 1733). Cited as Theobald, *WS*.

The Works of Shakespeare, 6 vols., 4to, ed. Thomas Hanmer (Oxford, 1744). Cited as Hanmer, *WS*.

The Works of Shakespeare, 8 vols., 8vo, eds. Alexander Pope and William Warburton (J. and R. Tonson [etc.], 1747). Cited as Pope–Warburton, *WS*.

The Plays of William Shakespeare, 8 vols., 8vo, ed. Samuel Johnson (J. and R. Tonson [etc.], 1765). Cited as Johnson, *PWS*.

Twenty of the Plays of Shakespeare, 4 vols., 8vo, ed. George Steevens (J. and R. Tonson [etc.], 1766). Cited as Steevens, *TPS*.

Mr. William Shakespeare his Comedies, Histories, and Tragedies, 10 vols., 8vo, ed. Edward Capell (J. Tonson, 1767–8). Cited as Capell, *MWSHCHT*.

The Plays of William Shakespeare, 10 vols., 8vo, eds. Samuel Johnson and George Steevens (C. Bathurst [etc.], 1773). Cited as Steevens, *PWS*. Revised and augmented by Isaac Reed, the edition was reprinted in 1778, 1785, and 1793. In 1780 Malone's two-volume *Supplement* was added.

The Plays and Poems of William Shakspeare, 10 vols., 8vo, ed. Edmond Malone (J. Rivington [etc.], 1790). Cited as Malone, *PPWS*.

The Plays and Poems of William Shakspeare, 21 vols., 8vo, eds. Edmond Malone and James Boswell (F.C., J. Rivington [etc.], 1821). Cited as Malone–Boswell, *PPWS*.

Introduction
Shakespeare's Apparatus

IT is impossible to imagine the study of Shakespeare without authentic texts for his works, historical accounts defining his period, facts about his life, chartings of his artistic and psychological development, and determinations of his meaning. These materials appear essential to our editorial and critical treatment of Shakespeare's works (indeed, of any author's works). It is my conviction that these requirements are not necessary in any absolute sense. They were accorded that status at a certain historical juncture known as the Enlightenment and have largely retained it since. Authenticity, periodization, individuation, chronology, and even interpretation are the interlocked imperatives of the study of Shakespeare, the exemplary author of the English canon. Yet if they emerged in history, they cannot be the timeless necessities of Shakespeare study; rather they are the determinate needs of a specific historical situation.

This study will investigate the emergence of these textual and critical imperatives in the late eighteenth century, stressing their incompatibility with earlier approaches and assuming throughout their continuity with those that subsequently became traditional. It seems only fair to admit at the start that this study does not purport to be a disinterested contribution to the history of Shakespeare scholarship. My purpose in defining the modern study of Shakespeare as an historical construct rather than a universal given is to question its viability and desirability in the present. Why does this construct emerge in England at the end of the eighteenth century? To what end? At what cost? Most urgently, why should it still prevail?

The very fact that it has become possible to interrogate the construct indicates that it has started to lose its former transparency. Its dictates can no longer be so readily assumed after the recent challenges, founded primarily on the work of Foucault and Barthes, to the modern notions of author and work, after the Oxford Shakespeare's recharacterization of the Shakespearean text as malleable, permeable, and even multiple, and after the new-historicist and cultural-materialist emphasis on the production and reproduction of Shakespeare as performance and as text within institutional, ideological, and political contexts. For the past generation of scholars, then, theoretical, textual, and critical practices have been skirting around the traditional Shakespeare, making it increasingly possible, even necessary, to begin imagining Shakespeare without the Enlightenment schema that is the subject of this study.

It is to the end of displaying and situating that schema that the following chapters focus on a single edition, printed first in ten volumes in 1790 and again in a slightly revised and greatly amplified form of twenty-one volumes in 1821. New interests emerged in this edition that became and remained fundamental to Shakespeare studies. It was the first to emphasize the principle of authenticity in treating Shakespeare's works and the materials relating to them; the first to contain a dissertation on the linguistic and poetic particulars of Shakespeare's period; the first to depend on facts in constructing Shakespeare's biography; the first to include a full chronology for the plays; and the first to publish, annotate, and canonize the 1609 Sonnets. While it is always possible to locate adumbrations of these interests in earlier treatments, it is in this edition that they are first clearly articulated—and articulated together as an integral textual schema. However unexceptionable they may seem now, it must be emphasized that none of these contributions had been made in previous editions. Until 1790, Shakespeare was published and read without materials and criteria that are now deemed basic to serious bibliographical and critical approaches.

The name of the edition is Edmond Malone's *The Plays and Poems of William Shakspeare*.[1] Yet to call it Malone's, as I will do throughout this study, might misleadingly suggest that Edmond Malone (1744–1812) was solely responsible for it, a suggestion which would make Malone's biographical particulars relevant: his Irish origins, for example, or his training in law, his immersion in scholarship after an unhappy romance, and a

---

[1] Malone's *The Plays and Poems of William Shakspeare* was published in 1790 in ten volumes and reissued in an expanded and revised edition of twenty-one volumes by James Boswell in 1821.

network of illustrious friends that included Hume, Burke, Johnson, Boswell, Reynolds, and Blackstone.[2] Yet both the need to credit Malone with his textual contributions and the appeal to his life and social context in order to do so fully belong to the very apparatus that is under observation. The apparatus structuring the author's relation to his work pertains also to the editor's relation to his edition.

A mere glance at the edition would reveal the inappropriateness of assigning it solely to Malone. The edition (and to a markedly greater extent the more comprehensive 1821 variorum version) includes the prefaces and notes of previous editors as well as comments from a wide array of contributors. Despite its innovative features, it is clearly indebted to a long line of eighteenth-century editors, beginning with Rowe in 1709 and extending through Pope, Theobald, Warburton, Johnson, Capell, and Steevens in 1773. The relation of these editors to one another might even be called dynastic, for the powerful Tonson publishing house commissioned each of them, extending its claim to ownership of Shakespeare's plays through a succession of related editions. Though Malone's edition appeared without the Tonson imprimatur, he was connected to this editorial line by his association with its last member. After Malone had in 1780 provided notes and a two-volume supplement for Steevens's 1778 edition, Steevens declared himself 'a dowager commentator' and bequeathed, for a time at least, his interest in Shakespeare to Malone.[3] Before his death in 1812 Malone named the younger James Boswell his successor, leaving him instructions for the completion of his second edition published in 1821; his father's proximity to Johnson gave Boswell junior further claim to the editorial title.

On the other hand, to suggest that the edition was the cumulative achievement of several generations rather than the

[2] On Malone's biography, see James Boswell, 'A Biographical Memoir of Edmond Malone, Esq.', in Malone–Boswell, *PPWS*, i. liii–lxxi; James Prior, *The Life of Edmond Malone, Editor of Shakespeare* (London, 1860); and J. K. Walton, 'Edmond Malone: An Irish Scholar', *Hermathena*, 99 (Autumn 1964), 5–26.

[3] By 1785, Steevens had broken with Malone and returned to editing under the superintendence of Isaac Reed, to produce a series of rival editions (in 1785, 1793, and 1803). Boswell pieced together an account of the rift from Malone's correspondence in his 'A Biographical Memoir of Edmond Malone, Esq.', Malone–Boswell, *PPWS*, i. lvii–viii.

work of a single individual would also be misleading, though in this case it would take more than a glance at the edition to tell why. It would imply that the edition was the result of a gradual process advanced by each successive editor and culminating with Malone. According to such an account, Malone's emphasis on authenticity, for example, could be traced back as far as the 1623 First Folio's claim to have been printed from the 'True and Originall Copies' and sustained through the first eighteenth-century editor's consultation of the First Folio and a few early quartos in 1709, Pope's preferring the early quartos to the Folio in 1725, Theobald's collecting of all available quartos in 1733, Johnson's dismissal of the Second, Third, and Fourth Folios in 1765, Steevens's publication of twenty early quartos in 1766, and Capell's return to the quartos for his copy text in 1768. In such a view, all these instances would be seen as steps in a steady progress towards obtaining what had always, more or less, been desired: the authentic text, the text closest to what Shakespeare put on paper. The emphasis on authenticity in Malone's 1790 edition would thus constitute simply a further advance along the same course followed by previous editions, and the whole of eighteenth-century Shakespeare study, with its gradual compiling of documentary materials and increasingly sophisticated implementation of scholarly principles, would then seem to culminate in the 1790 edition.

Although genealogical accounts appear as natural as growth itself, they are strongly biased against difference and change. In order to chart progression towards an end, they must postulate a single objective throughout time. A genealogical account of Shakespeare's text takes the desire for authenticity as axiomatic. Its very structure rules out the possibility of registering different purposes. But the 1623 Folio's 'True and Originall' and the 1790 edition's 'authentick' are, as we shall see, hardly synonymous terms; the early quartos were used not to supplant later editions but rather to supply possibilities for emendation; it was antiquarian curiosity rather than a quest for authenticity that motivated the preservation of the early quartos in print; Johnson thought the four folios basically interchangeable; Capell's definition of authenticity allowed for fifty-eight authentic plays by Shakespeare. When various editorial activities are fused into the advancement of a single purpose, subtle but crucial distinctions are lost. Differences are accommodated on a continuous trajectory as gradations of the same—in this instance, as phases, stages, and steps along a uniform and progressive course towards the authentic Shakespeare that could be extended further through the nineteenth-century Cambridge edition and its popular offshoot the Globe, all the way through to their standard modern descendants currently in use.

Twentieth-century histories of Shakespeare's texts invariably follow a chronological course, charting the various editions since the 1623 Folio or Rowe's 1709 *Works*. Malone always figures prominently in such accounts, generally by virtue of his historical research, his use of documents and archives, his respect for facts, and his rigorous accuracy.[4] On the basis of such distinctions, he is credited with raising eighteenth-century scholarship to a level from which that of the nineteenth century could proceed with its continuing project of approximating ever more closely to what Shakespeare wrote and what Shakespeare meant. Within such a narrative, Malone cannot introduce anything new: he simply participates, albeit notably, in the continuum that runs from Shakespeare's first publication to the most recent editions.

Yet Malone's overwhelming preoccupation with objectivity marks a significant shift in the focus of Shakespeare studies from what might be termed the discursively acceptable to the factually verifiable, from accounts whose validity was assured by continued circulation to information whose accuracy was tested by documents and records. This newly privileged objectivity called into being a commensurate subjectivity. Documented facts impinged themselves on consciousness, marking it with the responses aroused, shaping subjectivity, and thereby projecting a new mode of negotiating the outer and inner, the public and private, much in the manner of the contemporary *Bildungsroman* or novel of personal formation.[5]

As genealogical treatments discourage the recognition of

---

[4] For typical assessments of Malone's importance, see S. Schoenbaum, *Internal Evidence and Elizabethan Dramatic Authorship* (Evanston, Ill., 1966), pp. 21–6, *Shakespeare's Lives* (Oxford, 1970), pp. 162–248, and, more briefly, *William Shakespeare: A Textual Companion*, eds. Stanley Wells and Gary Taylor (Oxford, 1987), p. 55.

[5] On the *Bildungsroman* and the transmutation of events into personal experience, see Franco Moretti, *The Prose of the World* (London, 1986).

difference, so too they resist the representation of change. Malone's work is typically cast as developing earlier interests when in crucial respects it definitively broke with them. The authentic text pre-empted the received text; actual usage in Shakespeare's time superseded standards of correctness contemporary with the editor; factual accounts discredited traditional anecdotes; the order in which the plays were written replaced generic groupings; the 1609 quarto *Sonnets* supplanted the adulterated 1640 octavo; interpretations of Shakespeare's content overtook evaluations of his style. These innovations do not extend earlier interests, as the use of a graduated chronological scale implies; they render them obsolete.

Insensitive to difference and change, a genealogical account tends, paradoxically, to withstand history. Impelled by an inherent momentum of its own, it draws itself ever closer to realization without coming into contact with the processes it considers extraneous. Critical historical junctures are elided when they cannot be recast as periodic manifestations of what was always there. Thus, motivated above all by its own development, Shakespeare study appears immune even to what Edmund Burke considered 'of all circumstances, the most astonishing that has hitherto happened in the world': the French Revolution, the necessary bloody aftermath, for Thomas Paine, of a prior full-scale 'mental revolution'.[6] That Malone's 1790 edition came out during a time of conceptual and political upheaval— spectacularly staged across the Channel where 'the new order of things has naturally followed the new order of thoughts'[7] — does not appear to upset or even hinder its assured forward gait. Nor does the fact that Malone's edition of Shakespeare was published in the same year as Burke's *Reflections on the Revolution in France*, nor that the statesman and scholar exchanged copies of their respective works, nor that Burke was remembered as having equated Malone's 'admiration of Shakspeare' with his own 'perfect abhorrence of the French Revolution'.[8]

[6] Edmund Burke, *Reflections on the Revolution in France*, ed. A. J. Grieve (London, 1967), p. 8; Thomas Paine, *The Rights of Man: Being an Answer to Mr. Burke's Attack on the French Revolution*, ed. Moncure Daniel Conway (New York, 1894), p. 333.
[7] Paine, i.
[8] On the friendship between Burke and Malone, see Donald Cross Bryant, *Edmund Burke and His Literary Friends* (St Louis, 1939), pp. 233–55. Boswell published in the 1821

As we shall see, chronology was of crucial import in Malone's edition, both in organizing Shakespeare's life and works into a complete and consummate whole and in supposing the history of Shakespeare studies one streamlined course whose most advanced point was always the present. It is, however, resolutely avoided in this book, precisely because chronology lends privilege to uniformity, continuity, and universality. By comparing in Chapter 1 the earliest collection of Shakespeare's works to standard recent ones, I demonstrate that nothing as steady as development can account for the radical differences separating the original production from its distant reproductions. In the remaining five chapters, instead of following reproductions of Shakespeare's text sequentially through time, I focus on a single late-eighteenth-century textual and critical apparatus. While those chapters frequently look back to earlier junctures, they are centred on a period almost two centuries after Shakespeare wrote his works, for my interest in this study is not in what Shakespeare wrote but in how what he wrote came to be reproduced in a form that continues to be accorded all the incontrovertibility of the obvious. It became obvious only around the time of Malone's apparatus, a crucial historical moment that coincided with nothing less than those 'astonishing' revolutionary circumstances. And this is no mere coincidence, for as I will argue in the following chapters, Malone's apparatus accommodated the equally astonishing reconstitution of the subject which attended those circumstances. The practices applied to Shakespeare in Malone's edition defined him in terms of the very autonomy that newly enfranchised the bourgeois subject.

This autonomy took various reflexive forms: self-reliance, self-determination, self-containment, self-possession. It is perhaps best indicated through the change undergone by the word 'individual'. First used during the Middle Ages to express the

edition the letter in which Burke acknowledges Malone's gift of the 1790 edition and reciprocates with a 'small donum' of his own, a copy of *Reflections*: Malone–Boswell, *PPWS*, iii. 3–4; in his memoir of Malone, he also prints Burke's response to receiving Malone's disclosure of the William Ireland forgeries (Malone, *An Inquiry into the Authenticity of Certain Miscellaneous Papers and Legal Instruments*, 1795), i. lxii–lxviii. The elder Boswell recorded how Burke broke off his denunciations of the French Revolution to praise Malone's edition: *Letters of James Boswell*, ed. Chauncy Brewster Rinker, 2 vols. (Oxford, 1924), ii. 407.

8 *Introduction*

indivisibility of the three persons of the Trinity, it came to designate the inseparability of a member from a group, kind, or species. By the late eighteenth century, however, it referred to the absolute identity of the member, separate from and against the group. As Raymond Williams notes, 'we have learned to think of "the individual in his own right", where previously to describe an individual was to give an example of the group of which he was a member, and so to offer a particular description of that group and of the relationships within it.'[9] Though Williams sees the change as occurring slowly and gradually from the sixteenth century onwards, it is effectual by the end of the eighteenth. The French Revolution and its analogues in Europe and America, by dissolving the privileges of birth that determined wealth, property, rank, and education, brought a new order of subject into being. For Burke, that dissevered subject was no more than a pulverized substance, 'the dust and powder of individuality', irresponsible and irrational once unloosed from his inherited ties.[10] For Thomas Paine, he was a man free to define himself on the basis of 'the substantial ground, of character', possessing inborn natural rights rather than inert inherited ones.[11] In both views, the individual, cut off from past dispensations and dependencies, was encumbered or invested with new powers of self-determination. An extended form of this reflexivity assigned the subject ownership over himself, granting him property in his 'proper' self: in Locke's compelling dictum, repeated throughout the eighteenth century, 'every Man has a Property in his own Person'.[12] As owner of himself, the individual was entitled to various properties or possessions, both material, like goods and land, and immaterial, like rights to life and liberty.

Entitled to what he owned by virtue of his own relation to himself, the individual no longer depended on the ties that once made him an 'individual', that is, 'indivisible' from a larger body. Deriving from his proprietorship over himself entitlement to the material and immaterial benefits he possessed, he was under no obligation to render them up to others, an

[9] Raymond Williams, *The Long Revolution* (New York, 1961), p. 74.
[10] Burke, *Reflections*, p. 93.   [11] Paine, *The Rights of Man*, p. 10.
[12] John Locke, 'The Second Treatise of Government', *Two Treatises of Government*, 2nd edn., ed. Peter Laslett (Cambridge, 1967), v. 27.

obligation reflected as late as the seventeenth century in the
then homonymic 'own' and 'owe': in a semantics that located
individuality in solidarity, ownership entailed distribution.
Under the new dispensation, individuality was defined in terms
not of reciprocal obligations, but of self-interested rights that
included political representation or the franchise. The social
and political principle of autonomy emerging at the end of the
eighteenth century finds its philosophical equivalent in Kant's
postulation of consciousness in the form of an individuated
programme of self-representation gleaned from analysis of the
postulate 'my representation is my representation', a tautology
which bridges the expanse between the phenomenal and the
noumenal.[13] Socially, politically, and epistemologically enfranchised, the individual takes possession of language as well,
converting a discursive and transactional mode into a personalized and self-expressive one that makes language a convoluted
allegory of consciousness.

It is such a sovereign subject or consciousness, centred on its
own subjective self-reflexivity, that Michel Foucault saw as the
late eighteenth century's 'invention of man', an invention
sheltered by a massive reorganization of knowledge into anthro-
pological and humanistic disciplines. Literary studies rank
among those newly subject-oriented disciplines, instating the
authorial subject in the dominant position from which the
nature, history, coherence, and unity of writing are determined
and monitored.[14] Although the Enlightenment's ability to
make its constructs look natural or transparent now appears as
one of its distinctive achievements, recent commentaries on
that age have implicated its institutions of criticism in the
constitution and entitlement of a rising middle class over and
against the hierarchical prerogatives of an absolutist state.[15]
To include a textual apparatus among these cultural catalysts

[13] Immanuel Kant, *Critique of Pure Reason*, trans. and ed. Norman Kemp Smith
(New York, 1965), B138, 157.
[14] Michel Foucault, *The Archaeology of Knowledge and the Discourse on Language*, trans.
A. M. Sheridan Smith (New York, 1972), p. 387; 'The Order of Discourse', in *Untying
the Text: A Post-Structuralist Reader*, ed. Robert Young (Boston, 1981), pp. 55–77; 'What
Is an Author?', in *Textual Strategies: Perspectives in Post-Structuralist Criticism*, ed. Josue V.
Harari (Ithaca, NY, 1979), pp. 141–60.
[15] Peter Uwe Hohendahl, *The Institution of Criticism* (Ithaca, NY, 1982); Hans Robert
Jauss, 'Literary History as Challenge to Literary Theory', in *Toward an Aesthetic of*

—to suggest that it might function ideologically like an Althusserian state apparatus that shapes and positions subjects— might seem to be a grim exploitation of a pragmatic piece of nomenclature.[16] It must be allowed, however, that Shakespeare has, for centuries, been a very important and influential subject. As this study will demonstrate, the apparatus encasing Shakespeare in the late eighteenth century provided sanction, not for the ordinary subject—at least not at the start—nor even for the extraordinary subject of the author, but for the unique subject of Shakespeare. The apparatus protected Shakespeare from what Malone termed 'modern sophistications and foreign admixtures', providing a bastion against the forces of 'astonishing' change at home and abroad that threatened to undermine political and cultural stability.[17] The materials it collected and the use to which it put them uniformly insulated Shakespeare, enclosing him in his own experience, consciousness, and creativity. In Chapter 2 I discuss how 'authenticity' shoved him back into the remote world of documents and records; in Chapter 3, how the construction of an historical period lodged him in a relativized enclave; and in Chapter 4 how individuation by factual substantiation and psychological interiorization abstracted him into a private realm to which the chronology of his works gave design and totality. Thus removed from the sites that formerly sustained him—of discourse, production, and reception—Shakespeare became, as I will maintain in Chapter 5, an exemplary instance of the autonomous self, the self whose autonomy entitled him to his works both legally (as the product of his own capacities) and hermeneutically (as his own self-expressing representation). It may well be, though the possibility is beyond the scope of this study, that it is only after such practices have been codified through reproduction and institutionalization that it is possible to have a Shakespeare canon,

Reception, trans. Timothy Bahti (Minneapolis, 1984); Terry Eagleton, *The Function of Criticism from the Spectator to Post-Structuralism* (London, 1984); Pierre Macherey, *A Theory of Literary Production*, 2nd edn., trans. Geoffrey Wall (London, 1985).

[16] Louis Althusser, 'Ideology and Ideological State Apparatuses', in *Lenin and Philosophy and Other Essays*, trans. Ben Brewster (London, 1971), pp. 127–86; Etienne Balibar and Pierre Macherey, 'On Literature as an Ideological Form', in Young, *Untying the Text*, pp. 77–99.

[17] Malone, 'A Letter to the Earl of Charlemont', in *An Inquiry into the Authenticity of Certain Miscellaneous Papers*, pp. 2–3.

as opposed to *Shakespeares Comedies, Histories, & Tragedies, Shakespeare's Works*, or *Shakespeare's Plays and Poems*: a canon, that is, that consists not only of authentic works, like the canonical books of Holy Scripture, but also of regulating and binding tenets, like those of Church dogma, inferred from the very texts over which they preside and legislate.

Once it has been shown that what had appeared to be the necessary conditions for preparing and reading Shakespeare are in fact postulates securing a particular though abiding historical dispensation, it becomes possible to ask what alternatives this schema has precluded. This is not the same as looking for the antithesis to its postulates, for a hegemonic schema often permits, indeed, even encourages, its own inversion; and, as I will have occasion to observe at several points in this study, opposites are not alternatives, but rather mutually sustaining constituents of the same dialectic. Authenticity and inauthenticity (forgeries and counterfeits) subscribe to the same underlying principle of authority. Factual accuracy and inaccuracy appeal to the same criterion of truth. Psychological readings, whether intuitive or analytical, are committed alike to the disclosure of an interior source of meaning. Anti-Stratfordian and Stratfordian venerate the same authoritative figure of Shakespeare. The power of a configuration depends on its ability to reduce alternatives to polarities, to a recto and verso that constitute the same leaf.

It is the apparatus that holds the plays and poems to such circumscribing alternatives in delivering them anew. While appearing only ancillary to a text, a handmaiden dutifully attending its reproduction, it is precisely what makes that reproduction possible, retrieving or translating the alien past of a text's inception into the familiar present of its reception. The apparatus makes it possible for a text to come back—to make a comeback—on conditions it both prescribes and instantiates. In reproducing a text, in making it again available and accessible, the apparatus dictates the terms of its reception. Whereas it seems to be merely a useful tool for an informed and responsible reading, it in fact specifies a text's ontology and epistemology: what it is (and is not), how it may be known (and not known). In determining the text's identity, the apparatus predisposes the reader to specific modes of reading and understanding. Its bracketing preliminaries and appendices and its interpenetrating notes encode the rules by which the content is to be valued and understood. As its etymology suggests, an apparatus is not simply curatorial. It is preparatory: it prepares the text for the reader by submitting it to certain procedures, and it prepares the reader for the text by equipping him or her with certain kinds of information. Hence this preparation shapes both the textual object to be delivered and the cognitive spaces into which it is to be received. The first volume of the 1790 Malone edition and the first three of the 1821 are called 'Prolegomena', literally a 'speaking before' that articulates the terms by which the text to follow will be comprehended and silences others that might discomfit them. The apparatus, of course, need not be as conspicuous as Malone's; once its operations are in place, it can recede from view, absorbed by both the texts and its readers. The first standard Shakespeare, the 1864 Globe edition, in which Shakespeare was reproduced worldwide for over a century, contained and needed no explicit apparatus whatsoever.

As this study itself periodically testifies, it is hard to discuss not only Shakespeare but Malone's treatment of Shakespeare without appealing to the terms postulated by his edition and assumed by subsequent ones. I have therefore adopted numerous procedures throughout the book contrived to resist the very axioms that are its subject: its non-chronological logic that keeps turning back on itself rather than inexorably advancing through time, its odd identification of Malone with a paratextual schema, its tendency to quote rather than paraphrase in order to dissociate its own exposition from his, and, most obvious, its focus on a cumbersome and seemingly dated apparatus rather than on the generative and immortal Shakespeare.

On the other hand, its close kinship with its subject must be admitted. It is itself a piece of historical criticism, its core chapter divisions follow the key terms of the 1790 apparatus, its thesis depends on such positivistic mainstays as logic and evidence. Arguing against historical scholarship from a position within it, it can make no claim to outside authority either from another discipline or from theory. Its own commitment to the procedures it criticizes is itself testimony to their tenacity. Yet if these procedures can be used to disclose their own past construction in history, they can also be used to accelerate their eventual dismantling in history.

To recognize the synthetic and contingent nature of the Shakespearean apparatus is to allow for the possibility of its being otherwise. Once the apparatus is situated in relation to historical exigency, its conceptual grip begins to weaken. The very act of turning it into a subject of attention undermines its authority, for the apparatus can work only if it appears inert, optional; dispensable, even. It becomes possible to look for phenomena that have been minimized, transformed, or excluded by its preparation or 'speaking beforehand'. At many points in the book directions of inquiry will be signalled that have been discouraged or forestalled by the apparatus—and, indeed, by the politics it has so effectively supported.

This is not to suggest that Shakespeare will in the end be revealed in all his pristine and unmediated purity. For his texts have never appeared unattended, not even in the first quartos and First Folio, not even in editions featuring no apparatus whatsoever. Some mechanism, stated or unstated, will always prepare the way for their reading, though rarely as extensively and obtrusively as in Malone. There can, then, be no desire to recover Shakespeare in his own terms, Shakespeare as he was before the late eighteenth-century intervention, Shakespeare before the emergence of the sovereign modern subject; for this desire belongs to the very apparatus that is under investigation; before it, or beyond its pale, it cannot even be contemplated, much less retrieved.

The concern of this study is not necessarily to strip Shake-speare of his modern textual investiture, nor to prepare him for a post-modern redress. Its purpose is to bring into full view the schema in which he has been so effectively reproduced from the late Enlightenment to the present, so that the needs it has satisfied can be acknowledged and the possibilities it has elided can begin to be taken into account.

I

The 1623 Folio and the Modern Standard Edition

A long genealogy separates the first published collection of Shakespeare's plays, the 1623 First Folio, from standard twentieth-century editions of Shakespeare. In the seventeenth century, the kinship of later editions with the first was apparent even in their physical form: each of its issue—the Second (1632), Third (1664), and Fourth (1685) Folios—inherited its progenitor's distinguished monolithic format. While at the beginning of the eighteenth century that form was broken into multiple volumes, the contents, as preserved in the latest or Fourth Folio, were reproduced through a succession of editions: Rowe's (1709), Pope's (1723–5), Theobald's (1733), Hanmer's (1744), Warburton's (1747), Johnson's (1765), Steevens's (1773), and Malone's (1790). The text received by the nineteenth century, drawn primarily from those of the last two editors in this list, was monumentalized in the Cambridge edition of 1863–6, whose long and imperious sway, extended by its popular single-volume deputy, the 1864 Globe edition, passed in 1921 to the New Cambridge, from which current standard editions descend. From time to time throughout this history spurious materials have slipped in—as with the 1664 Third Folio's insertion of seven new plays—and legitimate ones have been expelled—*Titus Andronicus*, for example, which the majority of eighteenth-century editors excluded; in general, however, the line has remained pure. The pedigree of each edition could be traced, theoretically at least, back to the most authentic texts, either those of the Folio or those of the quartos that preceded it. Through the First Folio and early quartos, and the putative manuscripts behind them, the line is imagined to extend directly back to the ultimate begetter, Shakespeare. However attenuated, the lineage appears more or less unbroken from the progenitor to the numerous present-day editions through which he lives on. If the past continues to serve as prologue, the line should continue perpetuating itself in reasonably fair and smooth succession.[1]

It is only natural to expect continuity from this textual genealogy. When its two extremes are juxtaposed—when the seventeenth-century Folio is set against a typical twentieth-century Collected Works—we expect to see the likeness of the original reflected in its most recent descendant, faithfully transmitted by intervening generations. Yet, as this chapter will stress, the resemblance is far from exact. The difference is in part, as might be expected, superficial. The refinement of printing techniques and the standardization of English have changed the appearance of the page. Technical and philological improvements, though, cannot explain away more substantial differences pertaining to content and organization. While the succession of editions appears to stretch unbroken from the First Folio to the present, only something as decisive as a break can account for the sharp dissimilarities between the venerable patriarchal source and its filial issue.

When the first collection of Shakespeare's works, the 1623 Folio of *Mr. William Shakespeares Comedies, Histories, & Tragedies*, is compared to a representative modern edition like the Riverside, Signet, or Pelican Shakespeare, it is tempting to see the differences between them as the result of the gradual mechanical progress that occurred during the three and a half intervening centuries, the abundant anomalies of the 1623 Folio appearing as marks of a crude and early stage in the progress towards the polished modern edition.[2] To begin with,

---

[1] No alterations in the entire history of the 1623 Folio corpus compare to those introduced by the recent Oxford edition: *William Shakespeare: The Complete Works*, eds. Stanley Wells and Gary Taylor (Oxford, 1986). The number of plays has swelled from 36 to 40 (with the addition of not only *Pericles* and *Two Noble Kinsmen*, but also *Sir Thomas More* and a quarto *History of King Lear* as well as the Folio *Tragedy*). In addition, the edition allows for the possibility of further multiplication by positing 'two independent substantive sources, both apparently authoritative', for five other plays besides *Lear*: *Henry IV Part II, Hamlet, Othello, Richard II, Troilus and Cressida*; *William Shakespeare: A Textual Companion* eds. Stanley Wells and Gary Taylor, (Oxford, 1987), p. 17. Whether the Oxford's innovations will prove standard remains, of course, to be seen.

[2] Generalization about the modern editions of Shakespeare are based on the following: *Shakespeare: The Complete Works*, ed. G. B. Harrison (New York, 1952); *William Shakespeare: The Complete Works*, ed. Charles Jasper Sisson (London, 1954); *The*

the degree of typographic irregularity in the First Folio is extraordinary: some 600 different typefaces have been identified.[3] Spelling and punctuation are far from uniform.[4] Plays are erratically divided: seventeen are divided into acts and scenes, six are not divided at all, and the remaining thirteen are only partially divided.[5] Line arrangements do not consistently reflect the distinction between verse and prose.[6] There are numerous irregularities and misprints in the pagination, like the jump from page 156 to page 257 in the section of Tragedies and the numbering of the Folio's last page at 993 instead of 399.[7] At the end of only twenty-four of the thirty-six plays does the elaborate 'satyr ornament' appear, and the imprint varies depending on the inking as well as on the condition of the woodblock.[8] Different amounts of spacing occur around the titles of plays, stage directions, and act and scene divisions, the result primarily of the stretching and crowding of type required by the process of 'casting-off' or 'setting by formes'.[9] Twelve

Complete Works of Shakespeare, ed. Hardin Craig (Chicago, 1951, rev. David Bevington 1980); *The Complete Signet Shakespeare*, ed. Sylvan Barnet (New York, 1972); and *The Riverside Shakespeare*, ed. G. Blakemore Evans (Boston, 1974).

[3] Charlton Hinman identifies the different types in *The Printing and Proof-Reading of the First Folio of Shakespeare*, 2 vols. (Oxford, 1963), i. appx B. 25–61.

[4] On the disuniformity of spelling and punctuation in the printing house as well as among the various compositors, see Vivian Salmon, 'The Spelling and Punctuation of Shakespeare's Time', in *William Shakespeare, The Complete Works: Original-Spelling Edition*, eds. Stanley Wells and Gary Taylor (Oxford, 1986), pp. xlii–lvi. On how orthography could be determined by considerations of typographical spacing, see T. H. Howard-Hill, 'Spelling and the Bibliographer', *The Library*, 5th ser., 18 (1962), 1–28.

[5] On the inconsistency of act and scene divisions, see Alfred W. Pollard, *Shakespeare Folios and Quartos: A Study in the Bibliography of Shakespeare's Plays 1594–1685* (London, 1909), pp. 124–5 and T. W. Baldwin, *On Act and Scene Division in the Shakspere First Folio* (Carbondale, Ill., 1965), esp. pp. 45–56, 73–9, 95–105.

[6] On the necessity of compressing and expanding prose and long verse lines, see Hinman, *The Printing and Proof-Reading of the First Folio*, i. 186–7. The Oxford *Textual Companion* illustrates twelve different expedients for saving space within a single Folio page (Wells and Taylor, *Companion*, p. 44).

[7] For a register of the Folio signatures, see W. W. Greg, *The Shakespeare First Folio: Its Bibliographical and Textual History* (Oxford, 1955; repr. 1969), pp. 436–8.

[8] For the 'satyr ornament', see Greg, *The Shakespeare First Folio*, pp. 439–40; for the various ornaments and ornamental initials used in the Folio, see Pollard, *Shakespeare Folios and Quartos*, pp. 132–3 and Hinman, *The Printing and Proof-Reading of the First Folio*, i. 178–80.

[9] On the economics and difficulties of setting by formes, see Greg, *The Shakespeare First Folio*, p. 434 and Hinman, *The Printing and Proof-Reading of the First Folio*, i. 47–51.

blank pages are irregularly interspersed through the 908-page volume.[10] Running-titles atop some of the pages are set by more than one fount.[11] Only seven of the plays are followed by lists of the dramatis personae.[12] The speech prefixes and stage directions often give different forms of a character's name, sometimes substituting that of an actor.[13] And because proof-reading was, in the words of the twentieth-century editor who has most exhaustively studied the Folio, 'careless and sporadic', some stretches of the printing are more accurate than others.[14]

By modern standards, certainly, an extraordinary degree of physical or external disuniformity characterizes the Folio volume. More astonishing still, the disuniformity differs from one copy of the 1623 Folio to the next. Four pages of the preliminaries, comprising one unsigned sheet, have no deter-minate position, having apparently been printed as an after-thought.[15] But the most remarkable difference among the copies is the result of the practices by which corrections were made, practices so varied and erratic that they have recently been shown to challenge the traditional 'postulate of normality' assumed to govern printing-house production.[16] Because the

[10] See Greg's account of the 'Interruptions and Dislocations' that could result in blank pages: *The Shakespeare First Folio*, pp. 438–46.

[11] On the use and changing of 'standing type' that accounted for these variations, see Greg, *The Shakespeare First Folio*, p. 435 and Hinman, *The Printing and Proof-Reading of the First Folio*, i. 89–90.

[12] Lists variously entitled 'The Actors Names', 'Names of the Actors', 'The Names of all the Actors', and 'The Names of the Actors' are provided only at the end of *The Tempest, Two Gentlemen of Verona, Measure for Measure, The Winter's Tale, Henry IV Part II, Timon of Athens,* and *Othello.*

[13] On the actors' names that found their way into the Folio texts, see Greg, *The Shakespeare First Folio*, pp. 117–19. On variant nomenclature in stage directions, prefixes, and the text itself, see Randall McLeod 'The Psychopathology of Everyday Art', in *The Elizabethan Theatre*, ix, ed. G. R. Hibbard (Port Credit, Waterloo, 1986), 100–68, McLeod, 'UNEditing Shak-speare', *Sub-Stance*, 33/4 (1982), 26–55, and Baldwin, *On Act and Scene Division*, pp. 81–94.

[14] Charlton Hinman, ed., *The Norton Facsimile: First Folio of Shakespeare*, (New York, 1968; henceforth Hinman, *TNF*), p. xx.

[15] Greg, *The Shakespeare First Folio*, pp. 449–50.

[16] Peter Blayney throws the concept into question in his discussion of the proofing and order of printing undergone by the 1608 quarto of *Lear: The Texts of 'King Lear' and Their Origins* (Cambridge, 1982), i. 88–218. See also D. F. McKenzie's discussion of how the average rates of work performed by compositors and pressmen introduce so many variables that the principle of 'normality' must be replaced by one of 'the normality of non-uniformity': 'Printer's of the Mind: Some Notes of Bibliographic Theories and Printing-House Practices', *Studies in Bibliography*, 22 (1969), 1–75, esp. pp. 8–13.

Folio sheets continued to be printed while the proofing was done, various copies of the same page can represent various different states of correction. Some copies may be entirely uncorrected, others partially corrected, others fully corrected. Thus all individual copies of the Folio 'show an apparently random mixture of early and late states, and never quite the same mixture', so that 'no two copies will be found textually identical throughout'.[17] This situation presented a problem for the editor of the most recent Folio facsimile: without an authoritative Folio, without even a typical Folio, what criterion could be used for selecting the copy to be exactly reproduced?

In fact, the 1968 Norton facsimile is based on no existing copy of the Folio, nor on any one copy that ever existed. It is an idealized composite made up of the most legible and most fully corrected pages the editor could locate in his collation of the seventy-seven copies and one fragment in the Folger Library. Twenty-nine of those copies and the fragment are represented in the facsimile, each providing anywhere from 1 to 183 pages of the facsimile text.[18] The facsimile's editor announced that his aim was not to reproduce photographically a given copy of the Folio, but rather to give material form to what formerly existed only as an ideal: 'to give concrete representation to what has hitherto been only a theoretical entity, an abstraction: *the* First Folio text'.[19] Yet it must be emphasized that the 'theoretical entity' of a uniform Folio—*the* First Folio—is itself a later abstraction dependent on later modes of mechanical reproduction: not until 1807 was the First Folio produced in type facsimile; not until 1866 was it reproduced in photographic facsimile.[20]

By contrast, a modern edition of the Collected Works presents no such conspicuous inconsistencies. Orthography, punctuation, typography, and formatting are uniform from copy to copy. Over the centuries and in the hands of a long succession of editors, editions of Shakespeare have come to conform to the standards of correctness regulating the printed word. In fact, there may be some correlation between the advance of printing

---

[17] Hinman, *TNF*, p. xix.   [18] Ibid. 929.   [19] Ibid. xii.
[20] See George Walton Williams, 'The Publishing and Editing of Shakespeare's Plays', *William Shakespeare: His World, His Work, His Influence*, ed. John F. Andrews, 3 vols. (New York, 1985), iii. 599.

and the standardization of language. As numerous recent scholars have suggested, it may be that the regulation of language was the result of what has been called print's *esprit de système*, its tendency to systematize both thought and production in conformity with its own mechanical uniformity.[21] It is quite clear that the perfection of the printing process and the codification of language occurred at approximately the same time: the first book to be printed without errors, a 1760 edition of Catullus, more or less coincided with the degree of linguistic standardization or stabilization represented by Johnson's 1755 Dictionary.[22] Thus an account of gradual progress in both domains, of advancing print technology and increasing linguistic systematization, could explain the most salient differences between the 1623 Folio and a modern edition. Until technology advanced and standardization took place, compositors could not possess the expertise, nor editors and proof-readers master the rules, by which uniform pages could be printed.

So construed, the conversion of the seventeenth-century Folio into a twentieth-century Complete Works appears an inevitable development. The physical particulars of the printed page gradually became more uniform as printers became more skilled, proof-readers more literate, editors more conscientious, and techniques and machinery generally more efficient—in order finally to produce correct copy. Steps in this development could readily be charted and might include the following: the Second Folio's correction of the First's typographical errors and irregular pagination, Rowe's division of all the plays into acts and scenes and his insertion of lists of characters, Pope's regularization of distinctions between verse and prose, Johnson's modernization of punctuation, and the Cambridge edition's numbering of all the lines in the works, reproduced in the Globe

[21] On print's tendency to systematize thought and writing, see Walter J. Ong, *Ramus, Method and The Decay of Dialogue: From the Art of Discourse to the Art of Reason* (Cambridge, Mass., 1958); Marshall McLuhan, *The Gutenberg Galaxy: The Making of Typographic Man* (Toronto, 1966); Elizabeth Eisenstein, *The Printing Press as an Agent of Change* (Cambridge, 1985), pp. 80–8; Alvin Kernan, *Printing Technology, Letters and Samuel Johnson* (Princeton, NJ, 1987), pp. 48–62. See also Timothy Murray's important querying of this position as a confusion of writing and printing, signification and mechanical reproduction, *Theatrical Legitimation: Allegories of Genius in Seventeenth-Century England and France* (New York, 1987), pp. 58–63.
[22] Paul Korshin has pointed out in private conversation that the 1760 edition of Catullus is thought to be the first book to be published without typographical errors.

edition and ratified by the line references in the first complete concordance to Shakespeare.[23] In consequence of these editorial and typographical improvements, irregularities were eventually eliminated. Thus gradual progress over the centuries would account for the difference between the original Shakespeare volume and its modern descendants. It would then appear that the printed Shakespearean text had always been heading towards its present correctness and consistency, but had had to await certain advances in technique and usage in order to get there.

But what if the non-uniform seventeenth-century printed page were lifted out of its gripping history of progress and seen instead in relation to the work it duplicates? Would the reproduced copy say something about the nature of the original? Twentieth-century bibliographers have worked doggedly to determine the relationship between Shakespeare's manuscripts and the 'underlying' copies from which the Folio plays were set. By one conservative account there are at least thirteen different possible sources, including the actual holograph, transcripts, prompt-books, earlier printed quartos, theatrical reports, and composites of the various possibilities.[24] However numerous, these materials have been considered in relation to what is imagined as a stable original, Shakespeare's holograph, though none is known to exist. Yet the very instability of the printed page when viewed as a function of the original itself discourages such a quest for a single and fixed document. Its intractability implies an original resistant to the regimes of both script and print: an original involved in the vagaries of production. The inconsistencies of the printed copy itself attest to a fundamental incompatibility between a play's protean composition and print's or even script's systematic fixity: it reproduces the provisionality essential to written plays that remain malleable at every stage to the exigencies of performance as determined by the physical structure of the theatre, the number and types of actors, other plays recently in performance, topical events, the time of year, the nature of the audience, censorship, and so

---

[23] On the importance of concordance in stabilizing the Shakespearean text, see Wells and Taylor, *Companion*, p. 58.

[24] Fredson Bowers, *On Editing Shakespeare* (Charlottesville, Va., 1966), pp. 11–12. For Bowers's most sustained description of the search for Shakespeare's 'underlying copies' see his 'Authority, Copy, and Transmission in Shakespeare's Texts', in *Shakespeare Study Today*, ed. Georgianna Ziegler (New York, 1986), pp. 7–36.

forth. The disuniformities of the 1623 Folio could be said to be faithful to the provisionality and variability of the plays' 'original' production.

When we turn from differences on the surface to those in content, when the Folio preliminaries are compared to a standard modern introduction, again the differences between the two editions bear witness to more than progress. A different principle of classification operates in the two volumes. The 1623 preliminaries consist of a title-page with an engraved portrait (Pl. 1) attributed to Martin Droeshout ('Martin Droeshout sculpsit London'), whose subject the affixed verse identifies as Shakespeare ('It was for gentle Shakespeare cut'), a title ascribing the plays to Shakespeare (*Mr. William Shakespeares Comedies, Histories, & Tragedies*), the date and place of publication (London, 1623), and the names of the printers ('Isaac Iaggard, and Ed. Blount'). An 'Epistle Dedicatorie' follows, an address 'To the great Variety of Readers', and then, in different arrangements depending on the disposition of the unsigned pages mentioned above, a 'Catalogue' of the plays, a list of the principal members of Shakespeare's acting company, and four commemorative poems.

These preliminary items represent the different activities involved in the production and promotion of the book: the title-page (supplemented by the colophon at the end of the volume) records information pertaining to the publication of the book, approximating the entry in the Stationers' Register; the dedication appeals to the patronage of the Earls of Pembroke and Montgomery; the address exhorts readers to purchase the volume; one of the catalogues provides the names of the play texts and the other the names of the players in the company which performed them; and the commemorative verses consist of elegies by four poets variously connected with the performance and publication of the plays.[25] The preliminaries are thus

[25] Three of the poets who contributed commendatory verses were variously tied by other literary ventures to one another and to both the publisher Blount and the dedicatees Pembroke and Montgomery. Jonson and Digges contributed commendatory verses to Mabbe's translation of Aleman's *Guzman de Alfarache* (1622) and Digges made a translation of Gerardo in the same year that was dedicated to the same Pembroke and Montgomery as the First Folio; both these works were published by Blount, who dedicated his own translation of Ducci's *Ars Aulica* to the same 'paire of brethren'. See John Freehafer, 'Leonard Digges, Ben Jonson, and the Beginning of Shakespeare

organized to publicize the functions on which the Folio depends: publishing, patronage, purchase, performance, and acclaim. As Shakespeare's authorship is acknowledged by the title-page and throughout the preliminaries, so too additional activities contributing to the making of the volume are acknowledged in the dedication, address, catalogue of plays, list of actors, and panegyrics.

Because all the parties represented by these functions have contributed to the book's realization, each has an interest in the product. The title-page calls the volume *William Shakespeares*, yet the names of the publishers in the imprint publicize their ownership of the right to copy, as recorded in the Stationers' Register entry of 8 November 1623 and as licensed by, 'under the hands of', two wardens of the Stationers' Company. The dedication 'gives' the book to Pembroke and Montgomery ('the Volume ask'd to be yours'[26]), the first of whom was in 1623 Lord Chamberlain, the officer responsible for controlling all theatrical matters, including the publication of play texts. Readers are encouraged to purchase copies of their own ('But, what euer you do, Buy'[27]), thereby entitling themselves to pass judgement on its contents. The right to perform the plays remains with the acting company as represented by its two leading members, Heminge and Condell; their interest in both performance and publication had recently (in 1619) been protected by an injunction from the Lord Chamberlain, the dedicatee of the Folio.[28] The elegiac poets, Shakespeare's literary beneficiaries and trustees, might also be said to have a proprietary interest in the legacy, as is suggested by Jonson's apostrophes to 'my beloued, the Author', 'My Shakespeare', and 'My gentle Shakespeare',[29] as well as Holland's and Digges's

Idolatry', *Shakespeare Quarterly*, 21 (1970), 63–75; A. W. Secord, 'I. M. of the First Folio Shakespeare and Other Mabbe Problems', *Journal of English and Germanic Philology*, 47 (1948), 37–81; E. A. J. Honigmann, *The Stability of Shakespeare's Text* (London, 1965), note A, pp. 34–5; and Wells and Taylor, *Companion*, p. 36. Digges was also the stepson of the man Shakespeare chose to oversee his will, as Hallet Smith points out in *The Tension of the Lyre: Poetry in Shakespeare's Sonnets* (San Marino, Ca., 1981), p. 137.

[26] Hinman, *TNF*, p. 6.
[27] Ibid. 7.
[28] On the injunction protecting the King's Men, see Greg, *The Shakespeare First Folio*, pp. 15–16 and note D, pp. 24–6.
[29] Hinman, *TNF*, pp. 9, 10.

appropriative tributes drawn from Shakespeare's sonnets.[30]
Thus, while the book ascribes itself to Shakespeare, calls itself
Shakespeares, the preliminaries record a nexus of interdependent
offices and claims that both obligate and entitle the parties
involved.

Linking the book together are the financial contracts and
affective ties implied and stated throughout the preliminaries.
The munificence of the patrons is expected to be commensurate
with their appreciation of the author whose works they followed
'with so much favour'[31] in his lifetime. Readers are enjoined to
respond similarly with both approval and payment, especially
the latter: they are urged to draw on the capacities 'not of your
heads alone, but of your purses'; 'read, and censure . . . but buy
it first', their financial output entitling them to judgement of the
purchase. Although the publication was without question a
business venture, Heminge and Condell profess to having been
prompted by sentimental considerations, by the desire 'onely to
keepe the memory of so worthy a Friend, & Fellow aliue, as was
our SHAKESPEARE'. And while the verses written in Shakespeare's honour are commissioned, like the commendatory
'purchas'd Letters' mentioned in the address, they are also
tributes of friendship written by 'other of his Friends', like Ben
Jonson, who addresses Shakespeare with familiarity.[32]

These interdependent transactions among parties in their
social, professional, and economic positions and functions have
no place in the standard modern introduction: Shakespeare
himself occupies it fully. Rather than representing the various
activities analogous to those that went into producing the 1623

[30] Hugh Holland preserved Shakespeare's lines with the play on literary lines and
genealogical lines/loins in the couplet of his sonnet, 'For though his line of life went
soone about, | The life yet of his lines shall neuer out' (Hinman, *TNF*, p. 11), recalling
Sonnets 16, 18, 74. Leonard Digges's poem draws more abundantly on the sonnets,
once again using Shakespeare's references to the immorality of verse (cf. Sonnets 55, 65,
81, 107) to claim immortality for his book of plays:

>   This Booke,
> When Brasse and Marble fade, shall make thee looke
> Fresh to all Ages: when Posteritie
> Shall loath what's new, thinke all is prodegie
> That is not *Shake-speares*; eury Line, each Verse
> Here shall reuiue, redeeme thee from thy Herse.
> Nor fire, nor cankring Age, as *Naso* said,
> Of his, thy wit-fraught Booke shall once inuade. (Hinman, *TNF*, p. 15)

[31] Hinman, *TNF*, p. 5.   [32] Ibid. 6–7.

volume, the sections of a modern introduction represent the
diverse features contributing to Shakespeare's art: Shakespeare's
life, his times or background, his development, his style or
technique or language, his text, his stage, his critical history.[33]
Eliminating all materials not 'having immediate relevance to
the understanding of his mind and art',[34] they are hardly
encyclopedic in scope. Yet, like encyclopedia entries, they
function to deliver information, aiming 'to provide the reader
or student with the information he normally needs in order to
understand and appreciate Shakespeare', and 'to give authoritative answers . . . to the questions that are most frequently
asked by readers and lovers of the plays'.[35] A full experience of
Shakespeare requires that he be experienced as a totality: 'In
order fully to understand and appreciate Shakespeare, it is
necessary to see him as a whole.'[36] His completeness manifests
itself when his works are arranged or considered chronologically,
usually in four periods that roughly approximate his generic

[33] The new Oxford Shakespeare and *Textual Companion* have broken with all
standard Shakespeares in their commitment to the plays 'as they were acted in the
London playhouses' (Wells and Taylor, *Works*, p. xxxvii), rather than as they were
written by Shakespeare. As a result, the editors have attended to a wide range of
materials that have traditionally been dismissed as non-authoritative because non-
authorial, including memorial texts, eye-witness accounts, theatrically based stage
directions, a hypothetical unwritten 'para-text' that accompanied the play script
(*Companion*, p. 2), frequent theatrical revision (pp. 16–18), and systematic state
censorship (pp. 15–16). In their realization that 'dramatic texts are necessarily the
most socialized of all literary forms' (p. 15), they allow for the corporate and diversified
interactions that are represented by the 1623 Folio preliminaries.
   At the same time, however, the edition and commentary repeatedly invoke the same
sovereign Shakespeare that has presided over previous modern editions. The editors'
aim of reproducing the practical theatrical prompt-book ('the plays as they were
acted') periodically lapses into the desire to recover the idealized authorial holograph
('trying to determine exactly what the author wrote', *Companion*, p. 6); the 'para-text'
turns out to be what Shakespeare had in mind ('what Shakespeare assumed or spoke
but never wrote', p. 2); the texts are uncensored and unexpurgated in order to restore
Shakespeare's intended lines ('We have, wherever possible, put such profanities back
in Shakespeare's mouth', p. 16); revisions are predominantly authorial, and when they
are not, they are imagined to have been approved by him ('Shakespeare personally
suggested many or most of the alterations made in rehearsal, and he acquiesced in
others', p. 19); and, finally and most tellingly, the works are printed in chronological
order of composition rather than (as in Jonson's 1616 Folio) of performance, providing
thereby a 'notion of his artistic development' (p. 36). Thus Shakespeare retains his
traditional magisterial powers, but his mastery has been transferred from the text to
performance: 'he was himself, supremely, a man of the theatre' (*Works*, p. xxxiv).
[34] Bevington, *Works*, p. x.
[35] Craig, *Works*, preface; Sisson, *Works*, preface.   [36] Craig, *Works*, preface.

progress (from comedy to history to tragedy to romance) and that can accommodate stylistic, temperamental, and philosophical development as well.[37] The Complete Works thus provide a unique plenum encompassing Shakespeare's experience and consciousness: 'He has created a world of his own.'[38] Though his own exclusive creation derives from his own unique experience, the plays belong to all: 'We look into Shakespeare's plays and find ourselves; it is for this reason that he is of all writers the most universal.'[39] So self-sufficient is that world, that it is not always clear that the historical world evoked to put it into relief is indeed necessary: 'That Shakespeare is of the Renaissance is undisputed, but that a study of the economic, political, or religious background of the Renaissance greatly illuminates Shakespeare is arguable.'[40] What matters above all is that the autonomous totality that he constitutes 'be understood and appreciated' in all its richness, as the best modern criticism, however pluralistic, strives to do: 'to achieve a synthesis that is at once unified and uniform in its vision'.[41] While Shakespeare in the Folio is predicated on the collective activities recognized by the preliminaries, in the standard modern introduction he is represented as a cosmos, certainly influenced by externals such as his education, historical events, predecessors and contemporaries, traditions and conventions, but integrating them into an independent and essential completeness that is his own and that is reflected in his works: his 'mastery was the ripe attainment of an individual mind'.[42]

[37] Accounts of Shakespeare's chronological development figure in every modern standard edition. Craig actually prints the plays in four groups representing the four periods of Shakespeare's development as formulated at the end of the nineteenth century by Edward Dowden (*A Shakspere Primer*, 1877; *Shakspere: A Critical Study of His Mind and Art*, 1874; and *Introduction to Shakspere*, 1893), noting that while the divisions also reflect 'current fashions', 'it is nevertheless convenient, as well as customary, to divide his plays into four groups.' Peter Alexander's edition, widely used in England, follows the Globe arrangement of the plays which itself follows the Folio's loosely generic order, but his introduction divides Shakespeare's career into four periods with theatrical, historical, biographical, and psychological correlates. The new Oxford edition arranges the plays in the order of composition, though to have arranged them in the order of their performance would have been more consistent with their emphasis on the plays as theatrical performance. Although they claim Jonson's 1616 Folio as a precedent for presenting 'the plays in their order of composition' (Wells and Taylor, *Works*, p. 36), Jonson's plays are given in the order of their performance.

[38] Levin, 1.   [39] Harrison, *Works*, p. 8.
[40] Barnet, *Shakespeare*, pp. 28–9.   [41] Bevington, *Works*, p. 95.
[42] Levin, 21.

Reluctance to recognize the radical incongruity between the original and the modern prefatory units has led to the assumption that details from the former can be pressed into the service of the latter. For example, accounts of his life and education generally feature the assessment of Shakespeare's learning in Jonson's tribute—'thou hadst small Latine, and lesse Greeke'.[43] Discussions of the period find evidence of Shakespeare's favour at court both in the dedication's mention of Pembroke's and Montgomery's sustained interest in his work and in Jonson's allusion to Elizabeth's and James's admiration. Evaluations of Shakespeare's style generally refer to Heminge and Condell's comment on the ease with which Shakespeare wrote—'His mind and hand went together: And what he thought, he uttered with that easinesse, that wee haue scarse receiued from him a blot in his papers'—and in establishing Shakespeare's reputation among his contemporaries, Jonson's high ranking in relation to classical and British dramatists is frequently evoked. Descriptions of Shakespeare's text invariably feature the comparison in the address between the Folio copies and those of the previously printed quartos: 'as where (before) you were abus'd with diuerse stolne, and surreptitious copies, maimed, and deformed by the frauds and stealthes of iniurious imposters, that expos'd them: euen those, are now offer'd to your view cur'd, and perfect of their limbes, and all the rest absolute of their numbers, as he conceiued them'.[44] And the several allusions in both the address and the commendatory verses to the plays' success on stage are used to illustrate Shakespeare's popularity. On the basis of such examples, it might be thought that modern introductions have simply expanded, refined, and organized the details scattered throughout the seventeenth-century preliminaries. Just as modern printing techniques perfect those of three centuries past, so modern introductions develop their seventeenth-century prototype.

Yet the results of gleaning the preliminaries for the information proper to introductions have raised problems. The only Folio claim that has not been contested pertains to Shakespeare's acclaim and popularity in his lifetime, though even that has

[43] Hinman, *TNF*, p. 9.
[44] Ibid. 7.

been thought exaggerated.[45] Other assertions and implications have been more controversial. Is Jonson's assessment of Shakespeare's learning—'small Latine, and lesse Greeke'—to be trusted? Or should it be dismissed as an expression of Jonson's invidious need to belittle his rival? Did Heminge and Condell truly undertake the Folio project 'without ambition either of selfe-profit, or fame',[46] or was it rather a business venture? Is it true, as they testify, that they had 'scarse receiued from him a blot in his papers',[47] that the Folio was printed from Shakespeare's own manuscript pages, and that he wrote *currente calamo*, without revising, or is this claim intended to outface rival publications? Are the Folio copies indeed of higher authority than the previously published quarto copies, as the publishers' address maintains in contrasting earlier quarto publications to their own, or should this statement be discounted as an advertising ploy? With factual information about Shakespeare so scant, the Folio claims have themselves been treated as if they purported to be factually true. Whether verified or disproved, they have been influential in forming the received wisdom as to the nature of Shakespeare's genius, his method of writing, the sincerity of those responsible for the Folio, and the respective authenticity of the Folio and quarto texts.

Yet even when referring to its own contents, the Folio's statements do not appear to be concerned with accuracy. Ben Jonson's verse testifying that the Droeshout engraving 'was for gentle Shakespeare cut' cannot be taken on faith, for poets were routinely commissioned to write such verses, sometimes without seeing the engraving to which they were to be affixed.[48] Also on the title-page is the imprint 'Printed by Isaac Iaggard, and Ed. Blount', a misleading imprint since while both men were publishers, Iaggard alone was a printer. Not only does the imprint only partially correspond to fact; it does not even correspond to the list of printers in the colophon at the end of

---

[45] G. E. Bentley concludes, on the basis of examining seventeenth-century allusions to both Jonson and Shakespeare, that Jonson's reputation was greater: *Shakespeare and Jonson: Their Reputations in the Seventeenth Century Compared* (Chicago, 1945). Malone believed the previous century had overvalued Jonson and Fletcher at Shakespeare's expense: *PPWS*, i. lxxiii–lxiv.

[46] Hinman, *TNF*, p. 6.   [47] Ibid. 7.

[48] On the convention of such inscriptions, see M. H. Spielmann, 'Shakespeare's Portraiture', in *Studies in the First Folio* (London, 1924), 27–31.

the volume where, 'W. Iaggard' replaces 'Isaac Iaggard', followed by 'Ed. Blount', and then by two new names, 'I. Smithweeke, and W. Aspley'.[49] The names of Heminge and Condell are printed after both the dedication and the address, yet this attribution has been disputed since the end of the eighteenth century on the grounds that two men of the theatre could not have written such sophisticated prose; and more literary figures—Ben Jonson, Edward Blount, and Leonard Digges—have been proposed in their stead.[50] The Catalogue of plays does not entirely correspond to the contents: it lists *The Winters Tale* as beginning on page 304 when it appears on page 277, gives no listing whatsoever for *Troilus and Cressida*, which is printed between the last history and the first tragedy with only one of its pages numbered (page 79), and includes *Cymbeline* among 'Tragedies'. The list of 'The Names of the Principall Actors' is not of the actors but of the shareholders in the acting company, listed in only approximate order of their seniority.[51] At the head of this list, the title of the entire volume is repeated in a different form from that on the title page: this second title calls the book 'The Workes of William Shakespeare', a noteworthy variation in light of the ridicule prompted by Ben Jonson's having entitled his plays 'works' in the 1616 folio collection *The Workes of Beniamin Jonson*, an important precedent for the 1623 Folio.[52]

There are, then, substantial discrepancies in the Folio between signs and what they signify: between portrait and subject, ascription and author, imprint of printers and printers, table of contents and contents, list of actors and actors. Some of them can surely be dismissed as the result of error, ineptitude, the makeshift procedures within the printing house that have been referred to as 'the easy-going ways of London stationers at the

[49] On the discrepancy between imprint and colophon, see Hinman, *The Printing and Proof-Reading of the First Folio*, i, pp. 24–6.

[50] On Jonson and Blount as possible authors of the epistle and address, see Greg, *The Shakespeare First Folio*, pp. 17–21.

[51] On the inaccuracy of the List of Actors, see Hinman, *The Printing and Proof-Reading of the First Folio*, p. x and E. K. Chambers, *William Shakespeare: A Study of Facts and Problems*, 2 vols. (Oxford, 1930), ii. 78–89.

[52] On Jonson's presumption in calling his plays 'Works', see *Works of Benjamin Jonson*, eds. C. H. Herford, Percy Simpson, and Evelyn Simpson, 11 vols. (Oxford, 1929–52), ix. 13. In the lists included after the play, the actors are called, not 'players', but 'tragediaens' and 'comediaens'.

time'.[53] Anomalies were introduced by circumstantial and
mechanical exigencies, for example the 'interruptions and dislocations' that occurred during the two-year period in which
the Folio was printed, the practice of 'casting-off' copy, and the
varying habits and preferences of the several compositors. In
time, they were eliminated by the more systematic labours of
subsequent editors and printers.

Yet to what can the dubiety of the statements about Shakespeare, his manuscripts, and the circumstances of their printing
be attributed? It may be that their imperfect correspondence to
fact derives from the purposes of their respective writers:
Jonson perhaps minimized Shakespeare's learning in order to
amplify his own; the Folio editors may have exaggerated the
proximity of their copies to Shakespeare's papers and maligned
the status of the quarto copies in order to enhance the value of
their own edition. When a statement falls short of factual truth,
explanations are sought in the writer's motives. The search for
either type of correspondence, however, assumes that the Folio
claims are functioning referentially, pointing either to an out-
ward reality or to an inward intent. When the workings of the
preliminaries are considered, however, the question of correspondence appears strangely inappropriate. For the preliminaries
are not documents that record with accuracy or inaccuracy the
prior events that led to the Folio's publication. They are texts
that encode those events in a form that will give viability to the
book they are in the process of constituting. The modern
introduction assumes the identity of both the corpus and its
author that the Folio preliminaries are in the business of
constituting: it can therefore presume to contain and deliver
information that is understood to have an existence prior to and
independent of its documentation. The 1623 preliminaries
cannot presuppose the existence of the very identities that
depend on its own language and formatting.

After almost three centuries of taking Shakespeare's dramatic
corpus as a given, it is easy to forget that until the 1623 Folio
there was no such thing as a dramatic corpus. Before being
gathered, stitched, and bound into one bibliographic body, the

plays were a scattered and heterogeneous lot consisting of published quartos, unpublished sheets, and prompt-books. It is often forgotten, too, that had circumstances been different, another collection of Shakespeare, another corpus, might well have anticipated the Folio. In 1619 Thomas Pavier attempted to publish a collection of ten plays as Shakespeare's until, it appears, the Lord Chamberlain's injunction protecting the interests of the King's Men caused him to abandon the project and publish each of them individually.[54] This attempt, though aborted, serves as reminder that until the 1623 Folio the Shakespearean corpus had not been defined.

Heminge and Condell, the supervisors of the publication, three times refer to their function or 'province' as one of collecting or gathering dispersed and disparate 'remains' or 'seuerall parts'. Half of the plays they collected had been printed and of those several had been reprinted.[55] The other half, it must be assumed, existed in the form of authorial manuscripts (rough 'foul' copies or clean 'fair' ones), scribal transcripts, or prompt-book copies used for performance, or combinations of the three. Of the printed texts, while fifteen bore Shakespeare's name on the title-page, three—*Titus Andronicus*, *Romeo and Juliet*, and *Henry V*—did not.[56] None of them had been fully divided into scenes and only *Othello* into acts. The ownership of the plays, the right to copy them, was in various hands. While the unprinted plays were presumably the property of the acting company, the printed plays were variously assigned by the Stationers' Register and by the individual quarto imprints: the rights to one play had never been established, those to two others had reverted to the Stationers' Company, six

---

[54] On the discovery and identification of the 1619 Pavier quartos, see Pollard, *Shakespeare Folios and Quartos*, pp. 81–107; Greg, *The Shakespeare First Folio*, pp. 9–16, and *The Editorial Problem in Shakespeare: A Survey of the Foundations of the Text*, 3rd edn. (Oxford, 1967), pp. 131–4; Chambers, *William Shakespeare*, i. 133–7; Wells and Taylor, *Companion*, pp. 34–6.

[55] *Richard II* and *Henry IV Part I* were reprinted six times. On the frequency of quarto reprintings, see Chambers, Table of Quartos, in *William Shakespeare*, ii. appx G. 394–6.

[56] The 1623 Folio did not include five plays that had been ascribed to Shakespeare (*Pericles*, *Two Noble Kinsmen*, *A Yorkshire Tragedy*, *London Prodigal*, *Sir John Oldcastle*) and three that were ascribed to W.S. (*Locrine*, *Thomas Lord Cromwell*, and *The Puritan*). Seven of these were added to the 1664 Third Folio, the 1685 Fourth Folio, and Rowe's 1709 edition, removed by Pope in 1725 but reintroduced in his 1728 edition. See Chambers, *William Shakespeare*, ii. 206–7.

belonged to the syndicate of four named on the imprint and colophon, and the remainder were distributed among six independent publishers.[57] In fact, it is not certain that the Folio publishers, Jaggard and Blount, were able to obtain the copyownership to all the plays by the time of publication.[58] The different quartos had been printed at different printing houses, bearing the marks of the different type founts and compositorial hands, and had been sold by different stationers. Like the plays that had never been printed, the quarto plays also bore various relations to what the author had penned, having undergone different amounts of theatrical cutting, interpolation, abridgement, censorship, revision, as well as scribal, compositorial, and proof-readers' modifications—some accidental and others purposeful. Furthermore, taking into account the estimate that as many as half the plays by professional dramatists between 1590 and 1642 were co-authored, it is not unreasonable to admit the possibility of collaboration on some of the plays.[59] Indeed, as early as 1687 it was recorded that *Titus Andronicus* had been brought to the players 'by a private Author' and that Shakespeare had added only a few touches.[60] With such diverse and complex backgrounds, the plays collected by Heminge and Condell needed a strong principle of unification to authorize their enclosure in one massive book.

[57] For the ownership of the Folio plays, see Greg's bibliographical history, *The Shakespeare First Folio*, pp. 61–7 followed by a summary account, and Hinman's slightly revised recapitulation, *The Printing and Proof-Reading of the First Folio*, i. 24–30.

[58] On the special complications with the printing and copyright of *Troilus and Cressida*, see Greg, *The Shakespeare First Folio*, pp. 445–8, and 'The Printing of Shakespeare's *Troilus and Cressida* in the First Folio', in *W. W. Greg Collected Papers*, ed. J. C. Maxwell (Oxford, 1966), 392–401.

[59] G. E. Bentley, *The Profession of a Dramatist in Shakespeare's Time: 1590–1642* (Princeton, NJ, 1971), p. 199. Bentley also points out that 'of the 282 plays mentioned in Henslowe's diary (far and away the most detailed record of authorship that has come down to us) nearly two-thirds of the work of more than one man.' Chambers also allows for the possibility that the work are other playwrights might have found its way into the Folio: 'It is quite possible that [Heminge and Condell] saw no harm in including without comment a play which Shakespeare had only revised, one or two for which he had a collaborator, and one to which he had contributed little, but which had long been linked to other "parts" of an historical series', *William Shakespeare*, i. 207.

[60] Edward Ravenscroft was the first on record to question the single authorship of a Shakespeare play in the Address to his adaptation of *Titus Andronicus*, quoted in Chambers, *WS*, ii. 254–5. For a history of the disintegrationist activity triggered by this claim, see Chambers, *The Disintegration of Shakespeare's Texts*, Annual Shakespeare Lecture of 1924 (London, 1924).

As has frequently been noted, until the appearance in 1616 of *The Workes of Beniamin Jonson* publication in folio was reserved for classics or for contemporary works of serious import.[61] The monumental folio form itself announced that the content was of enduring significance, meriting preservation. Plays hardly seemed likely candidates for the honour, being above all ephemeral writings, scripts penned for immediate performance, associated with publications of passing or limited interest like almanacs, joke-books, and coney-catching pamphlets or chap-books. In 1611/12 Sir Thomas Bodley instructed the keeper of his Oxford library to exclude plays along with almanacs and proclamations from his library, deeming such 'riffe-raffes' or 'baggage bookes' too transient for a permanent collection.[62] The quartos in which eighteen of Shakespeare's plays had been previously published were certainly not made to last: their thirty or forty leaves were unbound and probably not even properly stitched. Unless bound up as part of a tract-volume, the life-expectancy of a play quarto was quite short: 'After it was read it lay around, the top leaf and the bottom leaf got dirty and torn, then the string broke, and it disintegrated and was thrown away.'[63] Needless to say, the unpublished manuscripts, transcripts, and prompt-books in which the remaining eighteen existed were more perishable still.

Writings published in sturdy folio form, however, were intended to endure and did endure: while there are no more than forty copies of any given Shakespeare quarto extant, over 150 of the 1623 Folio have survived.[64] The task of the 1623 publication was to unify the disparate and stabilize the trans-itory. It had to assume and posit grounds for presenting a collection of thirty-six ephemeral pieces in a venerable and durable format with a perimeter four times as large and a cost

[61] Bentley, *The Profession of a Dramatist*, pp. 54–61.
[62] *Letters of Sir Thomas Bodley to Thomas James, First Keeper of the Bodleian Library*, ed. G. W. Wheeler (Oxford, 1926), pp. 219, 222, cited by Bentley, *The Profession of a Dramatist*, pp. 52–3.
[63] T. A. Birrell, 'The Influence of Seventeenth-Century Publishers on the Presentation of English Literature', in *Historical and Editorial Studies in Medieval and Early Modern English for Johan Gerritsen*, ed. Mary-Jo Arn and Hanneke Wirtjes (Groningen, 1985), p. 166.
[64] Henrietta C. Bartlett and Alfred W. Pollard, *A Census of Shakespeare's Plays in Quarto 1594–1709* (New Haven, Conn., 1939); Sidney Lee, *Shakespeare's Comedies, Histories and Tragedies: A Census of Extant Copies* (Oxford, 1902).

forty times as high as the printed play quartos.[65] Yet on what grounds could it entitle itself to bibliographic permanence? There is indication that it was immediately successful in doing so. The very library that had ruled out play texts in the previous decade became the first purchaser on record of Shakespeare's collected plays. While the Bodleian did not acquire its vast collection of play quartos until 1821, when it received Malone's library, its accounts record that in 1623 a copy of *Shakespeares Comedies, Histories, & Tragedies* was 'fetched by William Wildgoose' for binding and returned; it was then entered into the hand lists and chained into the position on the library shelves in the Arts end of the Library assigned by the inscription on its spine (S.2.17. Art).[66]

Jonson, not Shakespeare, was the first playwright whose works were dignified by the folio form.[67] Published seven years before the Shakespeare Folio in the very year of Shakespeare's death, the 1616 Folio of *The Workes of Beniamin Jonson* had two important advantages over the 1623 Folio. First, it did not contain plays only. Although the plays are featured first and occupy almost four fifths of the contents, the volume also includes works in two more elevated genres: poems, often dedicated or addressed to prominent individuals and institutions, and

---

[65] 'The traditional price of a quarto was sixpence; the Folio upon publication probably cost a pound. (A schoolmaster in 1621 might earn only £10 a year—which was at the very top of the pay scales for London workmen.' Wells and Taylor, *Companion*, p. 49.

[66] *The Original Bodleian Copy of the First Folio of Shakespeare*, by F. Madan, G. M. R. Turbutt, and S. Gibson (Oxford, 1905), pp. 5, 14 and Sidney Lee, *A Catalogue of the Shakespeare Exhibit Held in the Bodleian Library to Commemorate the Death of Shakespeare* (Oxford, 1916), pp. xiv–xv. The latter contains a photograph of the Folio's original site. There is no record of Jonson's Folio being in the collection until 1674, though there is a catalogue for 1620 and an appendix in 1635, *Catalogus Universalis Librorum in Bibliotheca Bodleiana* (Oxford, 1620).

[67] An unusual number of intelligent articles discussing the significance of Jonson's 1616 *Workes* has appeared recently: for the Folio's appeal to 'high culture', see Richard C. Newton, 'Jonson and the (Re-) Invention of the Book', in *Classic and Cavalier: Essays on Jonson and the Sons of Ben*, eds. Claude J. Summers and Ted-Larry Pebworth (Pittsburgh, Pa., 1982), 31–55; for the Folio as assertion of print's constancy over and against theatrical counterfeiting, see Murray, *Theatrical Legitimation*; as assertion of bibliographical ego, see Joseph Loewenstein, 'The Script in the Marketplace', *Representations*, 12 (1985), 101–14. The assumption has also swayed bibliographical studies: for example, James K. Bracken contends that 'Jonson intended the Folio to be a clear statement of his integrity as an author,' and therefore sought out William Stansby as the printer who would most respect his artistic aspirations: 'William Stansby and Jonson's Folio, 1616', *The Library*, 6th ser., 10 (1988), p. 19.

masques written for royal entertainment. Second, and more important, Jonson's imposing reputation not as a playwright but as a poet, translator, and scholar qualified him for the honour, extending the tradition of the great humanist folio editions of the ancients to include the 'English Horace', as he is styled by one of the verses commending him in his folio.[68] Taking advantage of its author's association with classical learning, the 1616 Folio fashioned itself into a classic—the classic represented by the imposing monument that literally constitutes the title-page (Pl. 2). As its very title announced, the volume arrogated to itself the prestige and durability of ancient art: as Horace had his *Opera*, so the 'English Horace' had his *Workes*, though most of those works were, as contemporaries derisively noted, plays. That its publisher William Stansby had previously printed in folio form a number of major English and classical works, including Sir Walter Raleigh's *The History of the World* (1614), Richard Hooker's *Ecclesiastical Politie* (1614), and Seneca's *Workes* (1614), further dignified the enterprise.[69]

The title-page engraving by William Hole emblematically realizes what the volume itself was to effect: the immortalization of drama or the making permanent of the transient.[70] The task is accomplished and commemorated by the monument consisting of three superimposed constructs: a book, a proscenium

[68] Signed IC, in Ben Jonson, *Q. Horatius Flaccus: His Art of Poetry* (London, 1640). On Jonson's classicism, see Katherine Eisman Maus, *Ben Jonson and the Roman Frame of Mind* (Princeton, NJ, 1984).

[69] Bracken maintains that Stansby was building a reputation in folio editions, and lists thirteen folio printings between 1614 and 1616: 'William Stansby and Jonson's Folio, 1616', p. 22.

[70] Several recent studies have extended Jonson's control over the 1616 Folio publication to include the title-page engraving. Mary Corbett and Ronald Lightbrown read William Hole's engraving as Jonson's bid for poetic immortality: *The Comely Frontispiece: The Emblematic Title-Page in England 1550–1660* (London, 1979), pp. 145–50; Stephen Orgel identifies Jonson's idiosyncratic touches in its details: 'Shakespeare Imagines a Theater', *Poetics Today*, 5 (1984), 549–61; Timothy Murray sees it as 'an iconic symbol of Jonson's peculiar drive for authority', *Theatrical Legitimation*, pp. 64–70. By looking at a number of title-page and frontispiece portraits, Leah Marcus argues for the uniqueness of Droeshout's engraving in representing its subject without encasing adornment: *Puzzling Shakespeare: Local Reading and Its Discontents* (Berkeley, Ca., 1988), pp. 2–32. She accounts for this feature in the context of what she sees as the Folio's project of lifting the plays from their topical and historical situation into a universalized generalized realm of transcendent art. I would argue, however, that in so far as such an aesthetic realm was conceivable in the seventeenth century, it would have been represented by the very classicizing icons that the portrait conspicuously lacks.

stage, and a triumphal arch. The stage opens to reveal not a performance but a rectangular book; both book and stage are embedded within the triumphal arch that also contains statues, friezes, and reliefs representing the genres and history on which both book and theatre depend. All the inscriptions on the monument are in the enduring classical rather than the transitory vulgar tongue: the names of the allegorical figures for the various genres (*Tragi Comoedia, Tragoedia, Comoedia, Satyr,* and *Pastor*), the names of the original and ancient structures in which drama was performed (*plaustrum, visorium, theatrum*), the quotations from Horace's *Satires* on the frieze (*SINGULA QUAEQUE LOCUM TENEANT SORTITA DECENTER*) and from his *Ars Poetica* on the central aperture (—*neque, me ut miretur turba, laboro: Contentus paucis lectoribus*), and the ascription, *Guliel° Hole fecit.* Diminutive statues of Bacchus holding a thyrsus and Apollo with a lyre, in addition to obelisks, laurels, acanthus leaves, tragic and comic masks, and Corinthian columns, further contribute to the illustration's immortalizing and classicizing theme. The only writing in English is on the volume and on the escutcheon, identifying what the monument commemorates (*The Workes of Beniamin Jonson*), its builder ('printed by William Stansby'), and the date and site on which it was erected ('A. D. 1616, London').[71] By locating the origins of theatre in the ancient past, by representing its genres through classical icons and Latin names, by incorporating the proscenium stage into the monument's architectonics, the engraving visually converts the transitory play texts, the contents of the book, into enduring art. The pages that follow underscore the triumph typographically with the catalogue's columnar lists and the tomb-shaped commendatory verses. The plays themselves are elaborately 'interred' within classically ornamented individual title-pages each inscribed with the work's name and date and decorative concluding colophons. Thus each work is contained within a separate typographical monument as well as within the encompassing volume that like a family vault contains them all. The title-page and the layout of the volume itself thereby reify the tomb/tome homonym: the engraving depicts and

---

[71] Three different imprints appear on the escutcheon; see Herford *et al.*, *Works of Benjamin Jonson*, ix. 16–17.

accomplishes the artful interment of the bibliographic tome within the architectural tomb.[72] On the title-page of Shakespeare's Folio, the monumental masonry adorned with classical icons and Latin inscriptions has been replaced by something much less artful: a likeness of a man in contemporary dress (Pl. 1).[73] The engraver has strained to make it life-like or natural: 'the Grauer had a strife | With Nature, to out-doo the life'—or so the reader is informed by the accompanying verse from Ben Jonson, the very author whose 'graver' William Hole had striven to outdo Art with his title-page architectonics. While the 1616 title-page made plays permanent by immortalizing them as monumental Art, the 1623 title-page represents not the plays but the author in modest contemporary dress, without any of the exalting ornamental or iconic apparatus that typically encased such title-like portraits. Jonson's verse testifies that the face has been for 'gentle Shakespeare cut', the same Shakespeare described in his ensuing commendatory poem as having, despite his 'small *Latine,* and lesse *Greeke*' triumphed over 'all that insolent *Greece,* or haughtie *Rome* | sent forth', for only he was 'of Natures family'.[74] While the verse admits that Nature must not receive all the credit for Shakespeare's greatness—'Yet must I not giue Nature all: Thy Art, | My gentle *Shakespeare,* must enjoy a part'—the part assigned to art involves no great learning or sophistication but rather hard labour, like that of a smithy: 'he | Who casts to write a liuing line, must sweat | (such as thine are) and strike the second heat | Upon the *Muses* anuile.' Thus the poet whose own works entitled themselves to permanence as Art in 1616 establishes Shakespeare as the pride of Nature in 1623: 'Nature her selfe was proud of his designes.' While a self-styled bibliographic tomb commemorates the living Jonson, the dead Shakespeare survives without artificial marker—'Thou

---

[72] For the tomb/tome homonym in Shakespeare's Sonnets, see *Shakespeare's Sonnets,* ed. Stephen Booth (New Haven, Conn., 1977), p. 283.
[73] Chambers, *William Shakespeare,* ii. 241 and J. L. Nevinson, 'Shakespeare's Dress in his Portraits', *Shakespeare Quarterly,* 18 (1967), 101–6. An engraved portrait of Jonson by Robert Vaughan appeared in Jonson's 1640 Folio as well as being inserted at a later date in some copies of the 1616 Folio. See Herford *et al., Works of Benjamin Jonson,* iii. ix–x and Greg, *A Bibliography of the English Printed Drama to the Restoration* (London, 1957), iii. 1072.
[74] Hinman, *TNF,* pp. 9, 10.

art a Moniment, without a tombe'—through the vitality of his book: 'alive still . . . while thy Book doth live'.[75] The address to the readers similarly stresses Shakespeare's association with Nature, remembering the author 'Who, as he was a happie imitator of Nature, was a most gentle expresser of it'.[76] Not only was his subject Nature, his manner of writing was natural and spontaneous, free from constraining artifice: 'His mind and hand went together: And what he thought, he uttered with that easinesse. . . .'

As Shakespeare's Sonnets and their echoes in two of the 1623 Folio's commendatory poems proclaim, there are two traditional paths to perpetuity: artful creation and natural procreation.[77] The 1616 Folio had already followed the former 'mightier way', contenting itself with the approval of an élite few rather than the vulgar crowd (*Contentus paucis lectoribus*); the 1623 Folio took the latter, more accessible and popular course, appealing to the multi-headed 'great Variety of Readers', 'From the most able, to him that can but spell'. Through the engraving, epistle, address, and commendatory poems, the 1623 Folio makes what might be called a natural or dynastic claim on the future. The dedication to Pembroke and Montgomery refers to the plays as children who have lost their natural parent and need a legal surrogate. By gathering them together into a folio, Heminge and Condell hope 'to procure his Orphanes, Guardians', two paternal parents or patrons. The favour of those two patrons is the children's only inheritance, passing from the father to his surviving descendants, an inheritance the two self-appointed executors, Heminge and Condell, would secure for them, trusting that the benefactors 'will use the like indulgence toward them, [they] have done unto their parent'.[78] The stability of the two adopted parents, the 'incomparable paire of brethren', is thereby extended to Shakespeare's otherwise uncertain issue. The firm constancy of that couple, H.H. and L.L., symmetrical and identical pillars occupying stations of rank and virtue—'Both Knights of the most Noble order of the Garter, and our singular

---

[75] Ibid. 9.   [76] Ibid. 7.

[77] T. W. Baldwin discusses the classical and Renaissance topoi of immortality through procreation and art in *On the Literary Genetics of Shakspere's Poems and Sonnets* (Urbana, Ill., 1950), pp. 181–228, 261–77.

[78] Hinman, *TNF*, pp. 5, 6.

good Lords'—will support the otherwise unprovided-for
orphans, thereby also strengthening their own constancy by
remaining true to their former acts of generosity. The consec-
ration of Shakespeare's 'remaines' to the 'Temple' of that firm
'payre'—to 'the places your H.H. sustaine'—ensures the liveli-
hood of the otherwise frail and nondescript survivors, 'what he
hath left us'.

Thus the dedicatory epistle represents the contents of the
Folio as a family, all issuing from the same parent and entitled
to his sustaining legacy. Jonson's commemorative verse, too,
insists on common ancestry, emphasizing the family resemb-
lance of its members: 'Looke how the fathers face | Liue in his
issue, even so, the *race* | Of Shakespeares minde, and manners
brightly shines | In his well torned, and true *filed lines*'.[79] The
propagated 'lines' are both his genealogical and printed 'issue',
inseminated by the fecund ray that perpetuates the paternal
'race', 'filed' because stylistically polished and also arranged
within the book according to a system of affiliation that recog-
nizes them all as filial and racial sons or suns 'brightly' radiating
as they proceed in obedient, martial file: a hegemonic, brave
brood that become literal bearers of their warlike brandishing
patronymic as represented on Shakespeare's coat of arms
(*Hasti-vibrans*, or Shake-speare)—'In each of which, he seemes
to shake a Lance.'[80] Those forged 'lances' or 'speares' are also
styluses, precise simulcra of the very parenting pen that begot
them naturally, though it takes the studied virtuosity of Jonson's
art to describe their birth. The address to the reader bears
witness to the same strict and direct descent from the father,
another immaculate conception: 'His mind and hand went
together: And what he thought, he uttered with that easinesse,
that wee haue scarse receiued from him a blot in his papers.'
The issue is pure and uncontaminated, descending in a straight
line from head to hand to papers to the printed copy of the Folio
repository, a direct and undefiled line from the conceptions of
Shakespeare's mind to the printed issues of the Folio. The

---

[79] Hinman, *TNF*, 10; emphasis added.

[80] Thomas, Fuller, in *Worthies of England* (1662), makes the military connection in
maintaining that Shakespeare seemed to be 'compounded' of three eminent poets,
Martial, Ovid, and Plautus: '*Martial* in the *Warlike* sound of his Sur-name (whence
some may conjecture him of a *Military extraction*),' quoted in Chambers, *WS*, ii. 245.

conceit of Hugh Holland's commemorative verse, 'Upon the Lines and Life of the Famous Scenicke Poet, Master William Shakespeare', rests on the same continuity between the biological and biographical: Shakespeare's brief life-line gives way to the lines printed in the book and spoken on stage: 'For though his line of life went soone about | The life yet of his lines shall neuer out'.[81]

The 1623 preliminaries work to assign the plays a common lineage: a common origin in a single parent and a shared history of production that includes patrons, readers, printers, theatrical company, audiences, and praising poets. The plays are bound to one another by these natural and legal ties that establish their literal affiliation or consanguinity. The language of the preliminaries thereby confers a generic and genetic identity on the heterogeneous texts, a 'natural' pretext for their publication as a hegemonic text. 'Shakespeare' was the name that guaranteed the consanguinity and therefore the coherence of what might otherwise have been no more than a miscellany. It served as a rubric for the massive volume, a verbal equivalent to the threads and binding that physically fastened together its pages. The assignation 'Mr. William Shakespeare' and the engraved figure 'for gentle Shakespeare cut' on the title-page, combined with the preliminaries' repeated evocation of Shakespeare's memory, drew together those scattered and diverse dramatic 'seuerall parts' under a single name. The preliminaries translated the personal patronymic into a bibliographical rubric under which the heterogeneous printed and scripted textual pieces gathered by Heminge and Condell coalesced. The diverse functions that led to the production of the Folio—the various stages of scripting, acting, printing, selling, patronage—collapsed into that one name. As a bibliographical rubric rather than a proper name, 'Shakespeare' functioned synecdochally, the authorial part standing for the collective whole of production.

Yet that particular designation proved apt for the Folio for more reasons than because William Shakespeare was the

---

[81] Ibid. 11. For the homonymic 'lines' and 'loins', see −Shakespeare's Sonnets, notes, p. 579. See Richard S. Peterson's superb reading of Jonson's Folio tribute: 'Well-Turned and True Filed Lines: Jonson on Shakespeare', ch. 4 in *Imitation and Praise in the Poems of Ben Jonson* (New Haven, Conn., 1981), pp. 194–91, and Murray's discussion of the 'parented text' in *Theatrical Legitimation*.

primary writer of the plays. Shakespeare was the primary writer for the acting company which Heminge and Condell still headed; and, unlike other dramatists of the time, he wrote for that company and, as far as we know for sure, only for that company, from the time of its formation in 1594 as the Lord Chamberlain's Men (renamed the King's Men in 1603) until the time of his death in 1616.[82] In addition to being a writer for the company, he was also one of its actors and prime shareholders, something of a *Iohannes fac totem*, as Robert Greene's 1592 allusion styled him even before he became a shareholder.[83] And no doubt the name was also suitable because of the favour it had previously received from the two groups on whose endorsement the Folio depended: the aristocracy and the public. Dependent on both patronage and the market for success, the volume stood to benefit from its identification with a name that had been associated with the Earl of Southampton, to whom Shakespeare's first narrative poems were dedicated (and to whom the Sonnets may have been written) as well as with the popular acclaim to which the epistle of the 1622 quarto of *Othello* attested: 'the Authors name is sufficient to vent his worke.'[84] In addition, Shakespeare's status as a gentleman, alluded to by the title, by repeated references to him as 'gentle', and by his gentlemanly doublet in the portrait, no doubt elevated the status of his plays, *his* title literally incorporated into *its* title, thereby raising it above its common or vulgar theatrical milieu.[85] Even the fact of Shakespeare's death proved an advantage to the publication: in part, by commanding the respect due to the deceased; in part, because the termination of his natural body prescribed the limits of his textual corpus, the

---

[82] On Shakespeare's fidelity to the acting company, see Bentley, *The Profession of a Dramatist*, p. 279. On his dramatic activity before 1594 with the Lord Strange's Men, which regrouped as the Lord Chamberlain's Men in that year, see E. A. J. Honigmann, *Shakespeare: the 'lost years'*, (Totowa, NJ, 1985), ch. 6, pp. 59–76.

[83] *Greenes Groats-worth of Wit* (1592), quoted by Chambers, *William Shakespeare*, ii. 188.

[84] 'The Stationer to the Reader', *The Tragedy of Othello, The Moore of Venice* (1622), quoted by Chambers, *William Shakespeare*, ii. appx B. 227–8.

[85] On the definition of a gentleman in Shakespeare's time, see Laura Caroline Stevenson, *Praise and Paradox: Merchants and Craftsmen in Elizabethan Popular Literature* (Cambridge, 1984), pp. 83–6 and Andrew Gurr, *The Shakespearean Stage 1574–1642* (Cambridge, 1980), pp. 81–2; on the social status of other players, see Carol Chillington Rutter, *Documents of the Rose Playhouse* (Manchester, 1984), p. 5.

expiration of the former precluding, for a time at least, the change or growth of the latter.[86] All four commemorative verses allude to that dead body or corpse, consigned to the coffin, grave, tomb, and hearse, confined and stationed till doomsday but superseded by the perpetuating issue of the Folio tome. The Stratford Monument alluded to in one of the Folio verses supplied a validating precedent for the Folio memorial, 'to keepe the memory of so worthy a Friend, & Fellow aliue, as was our SHAKESPEARE', both tomb and tome enclosing their respective corporeal and literary 'remains', protecting them from dispersal, disintegration, and oblivion.

The dynastic language of buried fathers succeeded and perpetuated by surviving offspring runs through the prose and verse of the preliminaries with the design of affiliating its formerly miscellaneous contents. Issuing from one natural body, they are entitled to a single volume that, like a family vault, preserves their common ancestry and lineage, stretching it out till the end of time. Yet this self-entitling language reflects no prior truth or identity. Until the Folio's publication, there was no family or corpus, only disinherited 'Orphanes' and 'maimed, and deformed' limbs. The preliminaries function, then, not to document an existing reality but to constitute one retrospectively. The language of the preliminaries works performatively rather than referentially, simultaneously speaking and effecting. When the dedicatory epistle announces the gift of the volume to Pembroke and Montgomery, it simultaneously performs the giving. In the address to the reader, the exhortation to 'buy' would be similarly self-fulfilling, bringing about the purchase it urges. And the commemorative verses concurrently speak *in memoriam* and accomplish the remembering. Thus the content of the preliminaries refers to no outside and anterior reality, either in the outer world of fact or in the inner world of intent; it fashions one from within its own imaging discourse. Nor can the fashioning be said to be presumptuous, for it is backed by the combined authority of the present and future

---

[86] Seven plays were added to the 1664 Folio (see n. 56 above). Because Jonson's career continued beyond the publication of his Folio, the history of his Works is much more complicated. Additions to his corpus were made in the 1640 and 1692 Folios. See Herford *et al.*, *Works of Benjamin Jonson*, ix. 89–135.

Lords Chamberlain, the 'incomparable paire of brethren' who officiated over the production of plays on stage and in print, the acting company sponsored by and named for the King, a recent (1619) official injunction protecting the interests of that company, the publishers whose comprehensive claim was recorded in the Stationers' Register, the Master of Revels who had licensed its publication, and Ben Jonson, whose works had been commemorated by the Folio's only precedent.

The arrogational rhetoric of the preliminaries is backed up by the book's imposing form. The physical properties of that volume reify the corpus, making uniform its previously heterogeneous and dissevered members. Despite the irregularities of printing and formatting itemized above, the Folio's salient features bind its contents together. All plays are printed on pages of the same size and quality, consistently in double columns, with recurring act and scene divisions, exits and entrances, and stage directions. After being stitched and bound, they are all clasped between the covers of the Folio volume, occupying a single physical space, the volume of the Volume. Thus the consolidating efforts of the language in the preliminaries are reinforced by the physical dimensions of the book itself, not just for the 1623 publication, but for the 1632, 1664, and 1685 folios which also include them. After the interregnum, with three exceptions, the only texts that continue to circulate in stray quarto form are the 'players' quartos', often radically cut and adapted for theatrical performances;[87] the others remain safely encased within the Folio. When the Folio breaks into multiple volumes at the beginning of the eighteenth century, the preliminaries that once provided the volume's rationale are dropped. Johnson reintroduces the dedication and the address which he calls 'The Preface of the Players' after his own preface and before those of his predecessors Pope, Theobald, and Warburton. In Malone's 1821 variorum, they reappear not among the prefaces but in an appendix of various documents

[87] For an account of the 'players' quartos' and 'printers' quartos' in the seventeenth century, see George Walton Williams, 'The Publishing and Editing of Shakespeare's Plays', in *William Shakespeare: His World, His Work, His Influence*, ed. John F. Andrews (New York, 1985), iii. 493–4. Only three plays were reprinted in quarto after the interregnum: *Othello, Julius Caesar*, and *Henry IV Part I*, the first reprinted from the 1630 quarto, the other two from the Folio, both altered for performance.

that includes Shakespeare's will, excerpts from the Stratford register, and entries on the Stationers' Register.[88]

The classification of the preliminaries among documents prepared them for a new use: as documents, they came to provide information. In this capacity, they have given rise to enduring 'factual' truths or untruths. Perhaps no line of Shakespeare's has been more carefully scrutinized than Heminge and Condell's claim that the Folio replaced 'stolne and surreptitious' quartos with perfect copies received from the author's own hand. Malone's discrediting of their claim, based on his observation that the Folio had used the very quartos they repudiated in setting their own copy, precipitated what has been referred to as an age of 'textual pessimism' that was not reversed until the beginning of this century.[89] As textual pessimism set in after their claim was proved factually inaccurate, so textual optimism arrived when it was determined factually accurate. Since the later eighteenth century, nothing less than the status of the Shakespearean texts has depended on whether Heminge and Condell's claim has been regarded as factually true or false. Their related claim, 'we haue scarse receiued from him a blot in his papers', has also been influential both in ascertaining the authority of the Folio texts and in characterizing Shakespeare as an easy, spontaneous, and inspired writer who never revised.[90] Yet questions regarding the veracity, accuracy, and sincerity of the Folio's statements are irrelevant to its purposes. The preliminaries cannot be used like the Stationers' entries or legal instruments that record events and circumstances independent of and prior to the recording. The claim to the Folio's being

---

[88] Malone–Boswell, *PPWS*, i. i. xxi.

[89] Malone notes that the dedication's repudiation of the quartos 'was merely thrown out to give an additional value to their own edition', Malone, *PPWS*, i. xlii; compare Capell's view that the quartos rather than the Folio 'are the Poet's own copies', *MWSHCHT*, p. 10. On the centrality of Heminge and Condell's claim to New Bibliography, particularly in the work of Alfred W. Pollard, see Greg, *The Editorial Problem* and Margreta de Grazia, 'The Essential Shakespeare and the Material Book', *Textual Practice*, 2 (1988), 69–86.

[90] The issue of the unblotted papers has been crucial in debates over whether Shakespeare revised. Thus Pollard and Greg endorsed their claim in order to deny that Shakespeare revised (Greg, *The Shakespeare First Folio*, pp. 107, 109–10) and Honigmann has discredited it in making a case for Shakespeare's revision ('The Unblotted Papers', in *The Stability of Shakespeare's Text*, pp. 22–33), as has Taylor in defending the Oxford edition's recognition of 'intra-text' and 'inter-text' revision (*Companion*, p. 17).

based on unblotted papers, for example, has a long history extending back to the pre-print era of classical rhetoric, when a clean page was applauded as evidence of fluency of thought and expression.[91] Humphrey Moseley draws on the same tradition in his address to the next folio collection of dramatic works, Beaumont and Fletcher's 1647 *Comedies and Tragedies*, maintaining that Fletcher never blotted or revised, for he 'never touched pen till all was to stand as firme and immutable as if ingraven in Brasse or Marble'; a surviving holograph of one of Fletcher's plays, however, discloses that he did both rather freely.[92] This is not to say that such statements misrepresent or distort events and circumstances, but rather that they work them into the figuring dynamic of their ascriptive and constitutive accounts.

Still more determining has been the Folio's association of Shakespeare with Nature; in time, the pretext for the unification and integration of the heterogeneous plays became established as the most salient feature of both the author and his work.[93] In 1632, the Second Folio introduced commendatory verses that reinforced the connection: Milton praised Shakespeare because his 'easie numbers flow', shaming 'slow-endeavouring art'; in 1640, his poem was reprinted in *Poems: Written by Wil. Shakespeare Gent.*, along with one by Digges commending his 'Art without Art' that 'Nature onely helpt' and whose writings contained no borrowing from the Greek or Latin.[94] Not only

[91] Honigmann comments on the Roman rhetorical tradition that commends unblotted copy, citing Cicero and Ovid as examples: *The Stability of Shakespeare's Text*, pp. 23–5.

[92] 'What ever I have seene of Mr. Fletchers owne hand is free from interlining and his friends affirme he never writ any one thing twice: it seemes he had that rare felicity to prepare and perfect all first in his owne braine; to shape and attire his *Notions*, to adde or loppe off, before he committed one word to writing, and never touched pen till all was to stand as firme and immutable as if ingraven in Brasse or Marble': 'The Stationer to the Reader', *Comedies and Tragedies* (London, 1647). See also Greg, *The Shakespeare First Folio*, p. 92, n. 2.

[93] See also Jonson's criticism of Shakespeare for his lack of regulating Art in *Conversations with William Drummond* ('His Censure of the English Poets was this . . . That Shaksperr wanted Arte') and in *Timber or Discoveries* ('His wit was in his owne power; would the rule of it had beene so too'), both quoted in Chambers, *William Shakespeare*, ii. 207, 210. T. W. Baldwin traces the influence of Jonson's comments through the Restoration and eighteenth century in the first section of *William Shakspere's Smalle Latine & Lesse Greeke*, 2 vols. (Urbana, Ill., 1944), i. 1–74.

[94] For Milton's and Digges's commendatory verses, see Chambers, *William Shakespeare*, ii. appx B. 231–2, 235–6.

did Shakespeare write according to Nature, without effort or study; he also wrote about Nature: Dryden in his 1668 *Of Dramatick Poesy: An Essay* observed that 'he needed not the spectacles of books to read nature' and Johnson in the preface to his 1765 edition dubbed him 'the poet of nature' who faithfully held up a mirror before it rather than complying with the rules of classical art.[95] Writing in a natural manner about the subject Nature, Shakespeare educated himself by observing nature rather than studying books, particularly ancient ones. Richard Farmer concluded in his *An Essay on the Learning of Shakespeare* (1767) that 'his *Studies* were most demonstratively confined to *Nature* and *his own Language*'.[96] While this was perceived as a 'confinement' by Farmer and his predecessors, it was for Edward Young the enabling condition of his unrivalled genius: 'Who knows whether Shakespeare might not have thought less, if he had read more?' he asked in his *Conjectures on Original Composition* (1759) cited by Malone in 1790.[97] By the time of Schlegel and Coleridge, that natural 'irregular' genius was seen to possess principle of its own, not mechanical or artificial rules, but an innate 'organic form' that 'shapes as it develops itself from within.'[98] As this brief rehearsal of a topos suggests, the rationale of the 1623 Folio became indistinguishable from Shakespeare himself: the principle of Nature that unified and affiliated the hybrid plays collected by the Folio became the distinctive attribute of his work and genius.

Just as the 1623 Folio defined itself against its 1616 precedent, so too Shakespeare's identity was set into relief by Jonson's. Pope fully recognized the interdependency of their reputations:

[95] John Dryden, *Of Dramatic Poesy and Other Critical Essays*, ed. George Watson, 2 vols. (New York, 1962), i. 67; Samuel Johnson, preface to 1765 edition of Shakespeare, *Eighteenth Century Essays on Shakespeare*, 2nd edn., ed. D. Nichol Smith (Oxford, 1963), p. 106.

[96] Smith, *Eighteenth Century Essays*, p. 201.

[97] Edward Young, 'Conjectures on Original Compositions', in *English Critical Essays, Sixteenth, Seventeenth and Eighteenth Centuries* ed. Edmund D. Jones (London, 1961), p. 299. Malone quotes this passage on Shakespeare's unregulated and therefore unrestrained genius: Malone, *PPWS*, i. i. lxxvi.

[98] *Shakespearean Criticism*, ed. Thomas Middleton Raysor, 2 vols. (London, 1960), i. 198. For an example from the *Tempest* of Shakespeare's 'organic' as opposed to 'mechanic' regularity, see *Coleridge on Shakespeare: The Text of the Lectures of 1811–12*, ed. Reginald A. Foakes (Charlottesville, Va. 1971), p. 107. On the relation of Coleridge's 'organic form' to Schlegel's '*organische Form*', see Thomas G. Sauer, *A. W. Schlegel's Shakespearean Criticism in England 1811–1846* (Bonn, 1981), p. 89.

It is ever the nature of Parties to be in extremes; and nothing is so probable, as that because *Ben Johnson* had much the most learning, it was said on the one hand that *Shakespear* had none at all; and because *Shakespear* had much the most wit and fancy, it was retorted on the other, that *Johnson* wanted both. Because *Shakespear* borrowed nothing, it was said that *Ben Johnson* borrowed every thing. Because *Johnson* did not write extempore, he was reproached with being a year about every piece; and because *Shakespear* wrote with ease and rapidity, they cryed, he never once made a blot.[99]

The two major dramatists of the age have been locked into an Art/Nature opposition that was originally reified in their two monumental folio volumes. This is not to deny the reality of Jonson's learning or of Shakespeare's relative lack of it, but to suggest that these fundamental predicates owe their historical force and longevity to two monumental publications. The publications canonized the identities of the two dominant authors of the age not by preserving a prior and independent relationship but by retroactively designing and designating it.

Another folio collection of dramatic works participated in this same system of bibliographic semiotics, differentiating itself against its two predecessors. The frontispiece to Beaumont and Fletcher's 1647 *Comedies and Tragedies* features a classical bust of Fletcher; the bookseller explains that despite his best efforts, he could uncover no likeness of Beaumont. The single portrait, however, combines the features which the preliminaries assign to the collaboration. Fletcher's classicized bust is situated on two Parnassian wooded hills, marmoreal Art implanted in a Natural setting (Pl. 3); the preliminary addresses and several of the commendatory verses recommend the collection as the happy interweaving of Nature and Art, of natural gifts and university education, combining the separate virtues of Shakespeare and Jonson in order to form the third party of a 'Triumvirate of Wit'.[100] In this case, there can be no question that the attributes have been selected to give the volume

---

[99] Preface to *WS*, in Smith, *Eighteenth Century Essays*, p. 50.

[100] I. Denham, *Beaumont and Fletcher*. James Shirley's 'To the Reader' also stresses Beaumont and Fletcher's blending of Nature and Art, 'miraculously knowing and conversing with all mankind' as well as profiting from 'instruction of Libraries', as does Moseley's 'The Stationer to the Reader': 'It becomes not me to say (though it be a knowne truthe) that these *Authors* had not only High unexpressible gifts of *Nature* but also excellent *acquired Parts*, being furnished with Arts and Sciences by that liberal education they had at the *University*.' The same combination is stressed in the

integrity rather than to characterize its author or authors. It has been determined that fewer than twelve of the thirty-five plays included are the products of Beaumont and Fletcher's joint authorship; others have been identified as the unaided work of Fletcher or of Fletcher in collaboration with Massinger, or, on a recent estimate, of 'virtually every dramatist known to have been plying his trade in Jacobean London'.[101] The identity of this folio has to be seen in relation to the project of the publisher, Humphrey Moseley, to produce a 'canon' of English literature. By casting the 1647 collection in relation to its 1616 and 1623 predecessors, Moseley territorialized the native dramatic domain into Art, Nature, and Art plus Nature (sometimes termed 'Wit'), thereby forming a triumvirate of English dramatic writers. Having published the finest poetry in English —the first collected edition of Milton's poems, the poems of Donne, Vaughan, and Waller, for example—he no doubt wished to extend his publications to cover dramatic works as well, taking advantage of the time when, as a result of the closing of the theatres, drama could only be viable and vendible as material to be read.

The difference between Shakespeare and Jonson embodied in the preliminaries of their respective folios has become the basis for contrasting their biographical identities. Yet the history of the folios' production suggests the extent to which the issue at hand was the coherence of each book rather than the qualities of its respective author. Nevertheless, once that coherence can be assumed, the predicates on which it was based are recast to characterize an anterior and autonomous authorial source. The preliminaries are then treated as a more or less factual introduction rather than a performative act using the resources of book production to constitute and authorize itself.

This difference leads us back to the contrast with which this chapter began between the opening materials of the seventeenth-century Folio and those of a standard twentieth-century Collected Works. We have seen how they differ radically

commendatory verses by, for example, Thomas Stanley, John Web, and Jasper Maine. Dryden similarly commends them for their 'great natural gifts improved by study': *Of Dramatic Poesy*, i. 68.

[101] See Cyrus Hoy, 'The Shares of Fletcher and His Collaborators in the Beaumont and Fletcher Canon', in *Evidence for Authorship: Essays on Problems of Attribution*, ed. David V. Erdman and Ephim G. Fogel (Ithaca, NY, 1966), p. 204.

in both organization and content. The preliminaries of the original Folio were organized to represent the various agencies of dramatic and bibliographic realization, while the modern standard introduction was organized to reveal Shakespeare's self-absorbed creative process. Through its extended genetic and genealogical trope, the 1623 preliminaries ascribed a paternal matrix to the plays which conferred upon them the stability and uniformity of the monumental folio volume. The modern introduction, based on documentary research, provides the reader with information about Shakespeare's life and art in their historical and dramatic contexts. The difference is that between two different processes of artistic incorporation and development; and those different processes are differently encoded, the one by self-validating rhetorical arrogation and the other by externally verifiable documentation. In other words, neither the process that brings the plays into existence nor the way that process is represented is the same, or even congruous, in the two editions.

In attempting to account for the difference between the editions, no developmental trajectory can close off the conceptual and procedural hiatus between them. The discontinuity is the result of a reworking of the entire Shakespearean apparatus that introduced new criteria and new practices for establishing and reading the Shakespearean text. By examining Edmond Malone's 1790 edition and its 1821 variorum successor, the following chapters will display the interests and procedures that effected this break with the past. What must be emphasized from the start is that this reworking marks a sharp break with the past. The Malone edition's own construal of the past needs to be resisted, or it is a view in terms of precisely the continuity this present study avoids: that is, it imagines its predecessors dimly groping towards the very ends it pursues with vision and purpose. When its own aims are thrust as far back as the quarto and Folio publications, contingent needs appear as timeless and inalienable verities. It is to the end of dispelling this self-validating representation of the past as an underdeveloped version of the present that each of the following chapters proceeds, first displaying the imperatives of the Enlightenment apparatus and then moving back to earlier textual practices in order to stress the radical discrepancy between the two.

2

Authenticating Shakespeare's Text, Life, and Likeness

EVERY Shakespearean project Edmond Malone undertook throughout his thirty-five-year career involved the concept of authenticity. In 1780 he established without 'the smallest doubt' the authenticity of the 1609 quarto of the Sonnets which up until then had circulated, both independently and in editions of Shakespeare's works, in an eclectic 1640 edition.[1] Malone's 1790 edition of Shakespeare was the first to advertise itself as having been 'collated *verbatim* with the most Authentick copies'; the preface to that edition described his methods of ascertaining 'the authentick copies'; twenty-five pages of the same preface are devoted to disproving the authenticity of one of those copies, the Second Folio; a long dissertation on the authenticity of the three parts of *Henry VI* is also included.[2] In 1795, Malone disproved the claims to authenticity of various contemporary forgeries of Shakespearean and Elizabethan documents in a 400-page volume, *An Inquiry into the Authenticity of Certain Miscellaneous Papers and Legal Instruments*.[3] With equal enthusiasm, he entered into debates over the authenticity of the

[1] *Supplement to the Edition of Shakespeare's Plays Published in 1778 by Samuel Johnson and George Steevens*, 2 vols. (1780), ii. John Benson's edition of Shakespeare's poems was reprinted in editions of Shakespeare by Rowe (1710, 1714), Pope (1725, 1728), Ewing (1774), Gentleman (1771), and Evans (1775); see Hyder Edward Rollins's variorum edition of *The Sonnets*, 2 vols. (Philadelphia, Pa., 1944), ii. 29–32. Although the 1609 quarto was printed twice in the eighteenth century, by Bernard Lintott in 1711 and by George Steevens in *Twenty Quarto Plays* in 1766, it was not given an apparatus or established in the canon until Malone's *Supplement* and his two subsequent editions of 1790 and 1821; see Rollins, *The Sonnets*, ii. 36–8. For Benson's and Malone's editions of the *Sonnets*, see Ch. 4 below.

[2] Malone, *PPWS*, i. part 1.

[3] *An Inquiry into the Authenticity of Certain Miscellaneous Papers and Legal Instruments*, 1795. For a discussion of Malone's disclosure of the forgeries, see S. Schoenbaum, *Shakespeare's Lives* (Oxford, 1970), pp. 193–232. Malone also pronounced the Rowley poems forgeries in his *Cursory Observations on the Poems Attributed to Thomas Rowley* (London, 1782); see James Boswell's summary in 'A Biographical Memoir of Edmond Malone, Esq.', in Malone–Boswell, *PPWS*, i. lviii.

existing Shakespearean portraits and made arrangements to have the bust of Shakespeare on the Stratford monument brought back to what he believed to be its authentic 'stone-coloured' state.[4] And for the duration of his long career, he worked on a project which James Boswell the younger completed after his death and published as the second volume of Malone's posthumous 1821 variorum: 'an entirely new life of Shakespeare compiled from original and authentick documents'.[5]

As we shall see, Malone's new and pervasive emphasis on authenticity was not the overdue emergence of an obvious criterion. Rather, it was a compelling and novel response to the absence of a fixed and independent standard by which to prepare and present Shakespearean materials. Its validity was hardly self-evident, for it depended on a schema of interrelated textual imperatives that became clearly visible for the first time in the apparatus to Malone's 1790 Shakespeare. This chapter itself is evidence of their interconnectedness, for while it focuses on authenticity in regard to three of Malone's projects—the establishing of Shakespeare's text, biography, and likeness—it periodically anticipates the concerns of succeeding chapters with issues of history, factuality, self-identity, and literary property.

In introducing an external authority by which true and false could be positively and positivistically determined, the principle of authenticity worked to stabilize the preparation of Shake-spearean materials. The facts located in documents, records, and archives served to define what text and emendations were to be printed, what materials constituted the biography, and even what portrait was reproduced. Yet Malone's reaching back in time for authentic materials necessarily involved a large-scale rejection—and misunderstanding—of those con-

---

[4] On Malone's interest in the authenticity of the Chandos portrait, see Malone–Boswell, *PPWS*, i. xxiv–vii and ii. 507–16; James Boaden discusses the portrait in relation to other Shakespeare likenesses: *An Inquiry into the Authenticity of Various Pictures and Prints which . . . have been offered to the public as Portraits of Shakespeare* (1824; facs. repr. New York, 1975), pp. 39–48. On his conviction that the Stratford monument effigy was originally white, see Schoenbaum, *Shakespeare's Lives*, p. 187 and M. H. Spielmann, *The Title-Page of the First Folio of Shakespeare's Plays* (London, 1924), pp. 23–4 and David Piper, *The Image of the Poet: British Poets and Their Portraits* (Oxford, 1982), pp. 101–2.

[5] The biography was completed by James Boswell the younger who contributed the Advertisement, Glossary, and notes to the edition before bringing it to press. See Schoenbaum, *Shakespeare's Lives*, p. 246.

tributions which had been received and passed down over the generations linking his period to Shakespeare's. As Shakespeare studies became rounded in authenticity, earlier practices were increasingly categorized as merely subjective and arbitrary. By returning to the original and unmediated documents, bypassing the transmission from generation to generation, Malone lost sight of the successive traditional treatments which formerly endowed the study of Shakespeare with purpose and meaning.

Before Malone, texts professed to be based on copies that were 'genuine', 'original', 'perfected', or 'corrected', but not 'authentic'. Like so many crucial words, 'authenticity' underwent a sharp change in meaning during the final decades of the eighteenth century.[6] As the entries in the *Oxford English Dictionary* indicate, the term up to the middle of the eighteenth century was applied primarily to abstract principles: laws, reasons, rules, and doctrines. An item was 'authentic' when recognized as true by either consensus or authority. Seventeenth-century dictionaries defined the term as 'that which is undeniable and approved of all men . . . genuinely allowed or approved'.[7] By the end of the eighteenth century, however, the word had come to be applied to concrete rather than abstract items: texts, signatures, documents, and portraits.

And the criteria for applying it also changed. Objects were authentic not because they were accepted as true or right, but because they could be proven to issue from their professed origins by various types of external evidence: other documents, for example, the quality of ink and paper, watermarks, paleographic evidence, and typefaces. Counterfeiting a work at the end of the eighteenth century involved not simply imitating its style but also fabricating its material composition and corroborating documents. In 1728, Lewis Theobald argued for Shakespeare's authorship of *Double Falsehood* by citing a tradition that traced it back to him and by urging its Shakespearean manner and diction; in 1795, however, William Henry Ireland actually concocted ink and paper and forged script and attendant documents in order

---

[6] For lexical shifts in meaning during this period, see Raymond Williams, *Keywords: A Vocabulary of Culture and Society* (Oxford, 1976) and *Culture and Society: 1780–1950* (New York, 1958), intro., pp. xi–xviii. See also Hans Gadamer, *Truth and Method*, trans. Garrett Barden and John Cumming (New York, 1975), pp. 10–39.

[7] John Bullokar, *An English Expositor* (Menston, Yorks, 1967; first publ. 1616).

to pass off as Shakespeare's his own *Vortigern and Rowena*.[8] As techniques of counterfeiting changed, so too did the methods for detecting spurious works. Pope in 1725 excluded the seven plays introduced by the Third Folio because they impressed him as lacking 'all the distinguishing marks of [Shakespeare's] style, and his manner of thinking and writing'; Malone in 1780 excluded all of them except *Pericles* only after careful examination of what he termed 'external evidence', namely, the information provided by the Stationers' Register and title-pages.[9] The grounds for crediting materials had shifted in the course of the century from what authorities judged acceptable to what could be externally verified.

Until the later eighteenth century, the text selected for editing was the one closest to the editor rather than that closest to the author: the text that had undergone the most rather than the least mediation. Clearly this was the case in the seventeenth century when each new Folio was based on the one immediately preceding it: the Fourth Folio (1685) was based on the Third (1663–4), the Third on the Second (1632), and the Second on the First (1623).[10] Quartos, too, were as a rule based on the latest edition issued.[11] As a matter of course, changes introduced in an earlier edition, whether as minor as a spelling correction

[8] For Theobald, see Richard Foster Jones, *Lewis Theobald: His Contribution to English Scholarship* (New York, 1966; first publ. 1919) and Schoenbaum, *Shakespeare's Lives*, p. 90; for Ireland, see Schoenbaum, *Shakespeare's Lives*, pp. 211–12 and Charles Hamilton, *In Search of Shakespeare* (San Diego, Ca., 1985), pp. 231–6. On forgery in the period, see Bernard Grebanier, *The Great Shakespeare Forgery* (New York, 1965).

[9] On Pope's exclusion of the apocryphal plays, see S. Schoenbaum, *Internal Evidence and Elizabethan Dramatic Authorship: An Essay in Literary History and Method* (Evanston, Ill., 1966), pp. 9–10; Malone published these plays in his 1780 *Supplement* and evaluates the external evidence for each of them in a prefatory note.

[10] On the tradition of editors up to Malone, see Ronald B. McKerrow, 'The Treatment of Shakespeare's Text by his Earlier Editors, 1709–1768', Annual Shakespeare Lecture of the British Academy (London, 1933); Arthur M. Eastman, 'The Texts from which Johnson Printed his Shakespeare', *Journal of English and Germanic Philology*, 49 (1950), 182–91; G. Blakemore Evans, 'Shakespeare's Text: Approaches and Problems', in *A New Companion to Shakespeare Studies*, ed. Kenneth Muir (Cambridge, 1971), pp. 222–39. On Malone's relation to this tradition in establishing the composite text of *King Lear*, see Steven Urkowitz, ' "The Base Shall Top th'Legitimate": The Growth of an Editorial Tradition', in *The Division of the Kingdoms: Shakespeare's Two Versions of 'King Lear'*, ed. Gary Taylor and Michael Warren (Oxford, 1983), pp. 23–43.

[11] E. K. Chambers, *William Shakespeare: A Study of Facts and Problems*, 2 vols. (Oxford, 1930), i. 164.

or as major as the Third Folio's addition of seven plays, were
followed by the later. The later folios did not consult the
original 1623 Folio, much less the quartos printed before it.
Even if manuscript copies had survived the printing process,
and it is generally believed that they did not, they would not
have been retrieved for reprinting, primarily for economic
reasons: setting type from manuscripts rather than printed
editions was more difficult and therefore more expensive. Moreover, no particular authority or value was assigned either to the
authorial holograph or to the edition closest to it. Thus, emendations that the Second Folio introduced (1,679 according to
recent calculations[12]) were the result of its supervisors' or
editors' corrections rather than their consultation of earlier
editions or authorial manuscripts. In both the reprinting and
the correcting of the text, the earliest version was commonly
ignored, not necessarily because it was unavailable but because
no particular sanctity was accorded to the copy closest to the
author. Libraries displayed the same disregard for the oldest
editions, frequently replacing them with more recent ones: the
curators of the Bodleian Library, for example, ordered its First
Folio to be sold among other 'superfluous Library Books' as
soon as the enlarged Third Folio became available in 1664.[13]

In the eighteenth century, editions became more complex as
the textual apparatus expanded and more emendations and
notes were incorporated. Yet the same editorial tradition continued up to the last quarter of the eighteenth century. Each
new edition, with one important exception soon to be discussed,
took its immediate predecessor as its copy-text. The Johnson–
Steevens edition of 1773 was based on Johnson (1765) which
had been based on Warburton (1747) and so on down the line
back through Theobald (1733), Pope (1725), and Rowe (1709),
the first eighteenth-century edition which in turn derived from
the last or Fourth Folio. The tradition of using the most recent
Shakespeare edition as the basis for the new prevailed for a
century and a half.

[12] M. W. Black and M. A. Shaaber, *Shakespeare's Seventeenth Century Editors, 1632–1685*
(New York, 1937). Out of the 1,679 changes in the Second Folio, 623 are generally
accepted by modern editors and 213 restore readings of earlier editions even though
those editions were never consulted.

[13] *The Original Bodleian Copy of the First Folio of Shakespeare*, eds. F. Madan, G. M. R.
Turbutt, and S. Gibson (Oxford, 1905), p. 5.

In 1790 Malone's edition emphasized the necessity of returning to the earliest printed editions, whether the First Folio or the early quartos: 'Every reader must wish to peruse what Shakspeare wrote, supported at once by the authority of the authentick copies . . . rather than what the editor of the second folio, or Pope or Hanmer, or Warburton have arbitrarily substituted in its place'.[14] He was anticipated in this approach by Edward Capell, whose edition in 1768 was based on his own transcription by hand of the earliest substantive quartos, a labour of fifteen years. Though Capell's accomplishment has received high recognition in this century, his efforts were slighted and denigrated in his own century.[15] Various explanations for this have been proposed: the authority of Johnson's nearly contemporaneous edition, the fact that the notes and commentary to Capell's edition did not appear until a dozen years after the text, the convoluted and garbled prose of his introduction and notes, and the envy of rival editors. Yet what needs to be stressed here is that the importance of Capell's break with the received text was not discernible until it could be placed within a schema as comprehensive and consistent as Malone's. While intimations of that schema can retrospectively be read back into a number of Capell's practices, some of them are strikingly at odds with it: his fastidious concern with the 'unblemish'd' appearance of the page that caused him to separate text and notes; his idiosyncratic punctuation system that typographically distinguished ironic passages, 'a thing shown or pointed to', asides, and changes of address; his claim that Shakespeare had written fifty-eight plays; his 'suppression' of the names of the commentators who had contributed notes and emendations; and his dictum that improvement of a passage argued for its authenticity.[16] Each of these positions conflicts with the criterion of authenticity: by preferring aesthetic appearance to scholarly

[14] Malone, *PPWS*, i. liii.

[15] See Alice Walker, 'Edward Capell and His Edition of Shakespeare', in *Studies of Shakespeare*, ed. Peter Alexander (London, 1964), 132–48 and Brian Vickers, *Shakespeare: The Critical Heritage*, 6 vols. (London, 1974–81), v. 32–5.

[16] Capell, *MWSHCHT*, i. intro. For Capell's innovative punctuation, see pp. 28–9, n. 2; for his 'suppression' of other contributors' names, pp. 24–5, n. 10; on improvement as sufficient authorization for emendation, p. 21. See, however, Gary Taylor's assessment of Capell as revolutionizer of the editorial tradition: *Reinventing Shakespeare: A Cultural History from the Restoration to the Present* (New York, 1989), pp. 141–4.

lemma, by adulterating the text with modern markings, by confusing the apocryphal and the canonical, by failing to distinguish his contributions from those of his predecessors, by appealing to universal taste rather than textual recension.

Yet it is not to the end of giving credit where it is due that these considerations are raised, for proper acknowledgement, as we shall see, is one of the concerns of the very schema under discussion. Rather, it is to emphasize the importance of the unprecedented consistency of Malone's commitment to authenticity. When Malone's text claimed to be based not on the traditionally received copy but on the First Folio for those plays that first appeared there and on the earliest quarto for all those that had been printed previously, his entire apparatus buttressed that claim. Only within such a context could traditional treatments be definitively challenged and the foundation set for the orthodoxies of the next century—and indeed, for those of modern Shakespeare scholarship after that.

Capell was not the only eighteenth-century editor before Malone to demonstrate an interest in the early Shakespeare texts. The first of them, Nicholas Rowe, consulted the Second Folio and several late quartos and claimed in his dedication that he had worked 'to compare the several Editions and give the true Reading as I could from thence'.[17] Pope catalogued twenty-eight quartos at the end of his edition which he claimed to have used for the greater part of his readings and emendations.[18] The Tonson publishing house, which issued all but one of the major Shakespeare editions from Rowe in 1709 to Edward Capell in 1768, advertised for quartos printed before 1620 to be used in the preparation of subsequent editions.[19] Theobald announced that he had consulted the oldest copies in preparing his edition and provided a catalogue of editions at the end of his work.[20] George Steevens in 1766 published twenty quartos, most of them provided by David Garrick, thereby making them available to future editors.[21] Yet what must be stressed is that these editors consulted the older

---

[17] Rowe, *WWS*, i. dedic. A2ᵛ.   [18] Pope, *WS*, vi.

[19] On the Tonsons' control over Shakespeare publication for three generations, see G. F. Papali, *Jacob Tonson, Publisher: His Life and Work* (New Zealand, 1968), pp. 110–29. For the Tonson monopoly on Shakespeare, see Ch. 5 below.

[20] Theobald, *WS*, preface, i. lxviii.   [21] Steevens, *TPS*.

editions not as a matter of course, but only when difficulties arose. Where the received text was acceptable, it remained intact; when cruxes arose, the older texts were culled for variant readings.

Before Malone, eighteenth-century editors prized the older copies because they yielded alternatives to obscure or corrupt passages in the received text. Collation provided a new authority for emendation which had been lacking in the controversial 'conjectural criticism' associated with Richard Bentley and best demonstrated in his editions of Horace and Milton.[22] Theobald was careful to dissociate his 'literal criticism' from Bentley's 'intuitive' or 'conjectural' criticism, insisting that Bentley's intention had been to 'correct' Milton whereas his own was to 'restore' Shakespeare. Yet the distinction between correcting and restoring became blurred in the absence of an outside basis for the restoration.[23] Even Capell, who recognized the authority of the First Folio and quartos, maintained that 'one should look into the other old editions and select from thence whatever improves the Author, or contributes to his advancement in perfectness'.[24] For him, 'improving' and 're-storing' the author were synonymous: the improvement of a passage attested to its genuineness. By selecting emendations from the old copies, editors were less vulnerable to charges like those levelled by Thomas Edwards, who, in *The Canons of Criticism*, wryly pronounced peremptory emendation the first law of textual criticism: 'A Professed Critic has a right to declare that his Author wrote whatever he thinks he ought to have written with as much positiveness as if He had been at his Elbow.'[25] Yet what must be stressed is that these editors' collation of the old quartos demonstrated the same disregard for authenticity as did their acceptance of the received text. While variant texts increased the supply of possible readings,

[22] On Bentley's intuitive classical scholarship, see Rudolf Pfeiffer, *History of Classical Scholarship from 1300 to 1850* (Oxford, 1976), pp. 13–63 and E. J. Kenney, *The Classical Text: Aspects of Editing in the Age of the Printed Book* (Berkeley, Ca., 1974), pp. 71–4.

[23] Theobald, preface to *WS* (2nd edn.), *Eighteenth Century Essays on Shakespeare*, ed. D. Nichol Smith (Oxford, 1963; first publ. 1903), p. 75. References to the prefaces of Rowe, Pope, Theobald, Warburton, Hanmer, and Johnson will henceforth follow Smith's edition.

[24] Capell, *MWSHCHT*, i. 21.

[25] Thomas Edwards, *The Canons of Criticism and Glossary Being a Supplement to Mr. Warburton's Edition of Shakspear* (London, 1750), p. 1.

they offered no principle for ranking them. The editor's selection was based not on the authenticity of the quartos or Folios from which the variants had been taken, but rather on his own critically informed preferences.

Not until the later part of the century was the basic and simple principle behind modern collation formulated: 'An edition is more or less correct as it approaches nearer to or is more distant from the first.'[26] It has remained fundamental to twentieth-century bibliography: 'If a continuously touching line of direct descent can be worked out, and if no outside influence can be established as entering at any point, then only one document, the first printed edition, can be authoritative.'[27] In the collations for the 1733 edition, however, Theobald claimed to have consulted not only some of Shakespeare's early quartos but also Shakespeare's historical sources, English as well as Greek and Roman, 'comparing my Author with his Originals', believing that 'he was a close and accurate Copier where-ever his *Fable* was founded on *History*'.[28] Theobald's example suggests that in emending corrupt passages, collation provided a range of possibilities that were not the product of the editor's 'invention' or 'caprice'; the editor still had to choose among those possibilities, but at least the alternatives were not of his own devising. The eighteenth-century editor now considered to have done the most accurate and thorough collations for the six plays he edited, Charles Jennens, collated the major eighteenth-century editions as well as the four Folios and the available quartos and systematically recorded all possible variants at the bottom of each page.[29] Yet the resulting readings or 'alterations' were only occasionally from the oldest copy, indicating that he too assigned no special authority to the copy closest to the author: 'The several editions are a mutual help to each other.'

The modern textual scholar who first noticed this practice suggested that eighteenth-century editors simply did not reflect

[26] Malone, *PPWS*, i. i. xiii.

[27] Fredson Bowers, *On Editing Shakespeare and Other Elizabethan Dramatists* (Charlottesville, Va., 1966), p. 11.

[28] Smith, *Eighteenth Century Essays*, p. 77.

[29] On the accuracy and thoroughness of Jennens's collations for six of Shakespeare's plays, see *Shakespeare Variorum Handbook*, eds. R. Hosley, R. Knowles, and R. McGugan (New York, 1971), p. 66, entry 31.

on its illogicality: 'If they had thought for a moment, they would have seen that no reading which appears in a later text, but not in the one from which that later text was printed, can possibly have any authority. . . .'[30] To account for this 'failure to appreciate so obvious a fact', he suggested that editors may have confused Shakespearean quartos with classical manuscripts. Because classical manuscripts are polygenous (descending from multiple independent sources) rather than monogenous (descending from a single source), all manuscripts might be credited with equal authority. Even the most corrupt manuscript might in respect to some detail be more authoritative than a manuscript that was relatively intact. According to this explanation, Shakespeare scholars fell into textual habits applicable only to classical manuscripts: 'It appears . . . it simply never occurred to men like Pope, Theobald, and Capell that the Shakespeare quartos were not in the same position with respect to the author's original texts as the classical manuscripts were.'[31] In recent histories of textual criticism, the understanding of this distinction between classical manuscripts and printed texts, between manuscripts that are not descended from the same source and printed texts that are, marks the beginning of modern bibliography: 'The subsequent history of editing through the nineteenth century is one of growing realization that the conditions of manuscript transmission over the course of hundreds of years are essentially different from the conditions of printed transmission within relatively few years.'[32] It is assumed that editors, without this basic distinction, continued to select variants arbitrarily: until they understood it, editors simply continued 'to pick and choose among textual variants' without realizing that 'only those derived from the first edition are truly authoritative'.

Yet there are problems with attributing the earlier practice of collation to the neglect 'of so obvious a fact'. To begin with, while it might be conceivable that editors thought certain quartos descended from different manuscripts—Malone

[30] McKerrow, 'The Treatment of Shakespeare's Text', p. 20. See also Bowers, *On Editing Shakespeare*, pp. 83–6; Sailendra Kumar Sen, *Capell and Malone, and Modern Critical Bibliography* (Calcutta, 1960), pp. 1–22; F. P. Wilson, *Shakespeare and the New Bibliography*, rev. and ed. Helen Gardner (Oxford, 1970).

[31] McKerrow, 'The Treatment of Shakespeare's Text', p. 21.

[32] Bowers, *On Editing Shakespeare*, p. 85.

thought this was the case for the widely discrepant 1597 and 1599 quartos of *Romeo and Juliet*—it is inconceivable that they believed each of the four Folios, nearly identical in content and formatting, to represent a separate line of descent. The hypothesis that Shakespearean editors confused their printed texts with classical manuscripts is also problematic. While it is true that classical manuscripts generally derived from independent rather than common lines of descent, even in the cases when they were of the same line of descent, little attempt was made at this time to subordinate the more derivative. In classical textual criticism, it was not until the time of Malone that the first history of an ancient text appeared—Friedrich August Wolf's *The Prolegomena ad Homerum*, published in 1795; the first stemmatic diagram establishing the relations of surviving manuscripts as they descended from their source appeared in Carl Zumpt's edition of the *Verrines* in 1831.[33] Classical editors of this period appear to have been collating manuscripts with the same indifference as Shakespearean editors to the original source or its closest descendant.

It seems altogether unlikely, therefore, that editors thoughtlessly confused Shakespearean printed texts with classical manuscripts until they knew better. Only after the primacy of the text closest to Shakespeare had been established could the qualitative ranking of derivative texts occur. Among Shakespeareans, Johnson is usually credited with first articulating the principle of recension on the basis of a passage in which he objected to Theobald's high ranking of the first two Folios, maintaining that 'the truth is, that the first is equivalent to all others, and that the rest only deviate from it by the printer's negligence. Whoever has any of the folios has all. . .'.[34] But this passage clearly equates the four Folios, allowing for printer's errors, rather than privileging the First, as Malone was to do unequivocally a generation later: 'No person who wishes to peruse the plays of Shakspeare should ever open the Second Folio, or either of the subsequent copies';[35] 'Of all the plays of

---

[33] See Pfeiffer, *History of Classical Scholarship*, p. 174 and Kenney, *The Classical Text*, pp. 103–4. Though his earlier contributions were, like Malone's, adumbrated by earlier scholars, Karl Lachmann (1793–1851) is generally credited with establishing the genealogical method in classical and biblical texts; see Kenney, *The Classical Text*, pp. 102–5.

[34] Smith, *Eighteenth Century Essays*, p. 135.   [35] Malone, *PPWS*, l. xliii.

which there are no quarto copies extant, the first folio, printed in 1623, is the only authentick edition'.[36] Because for Johnson each folio contained all others, there was no point in consulting more than one: 'I collated them all at the beginning, but afterwards used only the first.'[37] As for his predecessors, collation of the Folio and the quartos yielded a stockpile of viable variants: 'In perusing a corrupted piece, [the editor] must have before him all possibilities of meaning, with all possibilities of expression'.[38] From these possibilities, the editor, on the basis of his Judgement or Taste, rather than of the text's genealogy, was to select the most suitable.

Malone by his own count introduced 1,654 emendations to Shakespeare's texts, not 'by capricious innovation, or fanciful conjecture, but by restoration of the poet's words as they are found in the only copies of authority'.[39] He strictly distinguished his use of 'restoration' from that of his predecessors, who believed that 'to alter Shakespeare's text and to restore it were considered as synonymous terms'.[40] They 'altered or amended as it was called, at pleasure', while he submitted to a 'task new and arduous': 'to collate word by word every line of his plays and poems with the original and authentick copies'. According to his preface, he had every proof-sheet of his work read aloud to him while he scrutinized the earliest printed copy, whether in quarto or the First Folio; for those plays existing in more than one edition, he consulted a table listing variations between them.[41] By this method, he purposed to remove the 'innovations' that had accumulated from the Second Folio through the modern editions. Several pages of his preface charting 'the gradual progress of corruption' undergone by passages as they passed through successive editions illustrated his rule that 'The first edition of each play is alone of any authority'.[42] For the first time, it was proposed that the First Folio without subsequent editorial accretions be printed and 'made the standard'. Malone

---

[36] Malone, *PPWS*, l. xix.

[37] Smith, *Eighteenth Century Essays*, p. 135.

[38] Ibid. 134.

[39] Malone–Boswell, *PPWS*, i. ix. Malone gave this figure in his *Letter to the Rev. Farmer* (1792), quoted by Bertrand H. Bronson, *Joseph Ritson: Scholar-at-Arms*, 2 vols. (Berkeley, Ca., 1938), ii. 520. It approximates closely the number of emendations (1,679) introduced by the Second Folio; see n. 12 above.

[40] Malone–Boswell, *PPWS*, i. xi.   [41] Ibid. xlv.   [42] Ibid. xiii, xviii.

saw his own 1790 edition as a more convenient alternative to such a reprint;[43] it was also more authentic, for in the case of those plays where earlier quartos existed, the First Folio itself had been invalidated by the contaminating process of transmission.

Malone's shift in textual priorities was accompanied by a new reassessment of the status of early quartos and the Folio. Earlier eighteenth-century editors had consistently lamented the corruption of the text, attributing it to diverse causes. Pope assumed the Folio text to be based on theatrical copies that had suffered greatly from theatrical mutations: they had 'from time to time been cut, or added to, arbitrarily' by actors who, 'ever a standard to themselves', 'know no rule but that of pleasing the present humour, and complying with the wit in fashion'.[44] He suggested that 'the Ignorance' and 'the Impertinence, of his first Editors', themselves both actors, were accountable for 'arbitrary Additions, Expunctions, Transpositions of scenes and lines, confusion of Characters and Persons, wrong application of Speeches, corruptions of innumerable Passages'.[45] Theobald attributed the text's 'Depravations' or 'Train of Blemishes' to their having been surreptitiously and haphazardly transcribed by short-hand during performance and from 'piecemeal parts' from playhouse papers.[46] Capell blamed the play's defects on Shakespeare himself: 'When the number and bulk of these pieces [fifty-eight, by his calculations], the shortness of his life, and the other busy employments of it are reflected upon duly, can it be a wonder that he should be so loose a transcriber of them?'[47] In the 1756 *Proposals* to his edition, Johnson found corruption at every stage of the text's history, from authorial manuscript to printed edition:

It is not easy for invention to bring together so many causes concurring to vitiate a text. No other author ever gave up his works to fortune and time with so little care: no books could be left in hands so likely to injure them, as plays frequently acted yet continued in manuscripts: no other transcribers were likely to be so little qualified for their task as those who copied for the stage at a time when the lower ranks of the people were universally illiterate; no other editions were made from

[43] Ibid. xliv.
[44] Smith, *Eighteenth Century Essays*, p. 48.
[45] Ibid. 56.   [46] Ibid. 74.   [47] Capell, *MWSHCHT*, i. 10.

fragments so minutely broken and so fortuitously reunited; and in no other age was the art of printing in such unskillful hands.[48]

For these editors, it was precisely because the text was so intractable that abundant corrections, alterations, and restorations were necessary. The multiple sources of corruption justified editorial intervention; in principle at least, the edition that had received the most editorial attention, the most recent edition, was the purest because the most purified.

Malone, however, after quoting Johnson's 1756 'Proposals', maintained that the corruption of the original text had been exaggerated ('our poet's text has been described as more corrupt than it really is'[49]), and that the problem lay not so much in the texts as in the ignorance and apathy of its editors. As a result, too much of the text had been sacrificed to easy emendation that instead should have been preserved by 'the labour required to investigate fugitive allusions, to explain and justify obsolete phraseology by parallel passages from contemporary authors, and to form a genuine text by a faithful collation of the original copies'.[50] Industrious and extensive research into the materials from the period would reveal that what subsequent editors regarded as corruptions were in fact customary uses of language before the reign of Charles I. The syntactic, lexical, and metrical irregularities Malone's predecessors had corrected were perfectly acceptable at the time the plays were first printed. As early as the Second Folio (1632), the language had undergone changes significant enough to leave its editor 'ignorant of our poet's language' and therefore too ready to correct him.[51] Malone provided ten pages of examples to prove that even Shakespeare's first editor, the anonymous editor of the Second Folio, 'was entirely ignorant of our poet's phraseology and metre',[52] not knowing, for example, that the double negative and double comparative were commonly used, and confusing 'I' as first person pronoun with 'ay' as affirmative particle. Similarly, he pointed out that what former editors, primarily Pope but also Steevens, had emended as metrical errors were entirely acceptable when accorded their

---

[48] 'Proposals for an edition of Shakespeare' (1756), in Vickers, *Critical Heritage*, IV. 269.

[49] Malone, *PPWS*, i. i. xi.   [50] Ibid.   [51] Ibid. xliii.

[52] Ibid. xx.

more flexible Elizabethan and Jacobean pronunciation. The identification of 'fugitive allusions' to outmoded customs also preserved the text from change, making apparent cruxes intelligible just as knowledge of 'obsolete phraseology' made grammatical and metrical anomalies acceptable.

It appears, then, that until the later eighteenth century, no principle of authenticity governed either the choice of text to be printed or the selection of variants by which to emend. As Malone noted, without it 'we have no criterion by which the text can be ascertained'.[53] In what he referred to as 'the era of conjectural criticism and capricious innovation',[54] the informed and practiced sensibility of the editor arbitrated textual decisions, establishing 'the genuine sense and purity' of the text. Although variants were compiled from the early quartos and First Folio, the copy-text remained the *received* rather than the *authentic* text, the most proximate rather than the most remote, the emendations were selected at the editor's discretion rather than by recension.

This should not be taken to mean, however, that earlier eighteenth-century editors were irresponsible or cavalier. For their objective was not the retrieval and preservation of what Shakespeare had put to paper. The process of establishing and evaluating Shakespeare served the broader cultural ambition of purifying English language, taste, and manners. Shakespeare was, in Pope's words, 'the fairest and fullest subject for Criticism' precisely because as Nature's child rather than Art's pupil, he provided the raw material for exercising Art, for defining and identifying 'Beauties and Faults of all sorts',[55] stylistic, moral, and social. The process of literary elevation and repression, of 'highlighting' and 'stigmatizing' by which certain passages were distinguished and others were degraded in the editions of Pope, Hanmer, and Warburton shaped ideas of correctness and incorrectness, the beautiful and defective, the proper and the improper. Indeed, the work of these earlier Shakespeareans needs to be considered in the context of the more general cultural project of regulating and refining the language in the absence of an Academy like the French or Italian, beginning perhaps with Dryden's complaint in 1693

---

[53] Ibid. xii. [54] Ibid. lv. [55] Smith, *Eighteenth Century Essays*, p. 44.

that English was still an 'illiterate' language: 'We have yet no
English prosodia, not so much as a tolerable dictionary, or a
grammar; so that our language is in a manner barbarous.'[56] In
his preface to Shakespeare written seventy-five years later,
Warburton remarked on the same need, but proposed that it be
met not by a state-supported institution, but by the 'critical
attention' due its 'many excellent Works':

And its being yet destitute of a Test or Standard to apply to, in cases of
doubt or difficulty, shews how much it wants that attention. For we
have neither GRAMMAR nor DICTIONARY, neither Chart nor
Compass, to guide us through this wide sea of Words. And indeed
how should we? since both are to be composed and finished on the
Authority of our best established Writers. But their Authority can be
of little use till the Text hath been correctly settled, and the Phraseology
critically examined. As, then, by these aids, a *Grammar* and *Dictionary*,
planned upon the best rules of Logic and Philosophy, (and none but
such will deserve the name) are to be procured; the forwarding of this
will be a general concern: for, as *Quintilian* observes; 'Verborum
proprietas ac *differentia* omnibus, qui sermonem curae habent, debet
esse communis.'[57]

As Warburton noted, the fixing of the language and the
establishing of the best texts were interdependent projects by
which language and letters would be reciprocally rectified and
purified; both Johnson's 1755 Dictionary and his 1765 edition
of Shakespeare directly addressed this 'general concern' by
devising a standard on the basis of the great writings in the
language which in turn would make it possible to reproduce
those writings in accordance with the standard.

Having overlooked the interrelation between these two projects, recent accounts have been rather appalled by what has
appeared 'a tradition of personal abuse that colored and dis-
figured the development of textual criticism throughout the
century'.[58] Indeed, it would be possible to chronicle the entire
period as a series of bitter disputes over authority, beginning

[56] John Dryden, 'A Discourse Concerning the Original and Progress of Satire', in *Of
Dramatic Poesy and Other Critical Essays*, 2 vols., ed. George Watson (New York, 1962), i.
152.
[57] Smith, *Eighteenth Century Essays*, p. 101.
[58] George Walton Williams, 'The Publishing and Editing of Shakespeare's Plays', in
William Shakespeare: His Life, His Work, His Influence, ed. John F. Andrews (New York,
1985), iii. 596.

with Theobald's criticism of Pope's edition in *Shakespeare Restored*,
countered by Pope's ridicule of Theobald in the *Dunciad*, continued by Warburton's grievances against Theobald's and
Hanmer's appropriations, and tapering off with Steevens's
personal and professional attacks on Malone.[59] On both sides
of the controversy, editors accused one another of arbitrary and
capricious treatments of the text. Pope insisted that he performed an editor's duties 'without any indulgence to my private
sense or conjecture', but with 'religious abhorrence of all
Innovation', 'preferring' passages into the text 'constantly *ex
fide Codicum*, upon authority'.[60] Theobald maintained that in
his edition 'nothing is alter'd but what by clearest Reasoning
can be proved a Corruption of the true Text',[61] and in such cases
'arbitrary or capricious' emendations were strictly avoided.
Hanmer recorded his resolution 'not to give a loose to fancy, or
indulge a licentious spirit of criticism'.[62] All the same, appeals
to consensual standards or to textual scholarship could still be
reduced to what one detractor called 'the legislative and dictatorial manner in which every succeeding editor has ushered
himself into the world'.[63] As Johnson's droll formula for writing
notes indicated, each new editor elevated himself by criticizing
his predecessors' high-handedness:

The work is performed, first by railing at the stupidity, negligence,
ignorance, and asinine tastelessness of the former editors and shewing,
from all that goes before and all that follows, the inelegance and
absurdity of the old reading; then by proposing something, which to
superficial readers would seem specious, but which the editor rejects
with indignation; then by producing the true reading, with a long
paraphrase, and concluding with loud acclamations of the discovery,
and a sober wish for the advancement and prosperity of genuine
criticism.[64]

    [59] For the Pope/Theobald conflict, see Jones, *Lewis Theobald*, chs. 2 to 4, pp. 61–
155. On Warburton's charges against Hanmer and Theobald, see A. W. Evans,
Warburton and the Warburtonians: A Study in Some Eighteenth-Century Controversies (London,
1932), ch. 9, pp. 143–55; on Steevens's and Malone's falling out, see Boswell's account
in Malone–Boswell, *PPWS*, i. x–xvii, lviii–lix, and Bronson, *Joseph Ritson*, ii. 533–40.
    [60] Smith, *Eighteenth Century Essays*, p. 57.
    [61] Ibid. 75; Theobald, *WS*, i. xlii.
    [62] Smith, *Eighteenth Century Essays*, p. 86.
    [63] Joseph Ritson, *Remarks, Critical and Illustrative on the Text and Notes of the Last Edition
of Shakspeare*, 1783 (New York, 1973), p. ii.
    [64] Smith, *Eighteenth Century Essays*, p. 146.

When nothing less than standards of literacy and manners depend on textual arbitrations, the authority of editors and commentators will necessarily be fervently disputed. In the seventeenth century, because the need for corrections was self-evident, any literate worker in the printing house could correct the text. When the authority of the text depended on the authority of the editor, however, the editor had to prove himself qualified to serve as both regulator of the text and dispenser of cultural standards. The Tonson publishers chose their editors carefully: Rowe was a poet and dramatist known for his adaptations of Shakespeare's plays, Pope a renowned poet and translator, Theobald a classical philologist and historian, Warburton a protégé of Pope's, Johnson a lexicographer, Capell a longtime Deputy Licenser of plays. These editors' most important contributions tended to be in their respective areas of expertise: the dramatist Rowe regularized act and scene divisions and prefaced each play with dramatis personae; the poet Pope extensively regulated Shakespeare's metre and commented profusely on the beauties and defects of Shakespeare's verse; the historian and classicist Theobald drew on his alleged familiarity with the classics and with earlier English literature in introducing emendations; 'Dictionary Johnson' applied his lexical expertise to the elucidation of obsolete or archaic terms; and Capell's official inspection of play texts prepared him to concentrate more on the details of staging than any of his predecessors. The very range of these editors' literary experience and expertise is sufficient to indicate that before the professionalization of Shakespeare studies, no fixed principle authorized the changing and glossing of the Shakespeare text.[65]

The antagonism among editors flared up also over the issue of acknowledgement or attribution. Despite their appeal to a consensual standard, editors were anxious to receive proper credit for their emendations and glosses. In the previous century, changes were introduced tacitly and anonymously. In the eighteenth century, however, editors who were selected by the

---

[65] Hugh H. Grady gives an important account of the development of the modern research university and modern English studies that extends Malone's positivism into the nineteenth century. I wish to thank him for allowing me to read his *The Modernist Shakespeare: Critical Texts in a Material World*, esp. ch. 1, 'Modernizing Shakespeare: The Rise of Professionalism' (Oxford, 1990).

publisher and named on the title-page increasingly expected to be credited for their contributions. Warburton in the preface to his edition accused his two predecessors Theobald and Hanmer of betrayal and fraud, 'trafficking in my Papers without my knowledge';[66] while forgiving Theobald 'who wanted money', he resented Hanmer, who, wanting only the 'Reputation of a Critic' took his conjectures 'and by changing them to something, he thought, synonymous or similar, he made them his own'.[67] So too, J. Collins, in his preface to the *Notes and Various Readings* to Capell's edition, accused Steevens of 'a regular system of plagiarism' in the 1773 Johnson–Steevens edition, maintaining that that edition had 'usher'd to the world upon credit of their names' comments belonging to Capell.[68] Editors, it appears, felt entitled to the same proprietary rights over their work that were being claimed on behalf of authors (see Chapter 5). Collins's preface to Capell's *Notes and Various Readings* referred to Capell as well as to Shakespeare as 'our author' and prefixed Capell's engraved portrait to the *Notes* just as Capell had prefixed Shakespeare's to his *Comedies, Histories, and Tragedies.* Johnson applauded one of Warburton's emendations because it 'set the critic on level with the author'.[69] Malone charged that the editions of Pope and Hanmer could 'with almost as much propriety be called *their* works as those of Shakspeare';[70] his 1790 edition featured not only Shakespeare's portrait but one of Johnson and three contributors to his edition. Boswell attributed Steevens's abuse of Malone to the 'jealousy of authorship'.[71] While purporting to restore Shakespeare's text and sense, the editor claimed ownership over his own restoration, as if his ascertaining and elucidating of the text made him co-proprietor with Shakespeare of the works. It is not simply the clash of irascible and petulant personalities that generated these conflicts, as is generally maintained, but rather a radical uncertainty about both the source of the editor's authority and the relation

---

[66] Smith, *Eighteenth Century Essays*, p. 91.

[67] Ibid. 92.

[68] Edward Capell, *Notes and Various Readings to Shakespeare*, 1783 (New York, 1970), a2[v].

[69] Johnson's praise was prompted by Warburton's emendation of 'Being a God, kissing carrion' to 'a good kissing carrion', *Hamlet* (II.2.180). See *Johnson on Shakespeare*, ed. Arthur Sherbo (New Haven, Conn., 1968), ii. 97.

[70] Malone–Boswell, *PPWS*, i. xxiii.   [71] Ibid. lx.

of his contributions both to those of other editors and to Shakespeare's text itself.

Johnson's decision to offer a text that included the important readings and variants of former editors might be seen as a solution to this crisis, described by Johnson as 'a spontaneous strain of invective and contempt, more eager and venomous than is vented by the most furious controvertist in politicks'.[72] Rather than contesting earlier contributions, Johnson adapted a format that would encompass them: 'The former editors have affected to slight their predecessors: but in this edition all that is valuable will be adopted from every commentator.'[73] Even when notes were in strident disagreement, the edition juxtaposed them as if they were in accord. This edition also provided the first system for attributing emendations and glosses to their source. Though Johnson's attributions have been shown to be less than complete, his principle was clear: 'Whatever I have taken from them it was my intention to refer to its original authour, and it is certain, that what I have not given to another, I believed when I wrote it to be my own'.[74] By bringing conflicting comments within the perimeter of the page and by systematically crediting them to their source, Johnson's variorum achieved something of a settlement. At the same time, however, it introduced a new area of instability. By providing an array of contributions, it effectively put the reader in the position of arbitrator formerly reserved for the editor. Equipped with 'all the observable varieties of all the copies that can be found', the reader could challenge the editor: 'If the reader is not satisfied with the editor's determination, he may have the means of chusing better for himself.'[75] Johnson's electorate of readers would have been unthinkable earlier in the century, as Hanmer's admonition in his 1744 edition indicates: 'This only the Reader is desired to bear in mind . . . the corruptions are more

---

[72] Smith, *Eighteenth Century Essays*, p. 140.

[73] Johnson, 'Proposals', in Vickers, *Critical Heritage*, iv. 273. While Johnson was the first to collect the prefaces and comments, the first variorum is usually considered the Johnson–Steevens–Reed edition of 1803, the second the 1813 edition of the same, and the third the Malone–Boswell edition of 1821. See Williams, 'Shakespeare's Plays', in Andrews, *William Shakespeare*, pp. 589–601.

[74] Smith, *Eighteenth Century Essays*, p. 139. On Johnson's sometimes unacknowledged borrowings from others, see Arthur Sherbo, *Samuel Johnson, Editor of Shakespeare* (Urbana, Ill., 1956), ch. 3, 'Johnson's Indebtedness to Others', 28–45.

[75] Johnson, 'Proposals', in Vickers, *Critical Heritage*, iv. 271.

numerous and of grosser kind than can be conceived but by those who have looked nearly into them.'[76] Johnson's transferral of authority to the reader is also evident in his objections to Pope's authoritarian 'privileging' and 'degrading' of passages, the former accomplished by marginal asterisks and commas, the latter by demotions to the bottom of the page. Johnson restricted his own examples of Beauties and Faults to what was necessary for demonstrating the precepts of Judgement and left their application to the reader, thereby supplying the initiate with the opportunity to exercise critical powers and the novice with the chance to develop them: 'Judgement, like other faculties, is improved by practice, and its advancement is hindered by submission to dictatorial decisions'.[77]

In the same decade in which Johnson's edition appeared, two other editors also invested editorial prerogatives in the reader by supplying the apparatus by which to evaluate emendations as Johnson had provided the precepts for adjudicating on and elucidating passages. The notes to Capell's 1768 edition were designed to put the reader in possession of all the 'readings of moment from quarto or Folio': 'Thus reader, you have before you in orderly manner, and so small a compass as possible, every single material that editions can furnish for whatever close examination you please. . . .'[78] Charles Jennens also intended to empower the reader with his notes; according to Boswell, he undertook 'to enable every reader to become his own Critick, by furnishing him with all the varieties which the folios, the quartos, or the suggestions of Commentators could afford.'[79] It was now the reader who was prepared to undertake what had been the 'dictatorial' editor's exclusive function of choosing from a stockpile of possibilities. The coveted privilege of 'perfecting' the Shakespeare text was taken from the 'dictatorial' editor and invested in the general readership unaccompanied by any stated principle of selection whatsoever.

Malone's edition, based on authentic copies and documents, posited a demonstrable standard that was neither self-evident nor dependent on either the editor's authority or the reader's

---

[76] Smith, *Eighteenth Century Essays*, p. 86.   [77] Ibid. 142.
[78] The notes to the 1768 edition were not printed until 1779–83: *Notes and Various Readings to Shakespeare* (New York, 1970).
[79] Malone–Boswell, *PPWS*, i. lx.

predilections. Objective documents were to provide concrete and independent criteria by which to govern editorial choices. The editor, therefore, no longer needed the credentials of a Pope or a Johnson to authorize his procedures. Malone had distinguished himself by no earlier accomplishments: trained in the law, his scholarly reputation depended solely on his 'researches', on his archival investigations and scrutiny of documents that led him ever back to the Shakespearean source. With the criteria for selection located in outside materials rather than within each editor's or reader's faculties, it was at least in theory possible to avoid what Johnson termed 'motion without progress', the flurry of contentious activity that ostensibly led nowhere.[80] For Malone, 'the era of conjectural criticism and capricious innovation' had 'given place to rational explanation', and Shakespeare studies could move forward progressively and cumulatively, like a science.[81] In his earliest editorial project, he looked forward to the gradual attainment of a perfect Shakespeare text, the result of relentless research into archives and documents.

Once the text with its variants could be selected on the basis of documents, it became lodged in the remote history recorded in those documents, removed from both the site of reception and the process of transmission and fashioned instead to its distant authorial and historical origin. Only after the farthest text was assigned this position of privilege could other derivative texts be ranked in relation to it. In addition to breaking the text from a tradition of transmission, the criterion of authenticity also broke it off from the standards by which it had formerly been prepared and understood. We can begin to see here how the emphasis on authenticity exempted Shakespeare's text from the warring judgements of earlier editors and positioned it within a new realm in which information pre-empted evaluation, factual scholarship phased out literary judgement. Authenticity provided an external principle for settling Shakespeare's erratic text; from the vantage of that principle, earlier editorial activity looked arbitrary and personal.

It has continued to look so still, so that what modern bibliographers disapprove of the most in earlier treatments of

---

[80] Smith, *Eighteenth Century Essays*, p. 137.
[81] Malone–Boswell, *PPWS* i. lv–vi.

Shakespeare, 'is that the editors almost invariably pick and choose among variants with no fixed principle except their literary taste.'[82] From this post-Malonean vantage, 'literary taste' appears a self-indulgent substitute for the 'necessary determination of the facts' rather than a responsible cultural project motivated by the desire to rectify and enrich language and literature and inculcate readers with critical values and their moral and social correlatives.[83] Yet from a pre-Malonean standpoint, Malone's concern with retaining the particulars of the most authentic editions would have appeared a retrograde throwback to 'barbaric' rudeness. Oblivious to former criteria and purposes, Malone abstracted Shakespeare from the process by which he had been made correct and comprehensible by Taste and Judgement and by which in turn Taste and Judgement had been enriched and fortified by Shakespeare. The new criterion of authenticity converted the Shakespearean texts into a new kind of object: one lodged in the past rather than integral to current cultural concerns. It is possible that the vitriolic cross-fire characterizing earlier Shakespeare studies provided the necessary structure for contesting contemporary values and, in the process, forging improved ones, just as Malone's cooler model of research allowed for the gradual accumulation of the information he identified with the bygone past.

The same preoccupation with authenticity characterized Malone's account of Shakespeare's life as it did his treatment of Shakespeare's text; and the same indifference to authenticity typified earlier biographical accounts as it did earlier textual treatments. Throughout the seventeenth century, separate biographical accounts of Shakespeare circulated in such compendia as Ben Jonson's *Timber*, Thomas Fuller's *Worthies*, and John Aubrey's *Brief Lives*.[84] No attempt was made to authenticate the incidents described in these accounts with documentary evidence. Because their ultimate sources were generally unacknowledged or inaccessible, their reliability could not be

---

[82] McKerrow, 'The Treatment of Shakespeare's Text', p. 30.

[83] Ibid.

[84] Chambers prints the traditional anecdotes in *William Shakespeare*, ii. 238–302. They are discussed by G. E. Bentley, *Shakespeare: A Biographical Handbook* (Princeton, NJ, 1961), pp. 6–15 and Schoenbaum, *Shakespeare's Lives*, pp. 75–143.

verified. Thus Aubrey, 100 years after Shakespeare's boyhood, claimed to have heard from some of Shakespeare's neighbours that Shakespeare would 'make a Speech' in his father's butcher shop while slaying a calf.[85] William Oldys, in the middle of the eighteenth century, learned of the deer-poaching incident from 'a very aged gentleman living in the neighbourhood of Stratford' who himself had heard it 'from several old people in that town'; from the same 'old people', the 'very aged gentleman' heard 'a bitter ballad' Shakespeare allegedly wrote to avenge himself on his prosecutor, 'which his relation very curteously communicated to [Oldys]'.[86] The validity of these accounts depended not on their factual accuracy as verified by documents, but on the circumstance of their having been accepted and transmitted from generation to generation.

The first eighteenth-century editor of Shakespeare, Nicholas Rowe, attempted to gather all the reports about Shakespeare in order to publish them in the preface to his 1709 edition. The result was a forty-page essay entitled 'Some Account of the Life &c. of Mr. William Shakespeare'. Towards the end of the account, Rowe acknowledged that most of the biographical materials had been collected by the actor Thomas Betterton, who had visited Shakespeare's birthplace and home 'on purpose to gather up what Remains he could of a Name for which he had so great a Value'.[87] Betterton had sought out these 'Remains' not in local archives, registers, and documents, but in conversation: in talking to people who had heard accounts from their ancestors who in turn had heard them from theirs and in some cases theirs before them. Any account that had been passed down over the generations from Shakespeare's relations, friends, and neighbours to their descendants was worthy of credit; if an account had been objectionable, it would have dropped out of circulation. Rowe, for example, admitted that he himself would have doubted and therefore omitted a report of Southampton's extreme munificence to Shakespeare were it not that Shakespeare's proclaimed dramatic heir and alleged natural son was supposed source: 'If I had not been assur'd that the Story was handed down by Sir *William D'Avenant*, who was probably very well acquainted with his Affairs, I

[85] Chambers, *William Shakespeare*, ii. 252–3.
[86] Ibid. ii. 279.   [87] Smith, *Eighteenth Century Essays*, p. 19.

should not have ventur'd to have inserted [it]'.[88] He apparently
did exercise such discretion in omitting the very report which
imputed Davenant's paternity to Shakespeare. According to
the account, related in Aubrey's *Brief Lives* and said to have
been repeated by Davenant himself, an Oxford townsman had
warned the boy Davenant not to 'take God's name in vain' by
referring to Shakespeare as his god-father; that the boy's mother,
'a woman of great beauty and sprightly wit', who owned the
tavern where Shakespeare often baited on his trips between
London and Stratford, had aroused suspicions that the relation
between the two Williams was more than a spiritual or literary
one.[89] Pope also excluded it from the preface, not because he
mistrusted his source, but because in biological no less than
stylistic matters he preferred that creation occur by the rules,
by legitimate 'regular production' rather than by adulterous
'grafting'.[90] The account's expurgation by the century's first
two Shakespearean editors marks the onset of a new piety that
disallowed the vagaries central to a number of the earlier
accounts. Yet it is not facts that invalidated certain reports, but
rather the reporter's discretion as directed by principles of
decorum and taste.

Rowe's 'Account' became the basis of every printed account
of Shakespeare's life until Malone's posthumously published
1821 edition, where it appeared not as biography but as one of
the editorial prefaces collected in that variorum edition. Like
the received Shakespeare text, the received life had been emended
—Pope omitted several passages and Theobald and Johnson
added some new materials. And like the received text, it was
criticized, though never for factual inaccuracy: Warburton
thought it insubstantial, 'a meagre Account . . . interlarded
with some common-place Scraps from his Writings'; and
Johnson complained of its stylistic infelicities: it was 'not
written with much elegance or spirit'.[91] Despite its faults,
nevertheless it was not supplanted until Malone's biography,

---

[88] Ibid. 5–6.
[89] Malone finds this account in William Oldys's manuscript notes and prints it after
Rowe's 'Account' in his 1790 edition (p. 158) and in the appendix to his own 'Life' in
the 1821 edition (p. 464). On the various accounts associating Shakespeare with
Davenant, see Schoenbaum, *Shakespeare's Lives*, pp. 98–108.
[90] Quoted by Malone, *PPWS*, i. 159–60.
[91] Smith, *Eighteenth Century Essays*, pp. 90, 133.

for as Johnson admitted, 'it relates . . . what is now to be known' of Shakespeare's life.[92] Not until Capell and Malone was the 'Account' considered trivial and inaccurate. Capell dismissed its 'traditional stories' as 'trifling in themselves, supported by small authority', and hoped 'to spirit some one up' to the writing of a new and 'masterly "Life of Shakespeare"' substantiated by documents: the title-pages of plays, his father's grant of arms, the patent granted by James, Shakespeare's last will and testament, and accounts of the monument to himself and his daughter.[93] In his first, 1790 edition Malone did not take up the task, although he did attempt 'to supply the defects [of Rowe's account] . . . by adding to it copious annotations . . . written for the purpose of demolishing almost every statement which it contained',[94] followed by documents many of which he himself had uncovered. Dissatisfied with the piecemeal result, he proposed in 1796 'an entirely New Life of Shakspeare Compiled from Original and Authentick Documents'. The advertisement for the edition urged readers to be on the alert for relevant documents and guaranteed that Shakespeare's life could be authentically reconstructed 'if Persons possessed of ancient Papers would take the trouble to examine them, or permit others to peruse them'.[95] For the remaining sixteen years of his life, Malone continued to collect all available source materials, combing through registers in Stratford and its environs, scrutinizing whatever documents fell into his hands, hoping additional ones would be unearthed. Glutted with documents, the biography remained incomplete at the time of Malone's death in 1812, and it fell upon James Boswell to bring it to press as the 525-page second volume of the 1821 variorum.

In his life of Shakespeare based on authentic materials, Malone dismissed the inherited anecdotes just as he had the received text of Shakespeare: he was 'not satisfied with receiving the aggregated wisdom of ages as a free gift'.[96] At the beginning of the biography, he ran through the anecdotes or 'traditionary

---

[92] Smith. *Eighteenth Century Essays*, p. 133.
[93] Capell. *MWSHCHT*, i. 72–4.   [94] Malone, *PPWS*, i. xix.
[95] Malone appended his 1795 'Proposals for an Edition of Shakspeare' to his 1796 *Inquiry*, so that 'by being more widely circulated [it] may perhaps be the means of . . . drawing from some hitherto unexplored Repository papers of a very different complexion from the miserable trash we have now been examining'.
[96] Malone–Boswell, *PPWS*, ii. 289.

tales' that had been circulating from the seventeenth century, measured them against the facts, and rejected them if they failed to correspond. Although at the beginning of the century it was agreed that Rowe's 'Life' had 'perfectly exhausted that subject',[97] Malone found it astonishingly inadequate. That for a period of eighty years, 'all the editors of his works, and each successive English Biographer, should have been contented with Mr. Rowe's meagre and imperfect narrative' was a circumstance which could 'not be contemplated without astonishment'.[98] What particularly shocked Malone about Rowe's account was that it consisted of so few facts, much less accurate facts: 'It is somewhat remarkable that in Rowe's Life of our author, there are not more than *eleven* facts mentioned; and of these, on a critical examination, *eight* will be found false.'[99] Of the remaining three, one was doubtful and the other two—records of his baptism and burial—were no further from general view than the Stratford parish register.

Malone attributed the inadequacies of the earlier accounts to his predecessors' lack of interest: had Shakespeare been appreciated 'in the same degree as he is now, the enthusiasm of some one or other of his admirers in the last age would have induced him to make some enquiries concerning the history of his theatrical career, and the anecdotes of his private life'.[100] Yet it was the kind of interest rather than its degree that set these 'admirers' apart from Malone. 'Traditionary tales', as their very paucity of factual information suggested, were not concerned with actual and verifiable occurrences. Rather than individuating Shakespeare by amassing particulars corroborated by facts residing in documents, the anecdotes set him in relation to the community, frequently in a public place of exchange—a shop, theatre, or tavern. Whether any incident had actually occurred may have been a matter of indifference, for what mattered was how that incident dramatized the peculiar problem posed by Shakespeare's art. The anecdotes repeatedly recorded occasions in which Shakespeare over-

[97] Charles Gildon, 'An Essay on the Art, Rise and Progress of the Stage in Greece, Rome and England', *The Works of Mr. William Shakespear* (London, 1725), aʳ. This volume, containing Shakespeare's poems, was spuriously appended to Pope's six-volume 1725 edition.

[98] Malone–Boswell, *PPWS*, ii. 11.

[99] Ibid. ii. 69–70.   [100] Malone, *PPWS*, i. i. lxxii.

stepped the bounds of propriety: the boy Shakespeare reciting verse while slaying calves in his father's butcher shop; the young Shakespeare writing a vindictive ballad to avenge the magistrate who prosecuted him for deer-poaching; the mature Shakespeare pre-empting Richard Burbage's tryst by claiming that William the Conqueror preceded Richard III; the older Shakespeare improvising in a tavern a scurrilous and unforgivable epitaph to a miserly friend. The repeated focus on Shakespeare in various indecorous and transgressive acts involving trickery, retaliation, deceit, and insult may have reflected a certain unease about his particular bent of genius: its unruliness, or, in the terms repeated in commentary of this period, his 'extravagance' and 'licentiousness'. The anecdotes portrayed Shakespeare's genius at various stages of his life put to merely personal or wilful use, invariably resulting in infractions of propriety, morality, and the law. They demonstrated the risible and minatory potential of 'natural' genius before it was idealized by Romanticism, the wayward tendencies of artistic power when not cultivated by education, classical models, or perhaps performance or publication. While the anecdotes may not have conformed with facts, they clearly conformed with how Shakespeare was perceived, as early as the Folio's influential characterization: short on education, original rather than imitative, natural rather than artful, spontaneous rather than industrious.

Three accounts seem to respond to the lack of legitimation expressed in the inculpatory *exempla*. In all three, Shakespeare's extravagant and vagrant genius yielded to high, even sovereign authority. In one, the Earl of Southampton rewarded Shakespeare with the lavish gift of a thousand pounds; in another, James I honoured him with a letter of high praise; and in a third, the most interesting in the present biographical context, Queen Elizabeth commanded Shakespeare to write a third part to *Henry IV* which would feature Falstaff—whose surname, like the author's *Hasti-vibrans*, had martial and heraldic overtones —in love, as if desirous to see the old fat rogue, extravagant by his own admission ('I liue out of all order, out of compasse,'[101]) get his comic come-uppance for romantic indecorums just as his namesake had received his historical put-down for political

---

[101] Hinman, *TNF*, 64.

transgressions. In these three transactions Shakespeare, rather than spurning societal norms and laws, is patronized, commended, and solicited by the ruling establishment.

'Extravagance' characterized accounts of Shakespeare's life just as 'irregularity' distinguished his works, during the Restoration and beyond. The roguish traditional tales and their inversions are the biographical corollary of the critical debate initiated by Thomas Rymer in 1693 concerning Shakespeare's violation of Aristotelian and Horatian precepts that did not taper off until, predictably, the end of the next century.[102] They also have a textual equivalent in Shakespeare's notoriously erring and erratic text. Even the long history of theatrical adaptation that begins in the Restoration addresses the same perceived need to bring Shakespeare within the bounds of decency, morality, and form.[103]

Committed to only those biographical materials which could be authenticated, Malone had little use for accounts which had been passed down first by word of mouth and then in written form. 'Traditionary tales' could be credited only if the facts were accurate to begin with and were then entrusted to responsible transmitters, only when 'handed down, by a very industrious and careful inquirer, who has derived it from persons most likely to be accurately informed concerning the fact related and subjoins his authority'.[104] Yet Malone still discredited accounts even when admitting their 'genealogy . . . very correctly deduced'.[105] Although, for example, the account of Shakespeare's holding horses outside the theatre upon his arrival in London had 'certainly a very fair pedigree' which could be traced from Davenant, Betterton, Rowe, Pope, Newton, Cibber, and Johnson, 'notwithstanding . . . I am utterly incredulous'.[106] While there may have been no evidence to corroborate this anecdote, it easily falls into relation with the anecdotes dealing with unbridled genius: rather than poaching deer in a private park, he reins in horses outside the public

---

[102] For a lucid account of the neo-classical debate over Shakespeare's eccentricities, see Vickers, *Critical Heritage*, ii. 1–12. On the supplanting of this debate by character study at the end of the eighteenth century, see Smith, *Eighteenth Century Essays*, xxi–xxxii and Vickers, *Critical Heritage*, vi. 16–33.

[103] See Vickers's list of the Shakespearean violations the stage adaptations were designed to remove: *Critical Heritage*, i. 6.

[104] Malone–Boswell, *PPWS*, ii. 119.   [105] Ibid. 158.   [106] Ibid. 159.

theatre (and for pay), as if his license in Stratford were brought under control in London. Malone mistrusted reports and reporters, querying the word of the Folio compilers Heminge and Condell concerning the authority of their copies as well as that of the editor Rowe in delivering unverifiable biographical materials based on Thomas Betterton's alleged but unverified trip to Stratford.[107] The process of biographical transmission was thus as suspect as that of textual transmission: both processes were seen to contaminate rather than to endorse the materials they conveyed, each successive step multiplying the possibility of error rather than testifying to its enduring acceptability and relevance.

In respect of the biography, too, the concept of authenticity protected Shakespeare from spurious materials, most of which, as we have seen and will see again, implicated him in socially transgressive acts. By linking Shakespeare to a past defined by facts and documents, Malone cut him off from the traditional context that had made his life relevant to those who discussed it, just as emendation and criticism made his texts relevant to current usage and values.

By reaching across the generations between himself and Shakespeare, by rejecting the traditional tales in favour of the authentic documents, Malone abstracted the life from broader social and moral concerns and sealed it in an historically remote past constructed of authentic papers. No longer a compilation of discrete exempla each illustrating a different facet or facets of the poet's relation to society, Shakespeare's life was on its way to becoming a self-contained narrative held together by its own causal and chronological design.

The same traversal of the received and inherited in order to retrieve the authentic can be charted through the portraits of Shakespeare featured in the major seventeenth- and eighteenth-century editions up to Malone. The first image to have been published was the now famous engraving by William Droeshout that appeared on the title-page of the 1623 Folio (Pl. 1). Since the engraving was taken after Shakespeare's death, it has been assumed that it was based on an extant likeness, either a

---

[107] Malone, *PPWS*, i. xii–iii; Malone–Boswell, *PHHJ*, ll. ʟ...

drawing or a portrait. The only evidence that the image indeed resembled Shakespeare is his colleagues' acceptance of the likeness for the publication, and Ben Jonson's conventional testimony in the accompanying verse 'To the Reader': 'This Figure, that thou here seest put, | It was for gentle Shakespeare cut; | Wherein the Grauer had a strife | With Nature, to out-doo the life.' Whatever its relation to what Shakespeare had actually looked like, the engraving passed as Shakespeare's likeness in all four seventeenth-century Folios, though the plate was not exactly identical for the four editions. Even for the First Folio, the plate went through at least two different states; after a few copies in the first state had been printed, Droeshout, it has been assumed, improved the plate by adding a shadow on the collar, thickening the moustache, and lengthening the right eyebrow.[108] In different stages of touching up and wearing out, the same engraved plate was used throughout the seventeenth-century folio series. The likeness was given more currency still when copied with slight variations and embellishments for the illustrations on frontispieces to other publications by or about Shakespeare: John Benson's 1640 *Poems* (Pl. 4), the 1655 edition of Shakespeare's *Rape of Lucrece* (Pl. 5), and John Cotgrave's 1662 *Witts Interpreter*.

The 'received' Droeshout image changed, however, just at the point when the massive single folio of the seventeenth century broke into the eighteenth century's multiple volumes; just at the point, too, when the Tonson publishing house announced its ownership of the collected Shakespeare by producing the first of what was to be a long line of Shakespeare editions. In 1708 a new image conveniently surfaced to replace the worn Droeshout plate: a portrait in the possession of Thomas Betterton, the Restoration actor sent to Stratford by Rowe to collect biographical materials; eventually it devolved to the Duke of Chandos by whose name it came to be known (Pl. 7). An engraving from this newly discovered painting appeared on the frontispiece of Nicholas Rowe's 1709 *The Works of Mr. William Shakespear* (Pl. 9). Along with the change from one folio volume to six octavo volumes, the substitution of

---

[108] On these changes, see Spielmann, 'Shakespeare's Portraiture', pp. 40–3 and Paul Bertram and Frank Cossa, ' "Willm Shakespeare 1609": The Flower Portrait Revisited', *Shakespeare Quarterly*, 86 (1985), p. 2.

'Some Account of the Life, &c.' for the Folio preliminaries, and the introduction of an engraved illustration for each play, the replacement of the Droeshout engraving by the Chandos image announced a major bibliographic event: the eighteenth-century volumes of the *Works of Mr. William Shakespear* had supplanted the seventeenth-century folio of *Mr. William Shakespeares Comedies, Histories, & Tragedies*. All subsequent major eighteenth-century editions of the collected works were in multiple volumes ranging from six to ten, all included in the prefatory materials a life more or less based on Rowe's 'Account', and at least up to the Johnson–Steevens edition of 1773, all of them and their re-prints included a likeness based on the Chandos portrait (Pls. 10–14). As a result of its reproduction in Shakespeare editions as well as in more general compendia, no picture in the century was more frequently copied.[109]

Yet the acceptance of the image as Shakespeare's did not depend on the establishment of its authenticity. In Rowe's 1709 edition, the same authority backed both the portrait and most of the materials for his 'Account of the Life': namely, the word of Thomas Betterton, who had both owned the portrait and gathered reports relating to Shakespeare in Warwickshire. In the same way that no documentation was required to support the materials mounted in the 'Account' until Malone, so too none was necessary to validate the portrait. In editions up to Malone's, repeated duplication and circulation would have been sufficient grounds for accepting the likeness, just as it had been for crediting the anecdotes. Despite its obvious deviation from Shakespeare's likeness in the Folio engraving and the Stratford Monument, the question of whether or not the Chandos portrait actually resembled Shakespeare seems not to have arisen any more than the question of whether the anecdotal incidents actually occurred. Furthermore, when the exact cor-respondence of the original portrait to its subject was of no concern, reproductions of that portrait did not strive for fidelity. After listing twelve engravings taken from the Chandos Shake-speare, Steevens noted with some exaggeration: 'No two of

---

[109] Spielmann, 'Shakespeare's Portraiture', p. 39. See Schoenbaum's discussion of 'Various Pictures', *Shakespeare's Lives*, pp. 279–94 and David Piper, '*O Sweet Mr. Shakespeare I'll have his picture*': *The Changing Image of Shakespeare's Person 1600–1800* (Washington, DC, 1964).

these Portraits are alike nor does any one of them bear the slightest resemblance to its wretched original.'[110] A glance at the sequence of engravings certainly reveals little attempt to be faithful either to earlier engravings or to the painting itself. In the same way as the earliest texts were assigned no special authority in the construction of new editions, so too the original portrait commanded no fidelity in the engraved reproductions. The earliest Folio and quartos were ignored, the documents remained buried in archives, and the portrait went unremarked: not because they were inaccessible, but because no need was felt to recover a remote text, life, and likeness when current ones remained in circulation. The earlier eighteenth-century editors were as little interested in ascertaining what Shakespeare in fact had looked like than what he in fact had done or what he in fact had put on paper.

The eighteenth-century engravings of Shakespeare did not resemble one another or the original closely enough to be considered accurate reproductions; they were familiar simulations rather than exact duplications. The question of whether the engravers possessed the skill to render exact reproductions obscures a more relevant consideration: the published images of Shakespeare did not after 1710 stand exclusively for the author of the *Works*, but also represented the publishing house that owned those works through most of the century. The image served as the house-mark of the Tonson publishing house, appearing on many of their title-pages as well as on the sign to their shop, which in 1710 had relocated to Shakespeare's Head in the Strand.[111] Approximations of Shakespeare's visage were inseparable from the claims of the institution that preserved, promoted, and distributed him as the most important dramatic author in the language.

The function of the frontispiece portraits was not to preserve

---

[110] Malone–Boswell, *PPWS*, i. 258. An Act was passed in 1735 to provide engravers with copyright protection; however, it was designed to protect original designs like Hogarth's rather than reproductions of a common subject, and so variation in the framework would have been sufficient to avoid commission of an infraction. See David Hunter, 'Copyright Protection for Engravings and Maps in Eighteenth-Century Britain', *The Library*, 6th ser., 9 (1987), 128–47.

[111] For the Chandos portrait as the Tonson trademark and colophon, see Harry M. Geduld, *Prince of Publishers: A Study of the Work and Career of Jacob Tonson* (Bloomington, Ind., 1969), p. 143.

what Shakespeare had looked like, but to celebrate the dramatic pre-eminence that the edition claimed for him. The engravings, rather than retrieving Shakespeare from the past, positioned him in a tradition of poetic and dramatic works as represented by various iconographic and ornamental devices. The space of the engraved frontispiece to the first eighteenth-century edition (Pl. 9) was dominated not by Shakespeare's portrait, but rather by the plinth on which it rests and the figures surrounding it: the overarching angel and the two flanking figures who crown Shakespeare's portrait with laurels, one of whom treads on abject Ignorance. That the frame was lifted from the 1660 Rouen edition of Corneille would have further enhanced the effect (Pl. 8).[112] By appropriating its ornate apparatus in order to crown Shakespeare, the engraving resolved the contest between French regulated Art and the English natural genius: the modern portrait of the English contender had usurped the classical bust of his French co-rival. Later engravers did not return to the actual portrait in making new plates any more than later editors returned to the First Folio and early quartos, but instead took recent engravings as their model. Throughout this succession of frontispieces, the engraving asserted Shakespeare's status as classical poet and dramatist rather than faithfully reproducing what he had actually looked like. Johnson's 1765 edition proclaimed that status further by the variorum format itself, the apparatus designed for ancient or classical works, as well as in the opening of his preface: 'The Poet, of whose works I have undertaken the revision, may now begin to assume the dignity of an ancient, and claim the privilege of established fame and prescriptive veneration.'[113] In editions up to Malone, a classicizing or monumentalizing apparatus always encased Shakespeare's likeness, conferring upon him the immortality ascribed to Jonson's works by the title-page engraving in the 1616 Folio. The engraving used various iconographic images—laurels, pens, masks, lyres, cornucopiae, books—in order to exalt Shakespeare within a tradition of dramatic and poetic works ratified by the publication itself.

Like the editions from 1709 to 1773, Malone's 1790 *Plays and Poems* instated the Chandos portrait but with a crucial

---

[112] On the origin of the frontispiece's framework, see Piper, *Image*, p. 52.
[113] Smith, *Eighteenth Century Essays*, p. 105.

difference (Pl. 16). Malone, as might be expected, *was* interested both in what Shakespeare actually looked like and in accurately producing that likeness. He was the first to provide a full pedigree of the portrait's 'authenticated possessors' from William Davenant, who he thought had purchased it from Shakespeare's colleagues themselves when 'reduced to great distress' after the theatres were shut down, all the way through to the Duke of Chandos in his own time.[114] In 1786, he arranged with the owner for the artist Ozias Humphry to do a drawing from the portrait itself, and it was from that drawing (Pl. 15), which Malone kept in his study, that the print prefixed to the 1790 edition was engraved. While the surrounding paraphernalia are more ornate than ever—the plinth opening up to picture Fame decorating Shakespeare's sarcophagus—the portrait is clearly a copy rather than a rendition of the portrait.

A more precise copy still appears on the frontispiece to the 1821 edition (Pl. 17) which included discussions of its authenticity in both the advertisement and the biography.[115] The resulting image, 'engraved with more than former care and elegance', is stunningly different from its predecessors. It breaks with the traditional likenesses, not only in its exacting fidelity to the original, but also in having removed all inherited iconographic trappings, including the oval cartouche. Without them, the picture no longer functions to situate and celebrate Shakespeare in the tradition of venerable ancient writing reflected and promoted by a powerful publishing house. Though a print taken from an engraving taken from a painting, this illustration gives the impression of being an unmediated image of Shakespeare as he looked in 1607, the supposed date of the portrait— an unmediated authorial image to accompany 'the author's unsophisticated text' and his unadulterated life.[116] And just as the editor had gone back to the 'authentick editions' in establishing his text and the 'authentick documents' in preparing his edition and life, so too his draughtsman returned to the Chandos portrait, the closest substitute for an encounter with Shakespeare himself. For the first time, we have a verisimilitudinous picture of Shakespeare rather than a coronation portrait. The divestment of the image implied no diminution in its subject's

---

[114] Malone–Boswell, *PPWS*, ii. 510–12.
[115] Ibid. i. xxiv–vii, ii. 511.   [116] Ibid. i. x.

status, but rather a different source for that status. No longer was it conferred upon him by the external critical acclaim symbolized by the classical icons, 'the privilege of established fame and prescriptive veneration' that, for Johnson, was bestowed by generations of critics and readers: 'Yet it must be at last confessed, that as we owe every thing to him, he owes something to us; that, if much of his praise is paid by perception and judgement, much is likewise given by custom and veneration'.[117] Shakespeare's status was now self-evident and self-ordained. At the end of the century, the primary issue was no longer whether Shakespeare could be considered a classic despite his violation of the rules of criticism, as it had been in the Tonson editions. Malone's concern was not with establishing Shakespeare's importance in relation to traditional prescripts and reception, but in preparing him, as we shall see increasingly, to appear as the well-spring of his own artistry.

The same authenticization and divestiture of Shakespeare's likeness can be traced through the sequence of engravings of Shakespeare's Stratford Monument (Pl. 18).[118] The first engraving appeared in William Dugdale's 1656 *Antiquities of Warwickshire* and deviated conspicuously from the monument itself, though it has been assumed that the engraver had observed the original in Warwickshire (Pl. 19). The deviations were so great—the cherubs are perched on the edge of the cornice instead of seated on mounds, Shakespeare sits poised before a pillow rather than pen in hand, leopards appear on either side of the frieze—that it was at one time thought that only an alteration of the actual monument sometime after 1656 could account for the difference between the seventeenth-century engraving and the monument as it stood in the next century.[119] In 1709, Rowe's engraver obviously looked at Dugdale's drawing rather than the monument itself, for he reproduced its innovations (Pl. 20)—as did the engraver for an edition in 1786. George Vertue in 1723 was more faithful to its details, though in addition to replacing the hour-glass and arrow in the cherubs' hands with burning tapers, he took the liberty of substituting the head on the monument with that of

---

[117] Smith, *Eighteenth Century Essays*, pp. 105, 130–1.
[118] Spielmann, *'Shakespeare's Portraiture'*, pp. 19–25.
[119] Chambers, *William Shakespeare*, ii. 185.

the Chandos portrait (Pl. 21), as did Gravelot for Hanmer's 1744 edition (Pl. 22). But Malone's engraver returned to the Stratford Monument, just as he had to the Chandos portrait, or at least to the plaster facsimile of the bust which Malone himself possessed.[120] In the engraving, Shakespeare's effigy appears once again without encasing ornaments and icons, to the same effect of untrammelled immediacy (Pl. 23). In Malone's eyes, no previous engraving could possibly have been authentic, for it was only in 1793 that he succeeded in persuading the authorities to return the monument to what he believed to be its original stone colour. In this instance, Malone's obsession with authenticity was indistinguishable from the very neo-classicizing impulse he deplored. The statue had never been monochrome; the original colours were restored in 1861.[121]

With both manuscripts and portraits, the emergent criterion of authenticity was attended by attempts to simulate that authenticity. William Henry Ireland's fabrication of Elizabethan and Jacobean manuscripts and documents was matched by the appearance of what was, in Malone's eyes at least, a counterfeit portrait of Shakespeare. Steevens, in the 1793 edition in which, as we shall see in the next chapter, he contradicted his some-time collaborator Malone on so many issues, denied not only the authenticity of the Chandos portrait but the likelihood that any authentic portrait had ever existed. Shakespeare, he claimed, had had no more interest in preserving his likeness through portraiture than his works through publication: 'As he was careless of the future state of his works, his solicitude might not have extended to the perpetuation of his looks.'[122] Though he consequently prefixed no image to his 1793 edition, in the following year he played so instrumental a role in bringing to light a new painted contender that he was suspected of being involved in its manufacture.[123] This was the Felton portrait, which Steevens insisted was the original from which the en-gravings of both the 1623 Folio and a 1640 octavo entitled *Poems Written by Wil. Shake-speare* had been taken. An engraving from

[120] Piper, '*O Sweet Mr. Shakespeare*', p. 10.
[121] See Chambers, *William Shakespeare*, ii. 184 and Spielmann, 'Shakespeare's Portrait-ure', pp. 23–4.
[122] Malone–Boswell, *PPWS*, i. 254.
[123] For Steevens's interest in the Felton portrait, see ibid. xxvii and Schoenbaum, *Shakespeare's Lives*, pp. 287–91.

this portrait was affixed with Steevens's endorsement[124] to both the 1803 Steevens–Reed edition and its 1813 successor. According to what remains the most thorough study on Shakespeare's portraiture, up until the 1790 appearance of the Felton portrait 'no fabrications of portraits of Shakespeare, painted with deliberate intent to deceive, were known'.[125] There were copies of paintings, certainly, and there were paintings like that prefixed to Pope's 1725 edition that were mistakenly taken to be of Shakespeare, but none which attempted to pass itself off as the real thing.[126] It appears, then, that at the same time as the authentic texts, documents, and paintings were established, inauthentic items and counterfeits began to emerge. The real proliferation of forgeries did not begin until the early nineteenth century, after the standard of authenticity was firmly in place.[127]

With respect to the selection of the portrait as well as to the establishment of the texts and the construction of the life, Malone bypassed generational transmission in order to get back to the authentic Shakespeare. He returned directly to his likeness painted in 1607, his life recorded in contemporary documents, and his texts preserved in the earliest printed editions, all in pursuit of the authentic Shakespeare—or rather 'Shakspeare' as he spelled it on the basis of 'instances from authentick documents', but above all Shakespeare's own autograph: 'he himself wrote his name without the middle e.'[128] As might be expected in an edition devoted to an unmediated text, life, and likeness, transcriptions of Shakespeare's name written in his own hand were printed from two documents—three from

---

[124] Malone–Boswell, *PPWS*, i. 281.

[125] Spielmann, 'Shakespeare's Portraiture', p. 46. Boswell himself was taken in by a miniature, which he had engraved for the frontispiece of vol. ii of the 1821 edition, believing that it 'bore the strongest Marks of authenticity': Malone–Boswell, *PPWS*, i. xxvii–vii; see Schoenbaum, *Shakespeare's Lives*, p. 292.

[126] For Shakespeare's portrait, Pope printed an engraving by George Virtue of an unidentified gentleman in a ruff (Boaden identified him as James I; *An Inquiry into the Authenticity of Various Pictures and Prints*, p. 131), a case of mistaken identity rather than of counterfeiting. See Piper, *Image*, p. 103.

[127] See Piper, *Image*, p. 102. On the appearance of 'pseudo-portraits' of Shakespeare in the late eighteenth and nineteenth centuries which culminated in the desire to open Shakespeare's grave and photograph his skull, see Schoenbaum, *Shakespeare's Lives*, pp. 464–73.

[128] Malone–Boswell, *PPWS*, ii. 14.

his will and one from his mortgage—and, also as might be expected, in facsimile, a new and more exact mode of reproduction developed in the last quarter of the eighteenth century.[129] It was from these facsimiles that William Henry Ireland based his forgeries of Shakespeare's signature, the faithful authentic reproduction serving here too as model for its fraudulent forged counterpart.[130]

In 1807 the First Folio itself was for the first time set in type facsimile. Delivering an exact copy of the original, the facsimile appears as the mechanical culmination of the late-eighteenth-century interest in authenticity that sought to eliminate the distortions and corruptions of mediations by preserving the exact physical features of the original manuscript, printed page, painting, and engraving. What must be stressed, however, is the curious incompatibility of that mode of reproduction with the sixteenth- and seventeenth-century materials to which it was applied. That all four extant signatures rather than just one had to be printed to exemplify Shakespeare's signing of his own name suggests the basic illogicality of exactly reproducing an unfixed and unstable original. The oscillating and malleable nature of the original radically casts into doubt the authenticity of the reproduction. If each of the signatures consisted of different letters and of differently formed letters, how could any one be singled out as the original? This is, of course, the same problem as that faced by the editor of the 1968 photographic Norton facsimile of the First Folio, who, rather than printing any one of the seventy-seven single copies of the First Folio available to him, printed a composite made up of the most correctly printed pages. Were the same principle adopted in reproducing Shakespeare's signature, the facsimile would consist of a similar composite based on the fullest spelling and clearest letters from each of the available signatures. Facsimile reproduction presupposes the uniformity of a stable original for both script and print, for both Shakespeare's signature and his plays' texts.

---

[129] Malone accompanied Steevens to the Prerogative Office to make tracings of the signatures; see Charles Hamilton, *In Search of Shakespeare* (San Diego, Ca., 1985), p. 41. The result is reproduced in Malone, *PPWS*, i. 190.

[130] Hamilton reproduces Steevens's tracings of the signatures on the will as well as Ireland's tracings of Steevens's: *In Search of Shakespeare*, p. 41.

In the case of the 1623 Folio, however, what *is* the original or 'originall'?

Though by no means consistent, seventeenth-century usage of the term 'originall' appears not to have referred to what Shakespeare originally wrote, his authentic manuscript. In the playhouse, the legal owners of the play referred to the author's pennings by the hardly honorific terms 'fowle papers' or 'foule sheet[s]'.[131] If indeed they had on occasion surrendered these papers to the printing house, as some bibliographers have maintained, it was precisely because they were of little value to them.[132] That not a single popular professionally performed play has survived in manuscript from between 1580 and 1642 also suggests that they may not have been much cherished in either the theatre or the printing house.[133] In the sixteenth and seventeenth centuries, the term retained an earlier sense that associated it with theatrical production rather than authorial creation. 'Originall' or 'rygynall' or 'regenall' were terms used throughout records of the medieval stage to refer to the copy that directed performances, replacing the *ordo* of the liturgical drama.[134] Variant forms resembling 'regenall' suggested an association with *regere* that in turn connected it with its synonymic *ordo*. As so often in this prelexical period, verbal confusions or fusions intimate semantic connections. The word frequently referred to the stage copy that regulated or ordered performance, to the copy that had the strongest relation to production, to the medieval 'ordinale' or 'play-book'; in Shakespeare's theatre it was known as the prompt-book or, more simply, 'the book', and contained the interlineations, deletions,

---

[131] A copy of a recently discovered folded 'foul sheet' is reproduced in *William Shakespeare: A Textual Companion*, eds. Stanley Wells and Gary Taylor (Oxford, 1987), p. 6. On the aptness of the term 'foul sheets', especially from a theatrical point of view, see Timothy Murray, *Theatrical Legitimation: Allegories of Genius in Seventeenth-Century England and France* (New York, 1987), pp. 33–5.

[132] For McKerrow's theory that the players released to the printers the foul copies rather than the prepared and official prompt-copy, see W. W. Greg, *The Shakespeare First Folio: Its Bibliographical and Textual History* (Oxford, 1955) pp. 96–7.

[133] 'The facts can be summarized in this way: no play by a professional playwright which was successful on the stage and which was printed before 1642 is known to have come down to our time or near it.' Giles Dawson and Letitia Kennedy-Skipton, *Elizabethan Handwriting* (New York, 1966), p. 3.

[134] Chambers, *William Shakespeare*, i. 97 and *The Mediaeval Stage* (Oxford 1903), i. 143; and Greg, *The Shakespeare First Folio*, p. 101, note E.

and marginalia that both directed and recorded production.[135]
Pope in the preface to his edition of Shakespeare made the same
correlation in glossing Heminge and Condell's reference to 'the
Original Copies; I believe they meant those which had lain ever
since the Author's days in the play-house, and had from time to
time been cut, or added to, arbitrarily . . . printed (at least
partly) from no better copies than the *Prompter's Book* or *Piecemeal Parts* written out for the use of the actors . . .'.[136] 'The book'
was also the text with the endorsing seal of the Licenser or
Master of Revels on its final page, the seal which regulated it in
another sense by bringing it under the rule of the law—'under
the hand'. Officially approved for production, it was referred to
as the 'allowed book'.[137]

'Originall', it then appears, denoted proximity to the script
regulating performance and itself regulated by official super-
vision, rather than to Shakespeare's own manuscript.[138] Indeed,
the quartos published before the First Folio based their authority
not on their proximity to the author's papers, but on their
fidelity to a given performance. Title-pages which were both
affixed to publications to identify their content and tacked on
walls and posts to advertise them almost invariably announce
their relation to a given production: 'As it hath been often (with
great applause) plaid publiquely, by the right Honourable the
L. of Hundson his Seruants', 'As it hath been lately Acted by
the Right honourable the Lord Chamberlaine his seruants', 'As
it was presented before her Highness this last Christmas'.[139]
Sometimes title-pages were more specific, naming not only the

[135] Scott McMillin, *The Elizabethan Theatre and The Book of Sir Thomas More* (Ithaca,
NY, 1986).
[136] Smith, *Eighteenth Century Essays*, p. 54.
[137] On 'The Hand of the Master of Revels', see W. W. Greg, *Some Aspects and Problems
of London Publishing between 1550 and 1650* (Oxford, 1956), pp. 103–12; on the censor's
'allowance' on the prompt-copy, see Chambers, *William Shakespeare*, i. 98, 104.
[138] The editors of the new Oxford Shakespeare have aimed to reproduce the kind of
'original' that the above account would endorse. 'We have devoted our efforts to
recovering and presenting texts of Shakespeare's plays as they were acted in the
London play-houses': *The Complete Works*, eds. Stanley Wells and Gary Taylor (Oxford,
1986), p. xxxvii.
[139] On the posting of title-pages for advertising, see Marjorie Plant, *The English Book
Trade: An Economic History of the Making and Sale of Books* (London, 1939), p. 248.
Citations are from *Shakespeare's Plays in Quarto*, ed. Michael J. B. Allen and Kenneth
Muir (Berkeley, Ca, 1981) and appear on the title-pages for 1597 *Romeo and Iuliet*,
p. 117, 1597 *King Richard the third*, p. 244, and *Loues labors lost*, p. 292, respectively.

acting company, but the place and occasion of the production.
The 1603 *Hamlet* and the 1608 *King Lear*, for example, offer
more details: 'As it hath been diuerse times acted by his
Highnesse seruants in the Cittie of London: as also in the two
universities of Cambridge and Oxford, and else-where'; and
'As it was played before the King Majestie at Whitehall upon S.
Stephans night in Christmas Hollidayes. By his Maiesties
servants playing usually at the Gloabe on the Bancke-side'.[140]
While Shakespeare's name was not, at least until 1598, necessary,
the title of an authorizing dignitary was—'Lord of Hunsdon',
'the Lord Chamberlaine', 'her Highness', 'the King Majestie'.
Noble and royal titles legitimized not only 'vagabond' actors
(the Lord Chamberlain's Men, the Lord Admiral's Men, the
King's Men) but also 'riffe-raffe' quartos.

If the printed play text bore allegiance to variable performance
rather than to a stable authorial manuscript, the inattention of
printers to the specifics of their copy becomes less surprising.
Compositors introduced their own spelling and punctuation
and proof-readers routinely did not refer back to their copy in
making corrections because no particular sanctity was ascribed
to the original. For the same reason, reprints of a play in either
quarto or folio form were based on not the earliest available
edition, but the latest: the ones closest, at least in theory, to the
most recent or perhaps most prestigious production. When the
authority behind a given text resided in its fidelity to ever-
changing production, no particular copy—the authorial 'fowle'
manuscript perhaps least of all—commanded particular respect. That Shakespeare's name did not appear on the title-
page of a play until 1598, whereas the circumstances of the
performances did, suggests the subordinate role of authorship
to performance.[141] The copy remained faithful not to the
relative determinacy of the written authorial word but to the
exigencies of theatrical production.

It should be remembered, too, that the term 'copy' did not at
this point carry the same obligation to reproduce its precedent

[140] Allen and Muir, eds., *Shakespeare's Plays in Quarto: Loues labors lost*, pp. 579, 663
[141] In his discussion of the ever-varying criteria for textual, theatrical, and pictorial
authenticity, Stephen Orgel distinguishes between the authenticity of 'the acting text'
of a Shakespeare play and that of its putative authorial manuscript: 'The Authentic
Shakespeare', *Representations*, 21 (1988), p. 6.

with fidelity.[142] Like 'model', 'copy' could refer to both an original and a reproduction: when a writing master penned a model for his pupil to follow, he 'set the copy'; the copy followed by printers was their source or original, not a duplicate of some other primary text.[143] Even when 'copy' is used to refer to a duplicate, its sense is complicated by its then active etymological relation to the dynamically charged concept of *copia*. As Terence Cave has illustrated, the concept, deriving from Latin antiquity, pertained to a wide variety of material, natural, and figurative riches (*co-ops*).[144] When the term subsequently passed into the vernacular, it applied to a specifically technological mode of multiplication or increase: duplication in manuscript or later in print. The still active Latin etymology of the word associated 'copy' with 'copiousness', suggesting that the primary function of 'copying' a text was to make it abundant rather than uniform. By the time of the Renaissance, the mechanical reproduction of 'copy' bore affinities to the rhetorical rubric of *copia*, a figure of peculiar importance to the Renaissance that amplified and dilated its source in repeating or imitating it.[145] Both mechanical 'copy' and rhetorical *copia* bore generative or 'copious' relations to their antecedents that perpetuated them through supersession rather than duplication: the printed copy frequently advertised itself as 'perfecting' or 'making whole' what it reprinted while the rhetorical *copia* recommended itself as 'replenishing' or 'supplying' its model. 'Originall Copies' like those which the Folio purported to contain, might then be filled-out copies of the 'originall' that directed and recorded

---

[142] Even in Johnson's 1755 *Dictionary of the English Language* (New York, 1967), 'copy' and 'model' mean both source and duplicate: 'copy' is both 'a transcript from the archetype or originals' and 'the autograph; the original; the archetype'; a 'model' is both 'A representation in miniature' and 'A copy to be imitated.' It is still the case today in publishing and printing that the original manuscript is 'copy' both for the copy-editor and the typesetter.

[143] On 'setting copy,' see *A New Booke of Copies 1574*, ed. Bertholde Wolpe (London, 1962), p. 10.

[144] See Terence Cave's spectacular book on this figure in French Renaissance literature, *The Cornucopian Text: Problems of Writing in the French Renaissance* (Oxford, 1979), esp. ch. 1, 'Copia', pp. 3–34.

[145] On *copia* as a mode of generating texts through language, see Marion Trousdale's discussion of Erasmus's influential *De Ultraque Verborum ac Rerum Copia* in *Shakespeare and the Rhetoricians* (London, 1982), 43–51. Patricia Parker gives a rich display of linguistic increasing and multiplying in 'Literary Fat Ladies and the Generation of the Text', *Literary Fat Ladies, Rhetoric, Gender, Property* (London, 1987), pp. 8–35.

performance. This may explain the frequently noted disparity between the average time a play took to be performed (two or three hours) and the length it would take to read out most printed plays (three to four and a half hours).[146] The spare lines representing performance, limited by the economics of production, would have been 'copied' and made 'copious' by the addition of the manifold possibilities representing other productions or possible productions. A 'perfect' or 'perfected' copy would have been one that had been made literally whole or complete—like the 1604 quarto of *Hamlet* that advertises itself as having been 'enlarged to almost as much againe as it was, according to the true and perfect Coppie'—increased or augmented in order to contain, not all that the author or authors had written, but all that had been produced or might be produced by the variable negotiations between enacted script and inscribed performance.[147]

The problems posed by the Shakespearean text might be formulated in terms of the incongruity between *copia*/abundance and *copia*/copy. How can an object that is amenable to continual expansion and modification be copied? How can a fundamentally pliable play text be reified by print? How can linguistic generativity be represented by precise mechanical duplication? The principle of authenticity presupposes a stable and unique manuscript behind the text, some type of document to which reproductions owe faithful homage. But if the 'original' was from the start variable—receptive to changes from actors, scribes, authors, revisers, censors, and accidental circumstances of all kinds—how could any particular copy be authentic? Walter Benjamin's observation in his influential essay 'The Work of Art in the Age of Mechanical Reproduction' proves strangely apt, though it concerns the irrelevance of authenticity to more modern modes of technical reproduction: 'The presence

---

[146] See Orgel's note on this discrepancy, 'The Authentic Shakespeare', p. 25, n. 11.

[147] Allen and Muir, *Shakespeare's Plays in Quarto*, p. 612. Both the Shakespeare and the Beaumont and Fletcher folios promise such a copious corpus: the former preferring plays 'cur'd, and perfect of their limbes' (*TNF*, p. 7) and the latter assuring that 'now you have both All that was Acted, and all that was not; even the perfect full Originalls without the least mutilation', *Comedies and Tragedies* (London, 1647), 'The Stationer to the Reader'. See Greg, *The Shakespeare First Folio*, p. 101 appx. E and Chambers, *William Shakespeare*, i. 98.

of the original is the prerequisite to the concept of authenticity.'[148] Like photography and film, the printed play text throws the possibility of authenticity into question by problematizing the existence of a separate and fixed antecedent; strictly speaking, there is no original behind any of these processes of reproduction. Malone's documents, records, and manuscripts (both putative and actual), substituted for the missing Shakespearean originals: the manuscripts he assumed behind the quarto and First Folio play texts, the documents he recovered preserving the events of Shakespeare's life, the verisimilitudinous portraits by which he visualized his likeness. Once an original had been postulated, an authentic representation could be presented (or, in the case of consequent forgeries and counterfeits, misrepresented).

Malone's authentic reproductions need to be seen in the context of the problem of copying *copia*, the impossible project of settling in reproduction what was never settled in production. Earlier editors had different tactics for regulating Shakespeare's proverbially unruly generativity, what Johnson anxiously described in the language of the *copia* tradition as a forest of 'endless diversity', a mine of 'unexhaustible plenty'. They corrected his anomalous texts, judged his stylistic vagaries, recounted his biographical excesses, reformed his dramatic indecorums. While the principle of authenticity appears to offer an objective solution to the absence of a precise standard by which to prepare Shakespeare, it too functions to manage Shakespeare's intractability by making it responsible to external criteria. Authenticity is thus no more and no less than a new mode of bringing Shakespeare under rule through a standard of historical objectivity which, as we shall see, has surprisingly determining implications for the subject Shakespeare.

[148] Walter Benjamin, *Illuminations*, trans. Harry Zohn (New York, 1969), p. 220.

3
Situating Shakespeare in an Historical Period

MALONE was involved in another project requiring authenticity, though this one was neither Shakespearean nor even literary. In 1782 he advised John Singleton Copley on a painting of *Charles I Demanding in the House of Commons the Five Impeached Members* (Pl. 24).[1] The painting was to depict a momentous confrontation between the King and Parliament, one which was thought to have precipitated the Civil War and its sequel up to the Glorious Revolution. Although Malone may also have suggested the subject, his primary interest was in the painting's style: every feature was to be based on authentic documents. The faces of Charles I, Prince Rupert, and the fifty-six members of the House were to be painted from likenesses taken in their lifetimes; if those likenesses had not been made in 1642, they had to be aged or rejuvenated accordingly. All fifty-eight individuals were dressed according to the style of the time; the architecture and furnishings replicated exactly those of the House; and an attempt was made to position the members in relation both to one another and to the King and Speaker as they would have stood on the afternoon of 4 January 1642 when the event occurred. In a letter dated 4 January 1782, 140 years to the day after the event, Malone provided Copley with written and pictorial sources for the painting.[2] He referred Copley to Hume's *History of England* as well as to the eye-witness

---

[1] Roy Strong discusses this painting as an example of a new school of historical painting, 'artist–antiquarian', 1780 to 1815, which based its representations on authentic documentation rather than vague and generalized evocations of the past: '*And When Did You Last See Your Father?' The Victorian Painter and British History* (London, 1978), p. 24–9, 137–8. For an identification of the portraits and an account of the circumstances of both the painting's inception and its reception, see Julius David Prown, *John Singleton Copley in England 1774–1815* (Cambridge, Mass., 1966). E. H. Gombrich notes the novelty of both the painting's method and its subject, as well as its political implications, in *The Story of Art* (Englewood Cliffs, NJ, 1984), pp. 381–3.

[2] Malone's letter to Copley is discussed by Strong, *The Victorian Painter*, p. 28, and Prown, *John Singleton Copley*, pp. 337–40 and is reprinted in Martha Babcock Amory, *The Domestic and Artistic Life of John Singleton Copley, R.A.* (Boston, 1882), pp. 450–3.

accounts of the Members of Parliament on which it had been based: Frankland, Clarendon, Rushworth, and Whitlocke, all of whom were depicted in the painting. Copley also drew on the illustrations for the 1717 edition of Clarendon's *History of the Great Rebellion* and had access to John Thane's collection of portraits and handwriting, *Autography*, before its publication in 1793; and in order to track down additional sources he journeyed to various private collections. When finally first exhibited at the Royal Academy in 1795, thirteen years after its inception, the painting was accompanied by a brochure documenting the sources of the major portraits and thereby attesting to its 'general authenticity and truth'.[3]

As Malone emphasized in proposing the subject, the King's peremptory entry into the House, 'a high breach of the rights and privilege of Parliament, and inconsistent with the liberty of freedom', had important consequences: 'From this day we may reasonably date the levying of war in England, whatever hath been since done being but the superstructure upon the foundations then laid.'[4] Charles's infraction of Parliamentary privilege precipitated 'all the ensuing disorder and civil wars', not to be resolved until William and Mary's happy ascent to the throne in 1688. Thus the depicted event led to the securing of the traditional constitutional liberties England continued to enjoy in 1782 when Copley undertook the project. The subject of the painting thereby participated in an historical continuum that could be traced back to the Magna Carta of 1215 and extended through the Glorious Revolution and beyond, up to the moment of the painting's execution and viewing.

Yet the painting's scrupulous fidelity to authentic materials had a different effect: rather than drawing the event into the grand sweep of English history, it locked it into a frame singularly its own. The painting's details gave precise definition to the event as something true to itself and distinct from all other historical occurrences. The particular furnishings of the House and the individuated physiognomy, clothing, position, and gesture of the King, Prince, and each Member established the uniqueness of the event in time and space. As the criterion of authenticity cut Shakespeare's text off from the tradition of

---

[3] Prown quotes the brochure: *John Singleton Copley*, p. 348.
[4] Amory, *Life of John Singleton Copley*, p. 452.

the received text, so too did it cut historical painting off from the tradition by which the past was represented through a stock vocabulary of columns, drapes, generalized antique architecture, and costuming.

The term 'artist–antiquarian' has been assigned to the school of later eighteenth-century historical painters who, like Copley, researched their subjects in order to paint them with exacting fidelity to minute historical details.[5] Clearly Malone shared their commitment to the past as it existed in documents contemporaneous with their respective subjects, whether Shakespeare or Charles I. His contemporaries referred to him as an antiquarian, and he referred to his own undertakings as 'antiquarian researches' that contrasted with the 'modern sophistications' of others. As these painters went back to documents coeval with the times they illustrated, so Malone returned to authentic materials in order faithfully to reproduce Shakespeare's text, his biography, and his likeness. As artist-antiquarian painting differentiated and characterized various episodes of past history through discrete particulars, so too Malone's antiquarian scholarship began to give specific and unique character to Shakespeare's time. In both cases, documentation provided the precise details by which historical differentiation might occur. Out of what had formerly been a uniform and generalized past, a distinct and free-standing period began to crystallize.

It is at this juncture that the word 'period' came to refer not only to a cyclical recurrence but to a singular and definite span of time. Like the word 'revolution', 'period' originally designated cyclic natural phenomena pertaining primarily to astronomical bodies; both words comprehended the notion of a return to a former state.[6] Again like 'revolution', 'period' towards the end of the eighteenth century broke from its earlier sense in order to denote not something that had happened before but rather something unprecedented: the breakdown of the pre-existing order in the former case and a distinct temporal unit in the

[5] Strong, *The Victorian Painter*, pp. 24–9.

[6] For a discussion of how 'revolution' evolved from an astrological to a political term, see Melvin J. Lasky's two chapters on 'The Birth of Metaphor', in *Utopia and Revolution* (Chicago, 1976), pp. 219–59 and Ronald Paulson's comments, *Representations of Revolution: 1789–1820* (New Haven, Conn., 1983), pp. 2–4, 38–40, and esp. 49–52.

latter. As the new sense of 'revolution' allowed for no cyclical revolving, so the new sense of 'period' suggested no periodic recurrence. The changes in both terms signalled the disruption of an homogeneous past, by unique cataclysmic upheaval in the first case and into discrete temporal divisions in the second.

Documents were fundamental and pervasive in both Malone's Shakespeares, in the 1790 edition and especially in the much amplified 1821 variorum completed by James Boswell. The documents Malone relied on in the essays in his edition as well as in his massive notes to the plays and poems supplied the factual details by which Shakespeare's age was to be differentiated from the composite that formerly constituted England's past in the comments of earlier Shakespeareans as well as in the monumental histories of David Hume and William Robertson.[7] Comprised of distinct and detailed characteristics, the time during which Shakespeare wrote came to possess a language, literature, institutions, customs, and practices of its own that were not answerable to subsequent standards and expectations. The various particulars emerging from documents coalesced into a period, an integral diachronic division distinct in character and standards from its temporal surroundings.

Because we take historical periods for granted—whether we refer to Shakespeare's as Elizabethan, Jacobean, Renaissance, Early Modern, or even Shakespearean—it is tempting to see the temporal structure emerging from Malone's researches as a welcome advance in the right scholarly direction, the result of the gradual accumulation of necessary source materials and of the development of sound methodological procedures.[8] What will become increasingly clear, however, is the extent to which the notion of an historical period served Malone's project of protecting Shakespeare from modification, his pressing 'solicitude', in

---

[7] According to J. R. Hale, the recognition, respect, and sympathy for historical periods was a Romantic phenomenon: *The Evolution of British Historiography from Bacon to Naumier* (London, 1967), p. 22. Compare David Hume's sense of temporal and human consistency: 'Mankind is so much the same, in all times and places that history informs us of nothing new or strange in this particular'; 'its chief use is only to discover the constant and universal principles of human nature', *A Treatise of Human Nature*, ed. L. A. Selby-Bigge (Oxford, 1949), i. iii.

[8] On the problem of periodization in Renaissance studies, see Margaret W. Ferguson's introduction to *Rewriting the Renaissance: The Discourses of Sexual Difference in Early Modern Europe* (Chicago, 1986), p. xvii and William Kerrigan and Gordon Braden, *The Idea of the Renaissance* (Baltimore, 1989), esp. preface.

his words, 'to keep Shakspeare pure and uncontamminated from modern sophistication and foreign admixtures.'[9] In Chapter 2, we saw how the criterion of authenticity served to curb what appeared to be peremptory treatments of Shakespearean materials. In this chapter, we shall see how the formation of an historical period similarly exempted Shakespeare from current standards of correctness and taste by attributing the ostensibly incorrect and distasteful to what was customary in Shakespeare's age. As the appeal to authenticity denied the variability of texts, so the construction of an historical period contained linguistic and cultural difference.

Like Copley's painting, all of Malone's Shakespearean projects involved extensive research. Though termed an antiquarian in his lifetime, recent Shakespeare scholarship credits Malone above all for 'laying down the foundation of modern documented study'.[10] Indeed, as Malone defined and practised it, editing at every stage depended on documents. The editor's threefold object was 'to support and establish what Shakespeare wrote, to illustrate his phraseology by comparison with his contemporaries, and to explain his fugitive allusions to customs long since disused and forgotten'.[11] The first of these functions was achieved by scrupulous examination of the oldest Folio and quarto documents, the 'most ancient copies'. The second and third required that all available documents contemporary with Shakespeare—printed or manuscript, literary or archival—be collected and investigated for what they might reveal about the language and customs of Shakespeare's age: 'The meanest books have been carefully examined, only because they were of the age in which he lived, and might happily throw a light on some forgotten custom or obsolete phraseology.'[12] In order to

[9] *An Inquiry into the Authenticity of Certain Miscellaneous Papers and Legal Instruments,* 1795; 'A Letter to the Earl of Charlemont', pp. 2–3.

[10] Charles J. Sisson, 'Studies in the Life and Environment of Shakespeare Since 1900', *Shakespeare Survey,* iii (Cambridge, 1950), p. 1. Other recent scholars who credit Malone for his modern scholarship include D. Nichol Smith, *Shakespeare in the Eighteenth Century* (Oxford, 1928), p. 56; Arthur Brown, 'Edmond Malone and English Scholarship', an Inaugural Lecture delivered at University College London, 21 May 1963 (London, 1963), p. 11; J. K. Walton, 'Edmond Malone: an Irish Shakespeare Scholar', *Hermathena,* 99 (Autumn 1964), p. 5; G. E. Bentley, 'Shakespeare's Reputation: Then Till Now', in *William Shakespeare: His World, His Work, His Influence,* ed. John F. Andrews (New York, 1985), iii. 713; S. Schoenbaum, *Shakespeare's Lives* (Oxford, 1970), p. 248.

[11] Malone, *PPWS,* i. i. lvi.   [12] Malone–Boswell, *PPWS,* ii. 289.

ascertain information relevant to any of his Shakespearean inquiries, Malone urged the most painstaking scrutiny of materials: 'Every circumstance . . . which may be found in any way applicable . . . should be sifted and examined with utmost industry and care; every hint, however slight, must be seized and investigated, and every allusion, however dark or mysterious, must if possible, be unfolded and explained.'[13] To this end, he visited Stratford and Worcester to consult legal records, examined the Records of the Courts of Chancery, and corresponded with those in a position to assist him in his archival research. Whenever possible, he examined the materials himself, fearing that intermediaries might distort information just as later editions had vitiated Shakespeare's authentic quartos and Folio.

Malone's efforts resulted in the retrieval of documents that have since remained basic to Shakespeare scholarship. In an old chest that had remained unopened for 130 years he discovered the Office book ('in a very mouldering condition' when discovered and having perished since[14]) of Sir Henry Herbert, Master of the Revels to James I and Charles I; and among the 'curious papers' he quarried at Dulwich College, he found a large folio volume of theatrical accounts kept by Philip Henslowe, proprietor of the Rose Theatre, a source that remains the most informative single document on the early stage.[15] So comprehensive was his familiarity with documents of this age, that he doubted the authenticity of any of which he was unaware. When William Henry Ireland first announced his discovery of numerous documents contemporary with Shakespeare, Malone suspected they were forgeries even before examining them: 'With all this ardour of inquiry, and all of this mass of information, I cannot believe that I had not known of so many original pieces.'[16] At the conclusion of his preface, he acknowledged his debt to those who had provided him with valuable documents, manuscripts, plays, and records. Yet these contacts possessed no special connection to Shakespeare, as had the alleged sources for the anecdotal accounts, Shakespeare's Stratford neighbours

---

[13] Malone–Boswell, *PPWS*, ii. 167.   [14] Ibid. iii. 59 n. 8.

[15] Ibid. iii. 295. Malone was the first to put *Henslowe's Diary* to scholarly use; see Schoenbaum, *Shakespeare's Lives*, pp. 183–4.

[16] Malone, 'An Inquiry', p. 4.

and their descendants. Nor did they connect to Shakespeare's works, as had the actor and playwright Thomas Betterton, sent to gather materials for Rowe's 1709 'Account', or the Restoration adapter and producer of Shakespeare's plays, William Davenant, whose authority as Shakespeare literary and perhaps biological heir was invoked to validate accounts. Nor did they have any special relation to Malone, as did the 'Friends' Theobald acknowledged for assistance in 'forwarding and compleating' his edition.[17] They were instead functionaries with direct access to archival materials. Thanks were extended to the 'librarian of Dulwich College for the Manuscripts relative to one of our ancient theatres'; to the 'Registrar of the diocese of Worcester, who . . . made many searches in his office for the wills of various persons'; 'to the Vicar of Stratford-upon-Avon, who most obligingly made every inquiry into that town and the neighbourhood . . .'.[18] His sources provided *information* rather than *accounts*, what had remained buried in official registers rather than kept in circulation through spoken and written reports. In the case of documents, only unmediated information transmitted by impersonal contacts could be trusted, whereas in the case of traditional accounts, mediation itself strengthened credibility by testifying to recurrent acceptance especially among those personally or professionally related to the subject.

Both Malone and Boswell were aware that the edition's reliance on documents would be criticized as 'too minute and circumstantial in collateral details'.[19] Yet it was, for them, precisely Malone's scrupulous antiquarianism—his indefatigable 'excursive inquiries' into documents, records, registers, printed and scripted materials of all kinds—that supplied clues 'which would otherwise have been lost, to more direct and important information'.[20] Repeatedly they defended his 'researches' against contemporary scoffers 'whose gross ignorance of the manners and customs of our ancestors, is such that they cannot even comprehend why the bequests of an ancient will are noticed, or how any useful information can be derived from circumstances apparently trifling and unimportant'.[21] The same blindness also characterized his predecessors: 'The truth

---

[17] Theobald, *WS*, i. lxv–lxvii.   [18] Malone, *PPWS*, i. lxxviii.
[19] Malone–Boswell, *PPWS*, i. lxi.   [20] Malone, *PPWS*, i. ixii.
[21] Malone–Boswell, *PPWS*, ii. 222.

is, our ancestors paid very little attention to posterity: they thought many things trifles, and unworthy of notice, which we consider important; and have left us in the dark about many other curious particulars.' As Shakespeare's biographer, Malone had special cause to lament their 'penury' in leaving nothing behind of the 'particulars of his private life, or dramatick history'.[22] His 'Life of Shakspeare' began with a long, exasperated disclosure of all the men and women between Shakespeare and himself who were in the position to record something of Shakespeare's life but failed to do so.[23] His satisfaction with the information he managed to retrieve through 'biographical researches, even at a remote period', was necessarily 'accompanied with a deep, though unavailing regret, that the same ardour did not animate those who lived nearer our author's times, whose inquiries could not fail to have been rewarded with a superior degree of success'.[24] Though he would have expected the townsmen of Stratford to 'have preserved some memorials of the domestic life and habits' of their most illustrious citizen,[25] owing to their 'lamentable neglect' all information had to be retrieved from scattered documents, the only reliable materials that remained for reconstituting Shakespeare's otherwise lost life and times.

The Shakespeare edition itself became a repository for preserving the documents Malone unearthed. In the 1821 variorum, the texts of Shakespeare's plays and poems were both encased and buttressed by documents and the facts they furnished. In addition to the prefaces of the major previous editors, a three-volume 'Prolegomena' contained four independent essays, all of which depended on documents: an examination of a letter pertaining to the literary and personal connections between 'Shakspeare, Ford, and Jonson'; 'An Essay on Phraseology and Metre of Shakspeare and his Contemporaries'; 'The Life of Shakspeare'; and 'An Historical Account of the English Stage'.[26]

---

[22] Malone, *PPWS*, ii. 211, n. 2.
[23] Ibid. 2–10.   [24] Ibid. ii.   [25] Ibid. 493.
[26] 'An Historical Account of the Rise and Progress of the English Stage and of the Economy and Usages of Our Ancient Theatres' first appeared in the 1790 edition, i. part 2. All three essays are included in the 1821 issue: 'An Enlarged History of the Stage with Additions and Appendix', ii. 7–409; 'Essay on the Phraseology and Metre of Shakespeare and his Contemporaries', i. 505–45; and 'The Life of William Shakspeare', ii. 1–525.

The third volume contained an appendix of transcripts from twenty documents referred to in the *Life*. Among them are a list of bailiffs at Stratford, the Will and Inventory of Shakespeare's wife's father, particulars relating to the Lucy family alluded to in *The Merry Wives of Windsor* and featured in one of the traditional anecdotes to be mentioned below, various legal instruments more directly relating to Shakespeare—the Grant of his Coat of Arms, a Conveyance, a Declaration of Trust by John Heminge and others, and Shakespeare's will—as well as numerous entries from both the Stratford Register, concerning Shakespeare's family, and the Stationers' Register, pertaining to his publications. Enclosed by documents, the corpus was upheld by footnotes containing information derived from documents; though set in smaller type, informative notes sometimes outweighed the text itself. As facts continued to accumulate, Malone's studies expanded.

'An Historical Account of the English Stage', first published in 1780, swelled into virtually a new work in 1790 'in consequence of the various researches since made, and a great accession of very valuable materials'.[27] In reprinting the 'Historical Account' for the 1821 edition, Boswell included Malone's subsequent revisions and additions and preserved in the final twenty-first volume an addendum of 'some valuable documents' that could not be worked into the final version. The influx of new materials also changed the size and shape of the 'Life of Shakspeare'. In the 1790 edition, it first appeared in the form of 'copious notes' affixed to what had been the standard biography, Rowe's 1709 'Account of Shakespeare', and supplying factual evidence that contradicted Rowe's narration; following Rowe's 'Account' were additional anecdotes Malone had collected as well as accounts of actors, legal instruments, and official records. As early as 1790, Malone intended one day to 'weave the whole into one uniform and connected narrative'; in 1796 he announced that he had 'amassed such an accumulation of materials' as to enable him to begin the project.[28] The resulting 525-page volume was hardly 'uniform and connected', for the account broke off just at the point when Shakespeare started writing for the stage; Boswell, without Malone's authorization, filled the

---

[27] Malone, *PPWS*, i. lxi.
[28] Ibid. i. lxiii; see Schoenbaum, *Shakespeare's Lives*, p. 238.

gap with the independent essay on Shakespeare's chronology which Malone had published in 1778 and revised in 1790: 'An attempt to ascertain the order in which the plays were written'. Though lacking the documents by which to reconstruct the crucial years of Shakespeare's life, the biography contained more materials than it could assimilate into a sequential narrative. Apologizing for his inability to integrate all the materials, Boswell published the remaining documents either in the appendix following the text or the addenda following the appendix. Even so some of Malone's papers were omitted altogether: because of the scattered state of Malone's papers, 'a number of curious matters of research are irrecoverably lost'.

In addition to the documents filed away in Malone's accounts, footnotes, appendices, and addenda, Boswell mentioned numerous key documents that were still to be uncovered: Heminge and Condell's account books; a treatise on the stage written by Sir George Buc, Master of Revels from 1610 to 1621; two projected but unpublished accounts of 'The Lives of the Poets' by Shakespeare's contemporaries, Thomas Heywood and Thomas Browne; any letters ('they must have been unquestionably voluminous') from Shakespeare's pen; information regarding the cause of Shakespeare's death; and the will of Shakespeare's daughter.[29] On at least two occasions, Malone advertised for information pertaining to Shakespeare's life, alerting the public to the kinds of documents that might be discoverable.[30] No doubt his conviction that further documents remained buried delayed the completion of the biography, preventing him from concluding it before his death twenty years after beginning the project.[31] Indeed, it might even explain his inability to finish the second edition of the Works during his lifetime, as if the whole could not be put forth before the missing documentary pieces could be assembled.

Documents determined not only the materials which belonged in the edition, but also those which did not belong. Long stretches of the apparatus were devoted to invalidating materials

[29] Malone, *PPWS*, i. ii. 191, 156 n. 5; Malone–Boswell, *PPWS*, ii. 6, 486, 505. On Malone's search for documents, see also Schoenbaum, *Shakespeare's Lives*, pp. 181–3.

[30] 'Proposals for an Edition' (1795) and appended to *An Inquiry*, 1795.

[31] On Malone's inability to complete the biography, see Schoenbaum, *Shakespeare's Lives*, pp. 241–2.

that could not be verified by documented facts: anecdotes, forgeries, and spurious attributions. Boswell maintained that the success of Malone's biography lay in its refutation of accepted materials as well as in its validation of new ones: 'he ascertained many particulars of that Poet's life and character . . . and detected the falsehood of many a traditionary tale that had been carelessly repeated by former writers'.[32] All materials concerning Shakespeare were checked against the facts; they were uniformly treated as information that could be validated or invalidated according to their correspondence with the facts registered in documents: 'Almost every circumstance that tradition or history has preserved relative to him or his works, has been investigated, and laid before the publick'.[33] As we have seen, Malone's biographical interest began with a nearly point-by-point refutation of the standard life of Shakespeare, Rowe's 1709 'Account', his copious notes on which were 'written for the purpose of demolishing almost every statement which it contained'.[34] Malone complained that Rowe had included only eleven facts, eight of which were false, one dubious, and the remaining two (the dates of Shakespeare's baptism and burial) no harder to find than the Stratford Register.[35] Rowe had maintained, for example, that Shakespeare came from a family of eight, though the register recorded the birth of only six; that he had given his son the name Samuel, though the register entered Hamnet; and that he had made an 'extremely inaccurate and erroneous' remark on the 'gentility' of Shakespeare's ancestry when 'neither the parish register, nor any other ancient document that I have met with there (and I have examined several hundred) furnishes the slightest notice of even his paternal grandfather'.[36]

Yet throughout the intervening decades, Rowe's report had been credited and repeated, often with the addition of new factual inaccuracies; as recently as 1773 Steevens had included in his edition 'an inaccurate and very imperfect list of Shakespeare's family'.[37] That a century should have passed before anyone even began a life of Shakespeare, that 'it should have been so imperfectly executed' once it was attempted in 1709,

---

[32] Malone–Boswell, *PPWS*, i. lxix.   [33] Ibid. ii. 289–90.
[34] Malone, *PPWS*, i. i. xix.   [35] Malone–Boswell, *PPWS*, ii. 69–70.
[36] Ibid. 118 n. 4, 19.   [37] Malone, *PPWS*, i. i. 171.

and that subsequent editors and biographers should have been contented with the scanty result for eighty years, were for Malone 'circumstances which cannot be contemplated without astonishment'.[38]

In refuting Rowe's received biographical materials, Malone measured the 'traditionary tales' against documented facts. His investigation of the deer-stealing anecdote accounting for Shakespeare's move from Stratford to London and the beginning of his dramatic career well illustrates his method of validation as well as the limitations of his factual criterion. He began by quoting the anecdote as printed in Rowe:

'He had,' says Mr. Rowe, 'by a misfortune common enough to young fellows, fallen into ill company; and, amongst them, some that made a frequent practice of deer-stealing, engaged him, more than once, in robbing a park that belonged to Sir Thomas Lucy, of Charlecote, near Stratford. For this, he was prosecuted by that gentleman, as he thought, somewhat too severely; and, in order to revenge the ill-usage, he made a ballad upon him. And though this, probably the first, essay of his poetry be lost, yet it is said to have been so very bitter, that it redoubled the prosecution against him, to that degree, that he was obliged to leave his business and family in Warwickshire, for some time, and shelter himself in London.'[39]

Malone's first step was 'to find out . . . the time when the supposed fact happened', always a difficult task: 'There is nothing in which stories of this kind are more deficient than dates'.[40] He determined that the date of the incident must have been after 1583–4, primarily because it would have had to precede a case recorded as having occurred in that year, arbitrated by the same Sir Thomas Lucy, between a friend of Shakespeare's and a farmer; had the case occurred after Lucy's prosecution of Shakespeare, Shakespeare's friend would have opposed the choice of Lucy as arbitrator. He continued to invalidate the tale by citing 'a tract of the age' and 'a quibbling verse' by a poet contemporary with Shakespeare, both illustrating that deer-stealing at the time was regarded as 'a juvenile frolick' rather than a criminal offence. According to William Fulman's slightly earlier account of the same incident, how-ever, Shakespeare had been repeatedly whipped for the mis-

---

[38] Malone–Boswell, *PPWS*, ii. 11.
[39] Ibid. 110–20.   [40] Ibid. 121.

demeanour: 'he was much given to all unluckinesse, in stealing *venison* and *rabbits*; particularly from Sir Lucy, who had him oft *whipt*, and sometimes *imprisoned*'.[41] But if the year were 1584, Shakespeare would have been twenty years old, and Lucy himself could not 'with propriety, punish the youthful trespassers by corporal chastisement'. Only the law would have inflicted such punishment on an adult; yet 'by the statute 5 Eliz. ch. 21', poaching was punished not by whipping but by fine and imprisonment. The vindictive ballad Shakespeare had allegedly written on this occasion Malone judged a forgery consisting of liftings from the first scene of *The Merry Wives of Windsor*. Finally and conclusively, he argued that Sir Lucy could have owned deer only if he owned a 'park' or a field that had by royal leave been enclosed and stocked with deer. That Lucy had no park was evidenced by the fact that the sixteenth-century antiquarian, John Leland, whose eye-witness reports Malone trusted, took no notice of any park belonging to the Lucy family during his itinerary through England between 1536 and 1542, though he 'never fails to take notice of every park that he passed by'.[42] That no park was subsequently formed either 'by prescription or immemorial usage' was proven by the fact that a royal franchise would have been required and 'no trace of such a grant [is] to be found on the patent rolls, during the whole reign of Elizabeth'.[43]

Malone's 'researches' invalidated the traditional account by demonstrating that the punishment, ballad, park, and deer featured in the account did not exist in Stratford at the moment of the alleged event. The deer-stealing account was therefore dismissed as 'unfounded calumny'.[44] Yet as the consistency of its inaccuracies suggests, the purpose of the account could not have been to preserve the facts of Shakespeare's life: how could an account purporting to be factual be wrong on every detail?

[41] Malone–Boswell, *PPWS*, ii. 123. Malone prints on the same page the earlier account (*c.* 1690), contained in a note from Richard Davies to William Fulman; see also E. K Chambers, *William Shakespeare: A Study of Facts and Problems* (Oxford, 1930), ii. 257.

[42] *The Itinerary of John Leland the Antiquary* (Oxford, 1770), 3rd edn., records Leland's travels and observations from 1536 to 1543 and includes notes on monasteries, archives, early inscriptions, etc. While Malone surely saw him as a kindred 'researcher', it should be mentioned that Leland also vigorously defended the authenticity of the Arthurian Legends against Polydore Vergil's skepticism (*DNB*).

[43] Malone–Boswell, *PPWS*, ii. 149.　　　　　　　　　　[44] Ibid. 119.

The anecdote was concerned not with recording facts but with commemorating 'the occasion' that introduced Shakespeare to his brilliant theatrical career. The sentence with which Rowe concluded the account specified its importance: 'It is at this Time, and upon this Accident, that he is said to have made his first Acquaintance in the Play-house.'[45] Yet in quoting Rowe's account, Malone omitted this concluding sentence; he also omitted the opening sentence, thereby removing the narrative frame that established the occasion's importance:

An Extravagance that he was guilty of, forc'd him both out of his Country and that way of Living which he had taken up; and tho' it seem'd at first to be a Blemish upon his good Manners, and a Misfortune to him, yet it afterwards happily prov'd the occasion of exerting one of the greatest *Genius's* that ever was known in Dramatick Poetry.[46]

The account recorded not an historical and datable event but a significant occasion: Shakespeare's passage from country to city, from youth to maturity, from offensive private pranks to acclaimed public plays. The 'Time' of the account was not the equivalent of the '4 January 1642' of Copley's painting, nor was the 'Accident' comparable to the King's momentous entrance into the House of Commons. The 'Time' of the account was Shakespeare's youth rather than a precise date; the 'Accident' was 'an Extravagance he was guilty of' rather than a singular event. The narrative conveyed neither correct information nor 'unfounded calumny', but rather dramatized the critical juncture of his life: his fortuitous conversion from pranks to plays, from wayward 'Extravagance' to motivated 'Genius'—an important reformation for a poet known for his 'extravagance', for his 'unruly' deviations from textual, critical, and biographical norms.

Malone used the same sort of evidence to examine forged documents. In his 500-page investigation of the Ireland forgeries, *An Inquiry into the Authenticity of Certain Miscellaneous Papers and Legal Instruments*, he brought forward countless documents

[45] D. Nichol Smith, ed., *Eighteenth Century Essays on Shakespeare* (Oxford, 1963), p. 3. References to the prefaces of Pope, Theobald, Warburton, Hanmer, and Johnson will also be to this collection.
[46] Ibid.

in order to expose Ireland's forgeries.[47] His 1790 edition contained a disclosure of a considerably less ambitious forgery: a letter allegedly copied from a 1631 pamphlet entitled 'Old Ben's Light Heart made heavy by Young John's Melancholy Lover'. In the letter, Ben Jonson accused Ford of having lifted *The Lover's Melancholy* from Shakespeare's papers with Heminge and Condell's assistance. Using 'those rules of evidence which regulate trials of greater importance', Malone was confident of being able to produce the testimony that would convict as the forger Charles Macklin, the actor who conveniently 'revealed' the letter just prior to his production of that play in 1748.[48] Malone's 'examination of its contents' began with his suspecting the title's reference to Ben as 'old': while the epithets 'judicious', 'learned', and 'immortal' had been applied to Jonson in the early part of Charles I's reign, he was not referred to as 'Old Ben' until around the time of his death in 1636; furthermore, on the basis of the register of the Middle Temple, his own collection of manuscripts, and the title-pages of plays and masques by Ford, he established that Ford would have been forty-five at the time of the pamphlet's publication, too old to be referred to as 'Young John'. Though subsequently known only as the result of Malone's arduous inquiries, these items (according to Malone) were in 1631 'facts of the greater part of which no writer of the time, conversant with dramatick history, could have been ignorant'.[49] More difficult to retrieve was the date of Jonson's birth: searches through two church registers revealed no baptismal record, though on the basis of a lacuna in the records for 1574, Malone inferred that he was baptized in that year.

The invalidation of the letter led Malone on to compose a more extended biography of Jonson which referred to additional documents refuting errors in traditional accounts of his life; those in turn led to a long digression on the title of 'poet laureate', conferred upon Spenser and Davenant as well as on Jonson, based on various grants from the signet-office, the chapel of the Rolls, letters patent, signed warrants—all dated,

---

[47] On Ireland's forgeries and Malone's examination of them, see Schoenbaum, *Shakespeare's Lives,* pp. 193–223.

[48] Malone, *PPWS,* i. i. 388. On Macklin's pamphlet, see Schoenbaum, *Shakespeare's Lives,* pp. 184–6.

[49] Malone, *PPWS,* i. i. 397.

all official. He also consulted Sir Henry Herbert's Office book in order to discredit the letter's claim that Jonson had charged Ford with stealing from his plays, as well as to establish that new scenes and acts were frequently added to old plays, a practice substantiated by John Lupton's 1602 account. Because Macklin's letter included verses assigned to Thomas May and Endymion Porter, Malone's examination provided information about their works too, as well as about their relation to Shakespeare and Jonson as witnessed by publications of the time. In the process of discrediting fabrications, then, Malone dug up factual particulars relating to Shakespeare's contemporaries: the authenticating of Shakespearean materials drew to the surface countless specifics regarding other writers of the period.

Malone used the testimony of documents to discredit works he believed spurious as well as those he believed forged, seventeenth-century works falsely attributed to Shakespeare as well as eighteenth-century counterfeits. The first texts he edited were all considered of questionable authorship: the seven plays incorporated into the 1667 Third Folio, the Sonnets, and the three *Henry VI* plays.[50] In 'vindicat[ing] Shakspeare from being the writer' of all these plays (with the exception of *Pericles* and revisions of the second and third parts of *Henry VI*), Malone introduced to Shakespeare studies the distinction between 'external' and 'internal' evidence: he produced 'external evidence' derived from title-pages and Stationers' Register entries to corroborate the 'internal marks' of diction, versification, allusions, and ideas.[51] As with the anecdotes, the facts residing in documents determined the validity of the material in question: verifiable evidence substantiated stylistic observations.

Malone unkennelled documents to defend Shakespeare from what he termed 'impositions' and 'fabrications': erroneous

[50] *Supplement to the Edition of Shakespeare's Plays Published in 1778 by Samuel Johnson and George Steevens* (London, 1780). On the *Henry VI* dissertation, see J. Dover Wilson's introduction to *Henry VI Part 2* (Cambridge, 1952), pp. 13, xiv–xix and his 'Malone and the Upstart Crow', *Shakespeare Survey*, 4 (1951), 56–68.

[51] For Malone's position in relation to a history of inquiries into Elizabethan authorship, see S. Schoenbaum, *Internal Evidence and Elizabethan Dramatic Authorship: An Essay in Literary History and Method* (Evanston, Ill., 1966), pp. 21–6. For an exhaustive account of the present state of the external/internal evidence distinction, see Stanley Wells and Gary Taylor, eds., *William Shakespeare: A Textual Companion* (Oxford, 1987), pp. 69–109.

facts, inaccurate legendary tales, forgeries, and spurious works. Facts—information provided or supported by documents, unmediated by transmission—became the ruling standard: 'The various extracts . . . from the Records of Stratford', for example, overthrew the testimony even of a 'a very fair pedigree' of authorities that included Davenant, Betterton, Rowe, Pope, and Cibber.[52] Archival remnants supplanted traditional legacies. Documents served to protect Shakespeare and his work from error and falsification, current forgeries and past misattributions.

Yet Malone's factual criteria were not always appropriate, as his examination of the biographical tales suggests. The exemplary tales made no claims to factual accuracy; as we shall continue to see in the next chapter, they encapsulated crucial encounters and conflicts that may or may not have had a basis in fact. Even the attribution to Shakespeare of seventeenth-century works was not, as we shall see in Chapter 5, fraudulent 'impositions', for it conformed with accepted practices of bibliographical classification before the prerogatives of authorship were defined and protected by law and recognized by printers and publishers. Factual criteria were appropriate only to the eighteenth-century forgeries, which, unlike the anecdotes and even the spurious works, were clearly intended to deceive readers by pretending to be what they were not. Thus, only if the Macklin letter were truly a forgery would Malone's repudiation of it on factual grounds be appropriate; if it were instead written in 1631, the incongruities Malone detected, in its casual use of diction for example, might have been characteristic of seventeenth-century writing itself, as Steevens observed in commenting on Malone's essay. What Steevens also understood was the interdependency of Malone's procedures for detecting forgeries and the forgers' techniques for producing them. He doubted whether there could have been any forgeries as early as 1748, believing that both forgeries and the 'antiquarian sagacity' required to detect them had developed later in the century: 'If Mr. Macklin was really the fabricator of these disputed authorities, he must be considered as the parent of literary impostures in England.'[53] As we have seen before, the

---

[52] Malone–Boswell, *PPWS*, ii. 159.
[53] Ibid. i. 432.

appearance of forgeries, written and painted, coincided historically with the very criterion of authenticity they attempted to replicate.

The process of retrieving documents for the purposes of establishing Shakespeare's authentic life and works and of denouncing their simulations resulted in a new focus on historical particulars. The factual details extracted from the documents provided the characteristic features of Shakespeare's historical milieu, features that were not constant but rather peculiar to the temporal duration in which Shakespeare had existed. Documents provided the facts that identified this span as a self-contained period with its own practices and customs. Malone's use of them, as exemplified in his scrutiny of both the deer-stealing anecdote and Macklin's letter, drew to the surface particulars peculiar to Shakespeare's time, particulars relating to customs, laws, poets, publications, and performances that would come to constitute the temporal construct later described as 'Shakespeare's world'.

As we have seen, Malone insisted that the proper elucidation of Shakespeare depended on knowledge both of the language and of the customs and manners of Shakespeare's time. The materials he collected on these two subjects informed his footnotes. He also projected an essay on each subject, but owing to the 'loose and disjointed state' of the materials on customs and manners, only 'An Essay on the Phraseology and Metre of Shakspeare and his Contemporaries' appeared.[54] Malone's comments on language in this essay, as well as in his preface to both the 1790 and the 1821 editions, pinpointed features unique to Shakespeare's time, unearthed from documents and records. For this purpose, literary materials functioned as documents: both emerged from 'antiquarian research'; both provided the evidence by which to define and establish the distinguishing characteristics of Shakespeare's age. Because Shakespeare's language and style reflected common usage, the works of his contemporaries provided parallels by which to illustrate and explicate his writing. Malone marshalled forth examples from scores of Elizabethan writers, many of them unread and even unknown,

[54] Ibid. xx. the Essay was completed by Boswell.

such as Barclay, Webbe, Griffin, and Watson, whose names he found in the compendious lists of British authors featured in the newly discovered *Palladis Tamia* (1598). In addition, while parallel passages from Shakespeare were used to establish his authorship of such works as *Pericles* and the Sonnets, parallels from other authors were used to prove that he was not the author of other works, for example *Locrine* and *The London Prodigall*.[55] In the cause of both illustration and attribution, the writings of hundreds of other dramatists and poets were culled for parallels and thereby raised out of obscurity to contribute to 'a general literature of the country'.[56]

Thus it was not only Shakespeare's reputation that benefitted from 'excursions into late sixteenth- and early seventeenth-century materials, but those of his contemporaries as well. By providing a single gloss on Shakespeare, any poet would rise from obscurity: 'The slightest references which can be drawn from the works of Shakspeare to a forgotten poet, has the effect of a stone thrown from the hand of Deucalion, and raised him at once into life.'[57] Lengthy glosses or disquisitions brought to light not only 'the most distinguished poets which England has produced',[58] but forgotten poets whose 'manners and usages' were now helpful in elucidating those of the distinguished. The ephemerality that had formerly consigned them to oblivion now won them recognition, for it was their very embeddedness in the historical moment that made them useful. In the process of ferreting out materials and references, the beginnings were laid for a unique sixteenth- and seventeenth-century English 'canon' with its own style, conventions, and usages—a native literature distinct from the French tradition so dominant in the eighteenth century.

This emergent corpus was distinct, too, from that of later English letters. Malone's emphasis on the degree to which phraseology and prosody had changed since Shakespeare's time reveals the interrelation of his authenticating and historicizing projects. His demonstration that what had appeared linguistic anomalies in Shakespeare's work were features customary in his period preserved the authentic quartos and Folio from emendation and censure. Malone particularly defended

---

[55] See Malone's 1780 *Supplement* for editions of the contested works.
[56] Malone–Boswell, *PPWS*, i. ix.   [57] Ibid. i. x.   [58] Ibid. ii. 223.

the authority of the 1623 First Folio against the claim of the 1632 Second Folio by demonstrating that the alterations introduced by the latter were the result of its 'superintendor's' ignorance of Shakespeare's phraseology. Almost a third of his preface to both editions consisted of specific examples of how the language had changed between the time of Shakespeare and the Second Folio: 'It should be remembered, that in the beginning of the reign of Charles the First many words and modes of speech began to be disused, which had been common in the age of Queen Elizabeth.'[59] Oblivious to these changes, the Second Folio's editor emended passages that Malone maintained were perfectly acceptable in Shakespeare's day, correcting grammatical, lexical, and metrical features perfectly consonant with usage of his time. 'The modern editors' followed his precedent in their 'wish to reduce our author's phraseology to a modern standard.' The 'Essay on Phraseology' further stressed the inappropriateness of applying to Shakespeare modern principles of writing and versifying: 'The language and modulation of Shakspeare were such as would have been considered unexceptionable in that Age of Elizabeth though deviating from the rules of George the Third or Fourth.'[60] A list of these obsolete conventions with examples appeared after the essay and included 'particles omitted', 'double comparative', 'double negative', 'plural substantive with singular verb', 'words differently accented from modern usage', and 'words either pronounced differently in those days, or lengthened, or shortened, by poetical license'.[61] Because its 'superintendor' corrected these irregularities as if they were errors, Malone deemed the Second Folio worthless, for 'when Shakspeare fell into these irregularities, he was countenanced by the practice of his contemporaries'.[62]

In stylistic as well as lexical and grammatical matters, Shakespeare's choices were customary rather than incorrect or infelicitous. Features that had been criticized and emended as stylistically defective—for example, the frequent incidence of redundancy and ellipsis—'perpetually occur in every writer of that age'.[63] Similarly, modern editors like Pope and Steevens who had attempted to regularize Shakespeare's metre were

---

[59] Malone, *PPWS*, i. i. xliii.   [60] Malone–Boswell, *PPWS*, i. 511.
[61] Ibid. 581–5.   [62] Ibid. 575.   [63] Ibid. 527.

ignorant both of how words were pronounced at this time and of how poets commonly shortened and lengthened syllables to suit the requirements of their verse.

Malone's predecessors, up to and including Johnson at least, had laboured to purge away what remained of such singular features rather than to retrieve and preserve them, especially in their treatment of Shakespeare's language. Pope tacitly extirpated passages he deemed defective or 'degraded [them] to the bottom of the page'.[64] Although later editors were less imperious in their judgements, they too in their preparation and criticism of Shakespeare's plays were concerned with refining the English tongue, which, as Theobald maintained, 'lisps and stammers as in its Cradle'.[65] In his 1733 preface, he hoped that English would receive the same advantages from his arbitrations as the Greek and Latin tongues had from their editors and critics, who had made it possible 'to write infinitely better in that Art than even the preceding Grammarians, who wrote when those Tongues flourish'd as living Languages'.[66] To the same purpose, Warburton in his 1747 edition acknowledged the importance of 'cultivating [our] own country idiom' by establishing Shakespeare's text, as Lycurgus, Cicero, Menage, and Selden had done by establishing the editions of Homer, Lucretius, Malherbe, and Drayton respectively.[67] Before the text of Shakespeare could be settled, however, English needed a Grammar and a Dictionary; on the other hand, as Warburton pointed out, no Grammar or Dictionary could be devised until there existed definitive texts of the most established writers, on whose authority vocabulary and syntax depended. Johnson's 1755 Dictionary and his 1765 Shakespeare jointly addressed this dilemma; impelling both projects was the belief that an essential English could be distilled from the great authors of the past and then codified, ideally for all time.[68] Quotes from Shakespeare, more than from any other poet, were used to determine and illustrate meaning and usage in the Dictionary; abundant

---

[64] Smith, *Eighteenth Century Essays*, p. 57.   [65] Ibid. 83.
[66] Ibid. 83.   [67] Ibid. 101.
[68] Alvin Kernan discusses both projects as symptomatic of print culture, imposing the fixity of print on both the vacillating Shakespearean text and the unstable English language: *Printing Technology, Letters and Samuel Johnson* (Princeton, NJ, 1987), pp. 164–172 ('Print Fixity and Editions') and 181–203 ('Language and the Literary Text: Johnson's Dictionary').

definitions from the Dictionary served to gloss the Shakespeare edition. Malone, by contrast, applied himself to dredging up the irregularities and anomalies that Theobald, Warburton, and Johnson would have filtered out as 'barbarisms' in their search for a purified and stable English. Johnson's purpose was not to excavate all past forms, but only those 'above grossness and below refinement, where propriety resides'.[69] Boswell himself contrasted Johnson's and Malone's purposes: 'the main object of [Johnson's] immortal work, was not [Malone's] archaeological inquiry into the state of our language as it anciently stood, but to ascertain in what its purity then consisted, that it might be fixed on a stable basis'.[70]

To Johnson the very locution 'state of our language as it anciently stood' would have been nonsensical: language in the past had never stood still, it never yet had attained a 'state'. It was precisely to release language from its past subjection to the vicissitudes of time, fashion, ignorance, and chance that he undertook his lexical, critical, and editorial projects: 'that it might be fixed on a stable basis'. In the preface to his edition, Johnson announced that Shakespeare's work could 'begin to assume the dignity of an ancient, and claim the privilege of established fame and prescriptive veneration' precisely because the passage of time had effaced the traces of its historical origin: 'personal allusions, local customs, or temporary opinions'.[71] Yet it was precisely Shakespeare's historical moorings that the antiquarian Malone wished to conserve and validate, thereby warding off 'modern sophistications'—the impulse of 'modern editors' to change and modify the Shakespeare of the authentic early quartos and First Folio according to their own standards.

It was only once Shakespeare was seen to occupy a specific time as distinct from a composite past that his irregularities could be defended as conventions rather than dismissed as errors or barbarisms. Up to the time of the Tudors at least, the past had been represented as a uniformly rude and undeveloped temporal expanse. In David Hume's 1763 *History of England*, for example, England only began to emerge from a massive irrational and

[69] Smith, *Eighteenth Century Essays*, p. 113.
[70] Malone–Boswell, *PPWS*, i. 509.
[71] Smith, *Eighteenth Century Essays*, p. 105.

barbaric past with the ascent to the throne of Henry VIII. It was from this vast darkness that Shakespeare had issued: 'Shakespeare was born in a rude age, and educated in the lowest manner, without any instruction, either from the world or books.'[72] Shakespeare's commentators before Malone attributed his defects to the misfortune of his having been born into this illiterate and vulgar time. As Rowe had stressed in his 1709 'Account', because 'in a State of almost universal License and Ignorance' Shakespeare had to depend entirely on the 'mere Light of Nature' for his direction; without any established standards, explicit or implicit, he necessarily wrote 'under the Dictates of his own Fancy'.[73] For subsequent editors, too, Shakespeare's primitive times excused his own lapses of taste and decorum as well as providing the bleak backdrop for his shining achievements. Theobald referred to the 'Vice of *his Times*' and '*reigning Barbarism*' that compromised Shakespeare. Hanmer evoked 'the Stage, rude and unpolished' and 'vicious taste of the age' in accounting for Shakespeare's lapses; finding that 'trash is frequently interspersed in his writings', he followed Pope and threw it to the bottom of the page. Warburton again defended Shakespeare's violation of dramatic laws and decorum, in terms of the circumstance that 'Public Taste was in its Infancy'.[74]

Johnson shared his predecessors' disdain for Shakespeare's historical situation: 'The English nation, in the time of Shakespeare, was yet struggling to emerge from barbarity.'[75] He could confidently venerate Shakespeare as an 'ancient' precisely because his plays had through the years cast off the accidents of their historical origin. Having 'long outlived his century', having outlasted the base standards governing past writing and taste, Shakespeare's works had proven themselves worthy to endure. In this context, Malone's project of retrieving lost allusions, customs, and opinions through the examination of documents only dragged back the particulars that were in Johnson's view best consigned to oblivion. While Shakespeare occasionally threw in circumstantial details 'to catch the attention

---

[72] David Hume, *The History of England, from the Invasion of Julius Caesar to the Revolution in 1688* 8 vols. (London, 1807), vi. 191–2.

[73] Smith, *Eighteenth Century Essays*, p. 15.

[74] Ibid. 68, 86, 95.   [75] Ibid. 122–3.

Pl. 1 *(above, left).* Droeshout, title-page, *Mr. William Shakespeares Comedies, Histories, & Tragedies* (1623)

Pl. 2 *(above, right).* Hole, title-page, *The Workes of Beniamin Jonson* (1616)

Pl. 3 *(left).* Marshall, frontispiece, *Comedies and Tragedies Written by Francis Beaumont and John Fletcher* (1647)

Pl.4 *(above, left)*. Marshall, frontispiece, *Poems: Written by Wil. Shake-speare. Gent.*, ed. Benson (1640)

Pl.5 *(above, right)*. Faithorne, frontispiece, *The Rape of Lucrece* (1655)

Pl. 6 *(left)*. Marshall, title-page, *Q. Horatius Flaccus: His Art of Poetry Englisht by Ben: Jonson* (1640)

Pl. 7. Chandos portrait, artist
unknown

Pl. 8. Paillet, frontispiece, *Œuvres
de Pierre Corneille* (Rouen, 1660)

Pl. 9. Vandergucht, frontispiece, *The
Works of Mr. William Shakespear*, ed.
Rowe (1709)

Pl. 10. Du Guernier, frontispiece,
*The Works of Mr. William
Shakespear*, ed. Rowe (1714)

Pl. 11. Duchange, frontispiece, *The Works of Shakespeare*, ed. Theobald (1733)

Pl. 12. Gravelot, frontispiece, *The Works of Shakespeare*, ed. Hanmer (1744)

Pl. 14. Miller, frontispiece, *Mr. William Shakespeare his Comedies, Histories, and Tragedies*, ed. Capell (1767–8)

Pl. 13 *(left)*. Vertue, frontispiece, *The Works of Shakespeare*, eds. Pope and Warburton (1747) and *The Plays of William Shakespeare*, ed. Johnson (1765)

Pl. 15 *(above, left)*. Humphry, sketch of the Chandos portrait (1786), owned by Malone

Pl. 16 *(above, right)*. Knight, frontispiece, *The Plays and Poems of William Shakespeare*, ed. Malone (1790)

Pl. 17 *(left)*. Fry, frontispiece, *The Plays and Poems of William Shakespeare*, eds. Malone and Boswell (1821)

Pl. 18 *(above, left)*.
Johnson, Shakespeare
monument, Stratford

Pl. 19 *(left)*. Shakespeare
monument, Dugdale,
Antiquities of Warwickshire
(1656)

Pl. 20 *(above, right)*.
Vandergucht, Shakespeare
monument, *The Works of
Mr. William Shakespear*, ed.
Rowe (1709)

Pl. 21 *(above, left)*. Vertue, Shakespeare monument with Chandos head, *The Works of Shakespeare*, ed. Pope (1723)

Pl. 22 *(above, right)*. Gravelot, Shakespeare monument, *The Works of Shakespeare*, ed. Hanmer (1744)

Pl. 23 *(left)*. Fry, effigy from Shakespeare monument, *The Plays and Poems of William Shakspeare*, eds. Malone and Boswell (1821)

Pl. 24. Copley, *Charles I Demanding in the House of Commons the Five Impeached Members* (1782–95)

of the rude', his focus was properly on the 'general impact', for 'a poet overlooks casual distinction of country and condition, as a painter, satisfied with the figure, neglects the drapery'.[76] It is for this reason that Johnson, after devoting a decade to editing Shakespeare, questioned—much to Malone's later consideration[77]—the validity of footnotes, for the bygone particulars they illuminated interfered with the lasting impact of the whole:

Particular passages are cleared by notes; but the general effect of the work is weakened. The mind is refrigerated by interruption; the thoughts are diverted from the principal subject; the reader is weary, he suspects not why; and at last throws away the book, which he has too diligently studied.[78]

Johnson's preface contained no such refrigerating footnotes; Malone's abounded with them.

Johnson went further and doubted whether editorial glosses and emendations had added anything to the understanding and recognition of Shakespeare. As Dryden's appreciation had demonstrated, 'he was read, admired, studied and imitated . . . while the reading was yet not rectified, nor his allusions understood'. For Johnson, as there was a language of style 'settled and unaltered' despite local and temporal permutations and 'personages . . . very little modified by particular forms', so too there was a general dramatic effect that could only be encumbered by the topicalities that footnotes revived.[79] The true value of a work would not become apparent until it was stripped clean of the contingencies once responsible for its popularity. Extraneous materials from the past or about the past tended to muddle rather than heighten the integrity of the work; by ensnaring the latter-day reader in its obscuring circumstances, it detracted from the experience of 'its full design and its true proportions', 'the beauty of the whole.' Footnotes that dredged up the past reversed the purifying forward movement of 'the stream of time' which had gradually washed away local and temporal impurities to reveal 'the adamant *Shakespeare*'.[80]

---

[76] Ibid. 109.
[77] Malone, *PPWS*, i. i. lvi, lxix.
[78] Smith, *Eighteenth Century Essays*, p. 148.
[79] Ibid. 149, 113, 112.
[80] Ibid. 113.

In his earliest work, Steevens was the first of the succession of Shakespearean editors to attempt just this reversal. In 1766 he published the first collection of Shakespearean quartos, *Twenty of the Plays of Shakespeare Being the whole number printed in Quarto During his Life-time, or before the Restoration*. Steevens, at the risk of injuring Shakespeare's reputation, published what he believed to be his rough, unpolished drafts in the hope that it would 'encourage others to think of preserving the oldest editions of the English writers, which are growing scarcer every day'.[81] In his first edition of the complete plays of Shakespeare in 1773, he propounded a new conservatism in textual preparation: what previous editors had rejected as 'theatrical maimings and interpolations of the age' he wished to preserve as instances of how Shakespeare and his contemporaries wrote and versified.[82] Rather than emending the text, he attempted to justify and clarify it by comparison with examples from Shakespeare's age. As the editor of two supplementary volumes to this edition in 1780, Malone followed Steevens's 'faithful adherence of the old copies' and refrained from 'unauthorized sophistications of the text'.

Yet in his 1793 edition, Steevens reversed his position dramatically, 'on a sudden wheeled round', apparently as a result of an emulous rift with Malone, and retracted what he had been propounding for thirty years.[83] Despite his initial commitment to defending the text according to the usage of Shakespeare's time, Steevens ended up maintaining that in some instances 'a blind fidelity' to the oldest printed copies was 'confirmed treason against the sense, spirit, and versification of Shakspeare';[84] he even prided himself on having introduced into his 1793 edition 186 corrections from the Second Folio that Malone had so ardently discredited in his 1790 edition.[85] He ridiculed Malone's historical inquiries into 'coeval productions' that had the effect of 'reviving the anomalies, barbarisms, and blunders of ancient copies', arguing that such attempts to conserve the

---

[81] *TPS*, i. 20.   [82] Steevens, *PWS*.

[83] Boswell pieces together an explanation for their conflict from correspondence: 'Biographical Memoir', Malone–Boswell, *PPWS*, i. lviii–ix; see also Bertrand H. Bronson, *Joseph Ritson: Scholar-at-Arms* (Berkeley, Ca., 1938), ii. 527, 533–42.

[84] Advertisement to 1793 edition, in Malone–Boswell, *PPWS*, i. 264.

[85] Malone's letter to Thomas Percy, ibid. i. 271–2, quoted by Bronson, *Joseph Ritson*, p. 539.

text by reference to contemporary usage and custom made it appear as if 'every casual combination of syllables may be tortured into meaning, and every species of corruption exemplified by corresponding depravities of language'.[86] The very 'modern sophistications' Malone resisted, Steevens embraced: according to Boswell, he unscrupulously discarded what could not be understood, and capriciously clipped and stretched the verse 'in order to make it perfectly consonant to our modern notions of metrical harmony'.[87] Boswell assured the reader of the 1821 edition that 'the numerous sophistications introduced by Mr. Steevens have been removed' and 'the author's unsophisticated text' restored.[88]

Like their predecessors, Johnson and the later Steevens had little use for the very sources and uses on which Malone depended in reconstructing Shakespeare's past. Their admiration for Shakespeare exacted the removal of his works from the contaminating conditions of the past. Malone's researches, however, fixed the works within an historical milieu defined by his enquiries. Once that milieu had been defined by practices and customs of its own, emendation and correction of the text by modern standards were no longer justifiable. Against Steevens's 'rage of emendation and the desire to reduce everything to a modern standard', Malone pitted his determination 'to show the propriety of preserving the integrity of the original text'.[89] It was to the end of demonstrating the initial acceptance of the vocabulary, diction, and metre criticized and corrected by succeeding generations that Malone cited Shakespeare's contemporaries to support his use of phraseology and metre. Passages which had been expunged or modified in the name of Reason, Taste, and Sense were shown to be perfectly consonant with customary usage in Shakespeare's time. Pronunciation, too, had become less flexible since Shakespeare.[90] As the emendations introduced in the 1632 Second Folio demonstrated, Shakespeare's language and modulation were thought deviant less than a generation after his death.

Malone's edition thus drew attention to the exclusive forms and applications of the written and spoken language of

[86] Malone–Boswell, *PPWS*, i. 523.
[87] Ibid. i. 511.
[88] Ibid. xxi, x.
[89] Ibid. 516, 517.
[90] Malone, *PPWS*, i. i. xxv–xliii.

Shakespeare's period. What had been supposed the result of printers' blunders, actors' interpolations, or Shakespeare's carelessness, appeared upon examination of materials from the period to be 'consonant to the universal practice of the age even among the learned'. This position encouraged the utmost fidelity to the authentic texts. Urging that no reader of Shakespeare's plays 'should ever open the Second Folio, or either of the subsequent copies', Malone entertained the possibility of sending the First Folio to the press, so that it would become standard, even in its original spelling.[91] The edition he settled on in 1790 was based on the most 'ancient copies' from the early quartos and First Folio, and attempted to preserve the advantages of such a transcript without its 'inconveniences'. He intended to preserve the original form of the Shakespeare text as far as possible, strictly adhering to its vocabulary, grammar, and versification even when these violated subsequent standards. By retaining 'many passages, which have heretofore been considered corrupt, and are now supported by the usage of contemporary writers,' the authentic texts might remain as they had been in Shakespeare's time. By providing an historical context for language and prosody, Malone simultaneously justified his objective of fixing Shakespeare's works in their authentic form.

Malone's awareness of the historical character of Shakespeare's writing decisively changed the function and responsibility of the editor. From Theobald through to Johnson, editors had defined their task as threefold: to establish the text, illuminate obscurities, and evaluate the author's style.[92] With Malone, and Capell before him, the latter function dropped out: 'The two great duties of an editor are, to exhibit the genuine text of his author, and to explain his obscurities.'[93] Once modern standards were shown to be anachronistic, the editor could claim no right to judge the quality of his author's writing. In questions pertaining to something as changeable and intractable as language, 'it may reasonably be questioned

[91] Malone, *PPWS*, i. i. xliii, xliv.
[92] On the three-fold duties of the editor before Malone—emendation, illumination, and evaluation—see Theobald (p. 76), Warburton (pp. 94–7), and Johnson (p. 140), all in Smith, *Eighteenth Century Essays*.
[93] Malone, *PPWS*, i. i. liv.

whether . . . we are entitled to say that we are right, and our ancestors were wrong'.[94] It would be proper to criticize Shakespeare for 'the faulty construction of his sentences' only if we claimed 'a right to try him by the rules which have been drawn by modern writers'. Malone's immersion in Shakespeare's distinct and discrete historical situation disallowed the evaluation of passages either in the form of Pope's and Hanmer's typographical ciphers and deletions, or in that of Theobald's and Johnson's critical strictures and notes applauding Shakespeare's Beauties and condemning his Faults. It had been precisely the 'judicial' aspect of editing that had allowed editors 'the utmost liberties' in both emending irregular passages and regularizing anomalous verse. By eliminating evaluation and concentrating on illumination, the editor could concentrate on his newly defined purpose: 'to support and establish what the poet wrote, to illustrate his phraseology by comparing it with that of his contemporaries, and to explain his fugitive allusions to customs long since disused and forgotten'.[95]

It might be said that criticism, under the pressure of Malone's differentiating historicism, ceased to be critical. Editorial comments became predominantly informative and, as we shall see, interpretative rather than evaluative. As Malone maintained in countering Johnson's observation that the succession of editors had added little to Shakespeare's 'power of pleasing', 'every author who pleases must surely please more as he is understood, and there can be no doubt that Shakspeare is now infinitely better understood . . .'.[96]

Situating Shakespeare in his period thus removed him from criticism according to posthumous and anachronistic standards of style and usage. Once aspects of Shakespeare's style which had formerly been regarded as offensive were seen as common to his age, they were protected from emendation and censure. For example, the wordplay that editors from Rowe to Johnson had condemned, Malone defended as 'an ancient paronomasy', 'congenial to the taste of the time', enthusiastically practiced by churchmen, other poets, and the King himself.[97] While Johnson regarded Shakespeare's puns as regrettable indulgences, detracting from the substantial force of his language, Malone

---

[94] Malone–Boswell, *PPWS*, i. 520.
[96] Ibid. i. i. lxix.
[95] Malone, *PPWS*, i. lvi.
[97] Ibid. ii. 207.

attempted to justify them as facets of Shakespeare's style in keeping with the period. While such features were for Johnson 'casual distinctions' that were best overlooked, they were for Malone 'the venerable reliques of our ancestors'.[98] While Johnson believed a painter who is 'satisfied with the figure neglects the drapery', Malone stressed the importance of such fabrics, both in Copley's antiquarian painting and in his own literary scholarship: 'There is a fashion in the works of the imagination, no less than in our cloaths, and equipage, and modes of life.'[99] While the trappings of a given time and place had formerly been held to trivialize and vulgarize a work, in Malone's practices they became essential to ascertaining its meaning.

We have seen in this chapter how Malone, in relying on documentary materials to fix and elucidate Shakespeare, drew to the surface the particulars from which he was able to constitute a discrete and contained historical division, replete with its own distinctive characteristics. In the search for illuminating parallels to passages in Shakespeare's plays and poems, hundreds of formerly neglected contemporary literary materials were scrutinized; these provided a body of works characteristic of a period that possessed a vocabulary, grammar, and poetics of its own. By granting the period its own idiom, Malone protected its works from both emendation and censure. Shakespeare's text could then remain faithful to the original printed form of the early quartos and First Folio; apparent irregularities and anomalies were allowed as normative linguistic and stylistic features of the age.

Malone's invocation of a discrete Shakespearean age appears an overdue advance over his predecessors' homogenization of the past. His historicism made Shakespeare's past an object of study separate from the subject studying it, an object that resided not in continuing discourse, practices, and institutions but rather in inert archives, records, and documents. To experience that remote object it was necessary to suspend present standards: 'We are not to be governed by our own judgments, but to transport ourselves two centuries backwards.'[100] The function of the apparatus was now, therefore, to change the

---

[98] Malone–Boswell, *PPWS*, i. 516.
[99] Ibid. ii. 206.   [100] Ibid. ii. 182.

modern reader rather than the ancient text. To gain access to the authentic and obsolete past, readers were required to waive their 'judgments' and inform themselves with the idiom of that past: 'We should always keep in our thoughts the manners, and habits, and prejudices of the age which produced the works we are reviewing.'[101]

Yet the prescribed change had its limits. While the past age was credited with characteristic 'manners, and habits, and prejudices', it was not deemed to have 'judgment' or 'reason' of its own: while particulars may have shifted with the times, universals remained constant. The 'customary' was so routinely evoked that Boswell appended an 'Index of Manners, Customs, Superstitions, etc. explained in the notes' in the final twenty-first volume of the 1821 edition. The entries, tidily alphabetized, represent all kinds of phenomena alien to the editor's sensibilities: 'fans worn sometimes by male fops', 'fumbling with the sheets, a sign of approaching death', 'Indians exhibited in London' 'lying at the feet of a mistress, a common fashion'. Practices which could not be brought within the confines of rationality and decency were explained by an appeal to the inexplicable usage and custom of the times. The historically contingent served as a repository for anything that fell outside the pale of the self-evidently true and right. Thus, while salvaging the past differences that his own universal standards could not comprehend, Malone's historicism still permitted those standards to appear universally valid.

Repeatedly Malone relegated to the category of the customary, phenomena that unsettled the norms and practices he took to be axiomatic. Aspects of language that subverted the 'modern standard' were countenanced as usage common to the age. Both the abbreviations of ellipsis and the repetitions of redundancy, for example, thwarted the referentiality Malone sought in the language of documents where sign and signified were assumed commensurate, one entry per event; and the puns or 'equivoques' Malone repeatedly allowed as fashionable, confused that same linguistic economy by generating multiple signifieds to a single sign. So, too, the phonetic overlappings that made one word interchangeable with another blurred

---

[101] Ibid. ii. 206–7.

latter-day lexical boundaries. Even the admissibility of the double negative unsettled the logic of affirmation and negation.

Assigned to the same category were incongruous theatrical practices pertaining to the plays' scripting, printing, and performance. Malone's 'Historical Account of the English Stage', an attempt 'to ascertain the real state of the stage, by the most authentick documents', paid particular attention to 'the internal economy and usages of the English theatres in the time of Shakspeare'.[102] By examining the financial transactions in Henslowe's Diary and Henry Herbert's Office book, he concluded that payment for a given play was not necessarily made to the author featured on the title-page.[103] The discovery of the Dulwich College papers established a related curiosity: revision and emendation of existing plays was common practice. As long as such facts could be attributed to the practices of the times, they were prevented from offsetting Malone's focus on Shakespeare's creative autonomy. The same might be said of his awareness that borrowing and imitation were customary among writers of Shakespeare's time. Though his prefatory remarks to each play revealed the extent to which Shakespeare's plots and phrases originated elsewhere, his belief in the originality of Shakespeare's genius remained firm.[104] The involvement of other hands—whether as sources, as collaborators, or as revisers—in the writing of plays was a feature peculiar to the times but irrelevant to Shakespeare's singular creativity.

With the same relativizing apology, aberrant mores were admitted, a large number of them pertaining to gender. The notes to the Sonnets, for example, excused the way in which the fair young man was addressed in terms only befitting a woman: 'Such addresses to men, however indelicate, were customary in our author's time, and neither imported criminality, nor were esteemed indecorous.'[105] The theatrical practice of having males impersonate females was 'a prejudice against women appearing on the scene' peculiar to England in the period, though it had Greek and Roman precedents.[106] Hamlet's 'in-

[102] Ibid. iii. 361; Malone, *PPWS*, i. ii. 2.

[103] Cf. G. E. Bentley, *The Profession of a Dramatist in Shakespeare's Time: 1590–1642* (Princeton, NJ, 1971), pp. 227–34.

[104] See Malone's endorsement of Edward Young's *Conjectures on Original Composition*: Malone, *PPWS*, i. i. lxxvi.

[105] Malone, *PPWS*, x. 207, n. 8.   [106] Ibid. i. ii. 126.

delicacy of language' to Ophelia was not to be condemned, for it merely dramatized 'the decorum of those times . . . even in the highest class', and 'undoubtedly represented the manners and conversation of [Shakespeare's] own day faithfully'.[107] So long as these 'improprieties' were categorized as no more than current fashions, modern determinations of what behaviour and attitudes were appropriate to the respective genders remained transparent.

In this way the category of the customary or the historically contingent served to protect Malone's present as well as Shakespeare's past. It provided a solution to the problem of intractable historical difference, difference that could not be translated into Enlightenment equivalents, as could, for example, the two hundred pounds at which Malone estimated Shakespeare's annual income: 'Equal to at least 1000 l. per ann. at this day: the relative value of money, the mode of living in that age, the luxury and taxes of the present time, and various other circumstances being considered.'[108] Linguistic and cultural practices that were not convertible, however, were consigned to the realm of the antiquated and obsolete. Thus Malone's sense of what was customary in Shakespeare's time was a convenient and commodious cache for what could not conform to Malone's standards, enabling him to countenance and condone what would formerly have been corrected or condemned. The strange particulars of the past could thereby coexist with the self-evident absolutes of the present.

Yet there was one type of strangeness, frequently remarked, that Malone was unable to excuse as characteristic of Shakespeare's times: indifference to factual truth, the very foundation of his historicism and scholarship. Repeatedly he inveighed against Shakespeare's contemporaries and their descendants for not having recorded the information and preserved the documents that would have served him in his historical and biographical reconstructions. It was not, he knew, because materials were then scarce, for the documents for which he had rummaged were then common fare; the early printed texts, for example, that he could 'scarce procure at any price' were just after the Restoration 'the furniture of the nursery or stall'.[109]

---

[107] Ibid. i. ii. 69 n. 5.   [108] Ibid. i. i. lxxi.   [109] Ibid. i. i. lxxi.

Only insufficient appreciation of Shakespeare could have accounted for such neglect: otherwise 'the enthusiasm of some one or other of his admirers in the last age would have induced him to make some enquiries . . . But no such person was found; no anxiety in the public sought out any particulars concerning him after the Restoration.'[110]

Shakespeare himself proved no more attentive to facts than those who neglected to preserve facts about him. While earlier critics had censured his violation of the Aristotelian unities of time and place, Malone repeatedly noted his inaccurate representation of the post-Newtonian particulars of historical time and geographical place. In *Othello*, for example, Shakespeare 'fell into an historical inconsistency' in referring to the Turks' intention to attack both Venice and Rhodes; yet in the year 1573 when the Turks prepared for such an attack on Venice, they were 'in quiet possession of Cyprus';[111] in *The Winter's Tale*, Shakespeare based an entire plot on the 'geographical error' that Bohemia had a sea-coast.[112] Shakespeare's carelessness with time and space accounted for dramatic as well as historical inconsistencies. Repeatedly Malone calls him to task for his 'careless . . . computation of time' as when, in *Cymbeline*, Imogen falls asleep at midnight and Iachimo enters immediately to the clock's striking of three (II. ii.) or for 'considering the very same spot, at one and at the same time, as the outside and inside', as when in one scene Othello interrogates Emilia and Desdemona within the castle yet Roderigo and Iago converse outside it (IV. ii).[113]

The factual errors that commanded most attention were anachronisms—the misplacing of events, persons, and customs in time. They were most offensive in Shakespeare's history plays—Greek, Roman, and British—though Malone complained that they pervaded all his writings: 'almost every page of his works shows that he was totally negligent' of chronological sequence; 'Shakspeare . . . perpetually offended against chronology in all his plays.' Their notes regularly drew attention to such offences: the Roman Lucrece's seventeenth-century superscription of 'more than haste' on her letter to Tarquin;

[110] Malone–Boswell, *PPWS*, ix. 290.
[111] Ibid. xiv. 301.   [112] Ibid. ix. 431.
[113] Malone–Boswell, *PPWS*, ix. 431.

Cleopatra's proposing a game of billiards; Brutus's reference to the sick wearing handkerchiefs on their heads; Cade's grievance against the abuse of printing in the reign of Henry VI; Hector's mention of Aristotle; Aaron's talk of monasteries and popish tricks in *Titus*; the prospect of death on the wheel in *Coriolanus*.[114] Malone's impatience with anachronisms was predictable, for Shakespeare's eclectic dramatizations of the ancient and British past muddled the historical discriminations that Malone's apparatus was in the process of constituting and establishing.

Despite the pervasiveness of these 'inaccuracies', however, Malone never consigned Shakespeare's disregard for facts to the custom of his times. While allowing philological and cultural aberrations, he unqualifiedly judged the historical deviations 'errors', 'mistakes', and 'inconsistencies', and scrupulously corrected them, in this respect resembling the editors he most disparaged: the 'superintendor' of the Second Folio, who corrected Shakespeare's syntax and vocabulary by his own standards, and Pope, who in his 1725 edition 'licentiously' emended, highlighted, and stigmatized Shakespeare according to his own peremptory taste. Earlier, less 'conservative' editors were less disturbed by anachronisms, either blaming them on the vulgar players and correcting them, like Pope, or allowing (and even applauding) them as 'poetic License', like Theobald.[115]

Malone attempted to blame Shakespeare's 'inaccuracies' on materials he had either rewritten or used as sources. In his 'Dissertation on the Three Parts of *King Henry VI*', for example, he argued that the abundant anachronisms in these works were committed by other playwrights and provided evidence that part one was the work of another playwright and parts two and three were Shakespeare's rewritings of two earlier plays.[116] Though in this essay he maintained that when Shakespeare himself consulted the sources, as in the writing of *Richard III*, he set 'the matter truly as it was', his notes to that play signalled numerous deviations from historical fact. For example, Shakespeare represented Clarence's imprisonment in the first scene and the funeral of Henry VI in the second, although the former 'in fact' occurred in 1477–8 and the latter in 1471.[117] Whenever

[114] Ibid. xxiii. 68, xx. 182, xii. 244, 47, xviii. 315, vii, 297, xxi. 355, xiv. 127.
[115] Smith, *Eighteenth Century Essays*, pp. 52, 81.
[116] Malone, *PPWS*, vi. 381–429.   [117] Malone–Boswell, *PPWS*, xix. 5.

possible, however, anachronisms were charged to Shakespeare's sources, to Plutarch or Holinshed. But since those sources were themselves mediated, it was difficult to determine at what stage of transmission the inaccuracy had been introduced: with Plutarch's English translator North, or Holinshed's source Hall, or Hall's source Sir Thomas More or Polydore Vergil. Anachronisms might have originated at any stage between the eye-witness account of an event and Shakespeare's dramatization of it.

The earliest illustration we have from a Shakespeare performance, the opening scene from *Titus Andronicus* attributed to Henry Peacham, suggests that they might also have slipped in during production. In the illustration depicting Tamora pleading with Titus, the costumes and weapons intermingle Roman, medieval, and Elizabethan styles. As the production had no concern for the progression of time in history, so the artist ignored the sequence of action in the play. The sketch, as the transcript beneath it notes, conflates two scenes from the play: Titus refusing Tamora's plea for mercy in Act I and Aaron refusing Lucius's (Titus's in the transcript) entreaty to penance in Act V.[118] While the conflation has confused modern commentators, it is quite purposeful: it synoptically puts two declamatory situations, each concerning execution, in chiasmic relation: in the first, a Roman denies a Goth; in the second, a barbarian rebuffs a Roman. The sketch thus possesses a rhetorical, political, and visual coherence that is independent of temporal sequence; indeed, it depends on its very disruption.

However pervasive 'inaccuracies' were among Shakespeare and his contemporaries, Malone could not have included them in the category of the customary without challenging the universality of his own criterion of factual exactitude. Yet the status, indeed the very definition of 'fact' had changed between Shakespeare's time and Malone's, sharply differentiating the two periods. The shift in the word's meaning during that two-century stretch is that between two radically different types of event. Throughout the seventeenth century a 'fact' was not a

---

[118] For a discussion and reproduction of the single sheet containing both the sketch and the 40-line text—the former routinely published, the latter almost never—see J. Dover Wilson '"Titus Andronicus" on the Stage in 1595', *Shakespeare Survey*, I (1948), 17–22.

unique piece of information determined by positivistic and objective evidence, but rather an exemplary deed of usually moral and often criminal consequence. That Shakespeare was born in Stratford in 1564 is a 'fact' in the later sense; that Shakespeare poached deer was a 'fact' in the earlier sense. One fact issued from documents, the Stratford register; the other circulated in various spoken and written accounts, among them those conveyed by Rowe, Betterton, and Fulman.

Malone expected the plays, no less than the biographical anecdotes, to evince verifiable facts. As he had read Rowe's tales and Macklin's and Ireland's forgeries, so he read the plays, particularly the histories, against documented facts. His bulky notes to the historical plays disclosed factual errors in the historical plays in just the same way as his notes to Rowe's 'Account'. So numerous were his corrections to Rowe, that he subsequently undertook his own account of Shakespeare's life; similarly, his refutation of the Ireland forgeries required the simultaneous publication of authentic documents and instruments. And in the case of Shakespeare's histories, the invalidation of incorrect materials laid the way for the institution of accurate ones. Corrected accounts of the events and customs misrepresented in the plays occur in the footnotes and endnotes, if not replacing Shakespeare's text, at least providing the factual record by which to set it straight.

Malone's apparatus situated Shakespeare within a self-contained temporal unity constructed on the basis of a positivistic standard that his work, and the work of his sources, could never satisfy. By repeatedly calling on facts as the ultimate arbiters of truth and meaning, the apparatus privileged their reality over the linguistic, fictive, and dramatic excesses of the text. The facts displayed in both the essays and the notes controlled the activity of the text, serving simultaneously to establish Shakespeare's past difference and to validate Malone's present epistemology.

Yet the standard of factual accuracy by which all materials were verified or rejected was itself peculiarly alien to its Shakespearean subject. It might even be called anachronistic, misplaced in a period indifferent to factual accuracy. Copley's painting of Charles I and Parliament once again proves analogous. Its most prominent subject certainly did not share

Copley's Malonean obsession with authenticity; Charles I, as Malone knew well, had read (and remarked on) Shakespeare in the notoriously inauthentic Second Folio.[119] Though disturbed that the monarch contented himself with that vitiated version of the playwright's works, Malone never considered the possibility that the very criterion of authenticity might be embedded in history, no less than the customs and manners registered in his edition and the furnishings and dress rendered in Copley's painting.

Fig. 1. Woodcut, *Edward III and Parliament*, Holinshed, *Chronicles of England, Scotland, and Ireland* (1577)

The criterion would have been more alien still in the reigns of Elizabeth and James, as an illustration of the King and Parliament published during the reign of the former suggests. The 1577 edition of the publication on which Shakespeare's British histories were largely based, Holinshed's *Chronicles of the Kings*

---

[119] Malone–Boswell, *PPWS*, ii. 659. Steevens possessed Charles's copy of the Second Folio. For Charles's jottings in the volume, see T. A. Birrell, *English Monarchs and Their Books from Henry VII to Charles II*, The Panizzi Lectures, (London, 1987), pp. 44–5.

of England, Scotland, and Ireland, was illustrated with a woodcut of the King and his counsellors (Fig. 3.1). The same woodcut was used twenty-six times to illustrate the reigns of kings from William the Conqueror to Edward VI.[120] It respected no singularity: not that of a given time, place, or person—not even that of the King. A chronicle history knows no anachronism because events repeat themselves without the uniqueness facts would later prescribe. The complementary relation between authenticity and forgery applies here too. History must take the form of unique phenomena falling into unique periods (with their own singular principle of cohesion) before a disregard for its characterizing difference can be considered ahistorical. The language in which Shakespeare's chronicle-based histories were written contained no word for 'anachronism'.[121]

---

[120] The woodcuts have been identified and counted by Ruth Samson Luborsky and Elizabeth Ingram, *English Books with Woodcuts*, 1536–1603, forthcoming. I wish to thank them for allowing me to see their manuscript.

[121] See Herman J. Ebeling, 'The Word Anachronism', *Modern Language Notes*, 52 (1937), 120–1.

4

Individuating Shakespeare's Experience: Biography, Chronology, and the Sonnets

JOHN Singleton Copley's painting of Charles I's entry into the House of Commons has relevance for this chapter as well as the last, suggesting how a commitment to authenticity encouraged the differentiation not only of a specific period but of individual identities. An authentic depiction of the chosen historical event required accurate representation not only of architecture, furnishings, and dress, but also of the fifty-eight participants in the event: Charles I, Prince Rupert, and the fifty-six members of the House.[1] We have seen how Copley, with Malone's guidance, delved into antiquarian publications and private collections in order to locate contemporary likenesses of the participants, making the necessary adjustments if they had been taken earlier or later than 1642. In the painting, each member is differentiated no less than the King and Prince by his appearance and, in so far as the available sources made possible, by his position in and reaction to the event depicted. Moreover, the differentiation is based not on formal considerations dictated by the composition of the painting, but rather on the particulars registered in documents. Each member is an identifiable individual possessing a distinct physiognomy and participating, from a specified position, in a unique experience that distinguishes him further still.

As Copley's painting individuated historical figures, so too Malone's textual and scholarly practices individuated Shakespeare. Yet it must be stressed at the outset that the individuality the painting confers on each of the fifty-six members depends on their common identity as Members of Parliament, the identity asserted at the very moment the painting represents by the Speaker's famous reply to the King's demand: 'I have, sire,

[1] For an identification of the portraits, see Julius David Prown, *John Singleton Copley in England 1774–1815* (Cambridge, Mass., 1966), fig. 600; see also Ch. 3 above, nn. 1 and 2.

neither eyes to see nor tongue to speak in this place, but as the House is pleased to direct me.'[2] In the painting, each member remains indivisible from the parliamentary group to which he belongs—and, in the case of the Speaker, which he represents. In contrast, by Malone's practices Shakespeare's individuality emerged independently of any collective body; it issued instead from his unique and self-contained genius. Like 'authenticity' and 'period', the key words respectively of the previous two chapters, the word 'individual' provides a semantic focus for the general change implicit in Malone's practices, in this case a decisive shift from individuation predicated on corporate political solidarity to individuation predicated on personal artistic complexity and growth.[3]

We will return to Copley's painting again in the next chapter to consider in what respect the individuation of persons implied both the privilege violated by the King's entry and the right to representation asserted by the Speaker. This chapter concerns how one extraordinary person, Shakespeare, came to be individuated through three of Malone's major Shakespearean projects; a biography, 'The Life of William Shakspeare'; a chronology, 'An Attempt to Ascertain the Order in which The Plays of Shakspeare Were Written'; and an edition of Shakespeare's Sonnets.[4] All three projects broke abruptly with traditional treatments. His documentary 'Life', not published until 1821 but occupying Malone throughout his career, replaced Rowe's unfactual 'Account of the Life, &c. of Mr. William Shakespear' which, as we have seen, had become the standard biography through the eighteenth century. His essay on chronology, first published in 1778 but revised for the 1790 and 1821 editions, was the first chronology of the works to be published.[5]

---

[2] Quoted in Roy Strong, '*And When Did You Last See Your Father?*' *The Victorian Painter and British History* (London, 1978), p. 28.

[3] Raymond Williams, *The Long Revolution* (New York, 1961), pp. 75–8 and *Keywords: A Vocabulary of Culture and Society* (Oxford, 1976).

[4] All three works are included in Malone–Boswell, *PPWS*.

[5] In the three-volume *Notes and Various Readings* (the first volume appearing in 1774 and all three volumes in 1783) to his edition (1767–8), Edward Capell scattered references to dates within plays; he also provided a list of their 'succession' based on the dates of the earliest impressions of the plays, Stationers' Register entries, and outside references to the plays: ii. 83–6. For recent assessments of Malone's chronology, see S. Schoenbaum, *Shakespeare's Lives* (Oxford, 1970), pp. 169–71, and Gary Taylor, *Reinventing Shakespeare: A Cultural History from the Restoration to the Present* (New York, 1989).

And his edition of the 1609 Sonnets conclusively supplanted
John Benson's 1640 *Poems: Written by Will. Shake-speare. Gent.*, the
hybrid edition in which Shakespeare's Sonnets had been read
in the late seventeenth and eighteenth centuries, and perman-
ently secured the sequence a position within the corpus of
Shakespeare's works.[6] From all three works Shakespeare's
identity was constituted, or rather reconstituted: on the basis of
new factual materials, according to a new temporal structure,
with a new focus on previously unprobed interiority. The
biography collected the facts distinguishing Shakespeare's life,
the chronology arranged the works to display the course of
Shakespeare's development, and the edition of the Sonnets
emphasized their importance as writing in Shakespeare's own
person.

After completing his annotations of Rowe's 'Account' for the
1790 edition, Malone resolved to write his own biography of
Shakespeare, integrating new materials with those he had
compiled for the annotations and weaving them all into 'one
uniform and connected narrative'.[7] Through the examination
of documents for the biography, he attempted both to recover
information that his predecessors had neglected and to test the
veracity of the reports which they had passed down. In Malone's
mind, the facts he compiled compensated, however imperfectly,
for the 'penury of [Shakespeare's] contemporaries' who had
failed to transmit 'any particulars of his private life or dramatick
history'. In the absence of their testimonies, Malone extracted
the information he considered relevant from parish and theatrical registers, title-pages, legal instruments, and publications of
the period. Research provided new criteria by which to evaluate
reports that had circulated in various compendia, many of
which Rowe had gathered. A large part of the biography was
devoted to the kind of scrutiny to which we have seen the deer-
stealing anecdote subjected. Reports were credited or dismissed
after having been tested against what could be gleaned from

---

[6] John Benson, *Poems: Written by Wil. Shake-speare. Gent.* (London, 1640). See Ch. 2
n. 1 above.

[7] 'Prospectus for an entirely New Life of Shakspeare compiled from original and
authentick documents', published separately and with *An Inquiry into the Authenticity of
Certain Miscellaneous Papers and Legal Instruments*, 1795.

documents contemporary with Shakespeare. Both processes, introducing new materials and reassessing the old, yielded a wealth of factual details that more thoroughly and finely articulated Shakespeare's life. Before Malone's undertaking, the facts about that life could be summarized in one sentence: 'All that is known with any degree of certainty concerning Shakespeare, is—"that he was born at Stratford upon Avon, married and had children there, went to London, where he commenced actor, and wrote poems and plays,—returned to Stratford, made his will, died, and was buried".'[8] Investigation into all available documents expanded that single sentence into a 525-page 'Life of Shakspeare' with a 175-page appendix 'compiled from Originall and Authentick Documents'. What was known about Shakespeare was amplified by information concerning such particulars as his ancestry, the profession and status of his father, the number of children in his family, and the precise terms of the legal instruments in which he was named. This is not to say that Shakespeare's parentage, family, profession, and legal transactions were previously of no concern, as a glance at the anecdotes current earlier demonstrates. One anecdote identified Shakespeare's father as a butcher, another implied an adulterous relationship between him and a vintner's wife, numerous accounts involved him in theatrical production, and still another subjected him to prosecution and whipping.[9] It was not, as Malone supposed, that there had been no earlier interest in Shakespeare's life, but rather that it was not then to be satisfied by uncovering and scrutinizing documents.

The majority of the materials featured in Malone's biography documented the bettering of Shakespeare's literary, social, and economic status. No less than three accounts established that Southampton, Elizabeth, and James had all bestowed special

[8] *Supplement to the Edition of Shakespeare's Plays Published in 1778 by Samuel Johnson and George Steevens in Two Volumes* (London, 1780), ii. 653.

[9] The anecdotes discussed in this chapter are all included in Nicholas Rowe's 'Some Account of the Life &c. of Mr. William Shakespeare' (1709), in *Eighteenth Century Essays on Shakespeare*, ed. D. Nichol Smith (Oxford, 1963), 1–22. Subsequent references to Rowe will be from this edition, as will those to the prefaces of Pope (1725), Theobald (1733), and Johnson (1765). Earlier versions of these accounts, as well as excerpts from Rowe, can be found in E. K. Chambers, *William Shakespeare: A Study of Facts and Problems* (Oxford, 1930), ii. appx C, 'The Shakespeare-Mythos', 238–302. Schoenbaum comments on them in *Shakespeare's Lives*, part 2, 'Shakespeare of the Legends: The First Biographers', pp. 75–143.

attention and favour upon him. In proving that the encomium to 'Willy' in Spenser's 'Tears of the Muses' was not addressed to Shakespeare, Malone determined that Spenser did none the less revere and honour him, as did all men elevated by either class or literary accomplishment: 'The gentle Shakspeare enjoyed the favour of all the most accomplished men that adorned the period in which he lived'; 'The patronage of Lord Southampton, the valour of the court, his own splendid genius and amiable manners, must have made his company sought after by all who were distinguished for their rank or literature'.[10] The only figure of note who did not seek him out was, according to Malone, Ben Jonson; but this very hostility testified further to Shakespeare's success, for it was precisely that success which kindled Jonson's resentment and envy.[11] Nor did Shakespeare's familiarity with the gifted and powerful interfere with his domestic attachments, for in addition to associating with the most powerful and accomplished, he also 'must have been perpetually engaged in amicable discourse with his family'.[12]

At the same time that he acquired a reputation for himself, Shakespeare also gradually increased his wealth and rank. He began his career, according to Malone, not to escape criminal prosecution for deer-poaching, 'not under the degrading circumstances which unauthorized tradition had handed down', but under financial duress, his father being 'in pecuniary difficulties'; by the time of his death, however, he was able to leave his family 'in a state of comparative affluence'. Thanks to his distinguished patrons, as well as to his own prudence, he quickly 'placed himself in circumstances of ease and comfort'. Malone had scrupulously examined documents to determine exactly 'the pecuniary benefit which he derived from [his] situation'. Among thousands of documents in the Stratford archives, he had discovered a letter to Shakespeare requesting a loan of thirty pounds, 'no inconsiderable sum in those days'; 'such a request could not have been made to a person who has not possessed of means . . .'.[13] The coat of arms 'obtained by his

[10] Malone–Boswell, *PPWS*, ii. 487.

[11] Malone's treatment of both Jonson's character and his work was so consistently disparaging that Boswell felt obliged to apologize for it (Ibid. i. xxxi–xlvii) and revise it (xlviii–l).

[12] Ibid. ii. 486.

[13] On the discovery of this document, see Schoenbaum, *Shakespeare's Lives*, p. 247.

father in consequence of the poet's celebrity' testified to another form of achievement. At the conclusion of the biography, calculations determined how much his share in the King's Men was worth at his death, what his earnings were during his lifetime, and the value of his estate—taking into consideration 'the relative value of money, the mode of living in that age, the luxury and taxes of the present time, and various other circumstances'. Because his home in Stratford housed the Queen and her company for three weeks during the Civil War, 'we may reasonably suppose it then was the best private house in the town'. In so far as the biography can be said to be woven into the 'uniform and connected narrative' Malone intended, it tells a story of the gradual acquisition of fame, wealth, and status as documented by legal instruments and official records. While temporal progression as charted by dated documents strung the factual bits and pieces together, the gradual attainment of prosperity provided the rationale for the whole: 'He had the good fortune to gather an estate equal to his occasion.'[14]

To some degree, the emphasis on Shakespeare's finances reflected the limitation of the documentary sources—largely records of Shakespeare's assets and purchases. Yet there was another sustained emphasis through the whole for which there was no warrant in factual materials. In applauding the success of the biography, Boswell named the one overarching verity assumed and confirmed by the entire account: 'The greatest genius which this country has produced, maintained, from his youth upwards, that respectability of character which unquestionably belonged to him in after life.'[15] In every instance, the traditional accounts that conflicted with Shakespeare's respectability were rejected as factually inaccurate while those which confirmed it were validated. Yet, as we have already seen, the anecdotes regularly featured Shakespeare in indecorous or transgressive acts: versifying in a butcher's shop, poaching deer, pre-empting his colleague's tryst, begetting William Davenant of a vintner's wife, offending an usurious friend with a stinging epitaph. In utter contrast to the anecdotes that cast Shakespeare as thief, adulterer, and carouser, Malone's 'Life of

---

[14] Malone–Boswell, *PPWS*, ii. 484–7, 518–20.
[15] Ibid. 472.

Shakspeare' from beginning to end uniformly displayed Shakespeare's 'respectability of character'.

Malone takes particular pains to refute two of the accounts
that appeared in Rowe. In the first, already discussed in
Chapter 2, Shakespeare committed a legal infraction—he stole
deer; in the latter, he committed a social, moral, and religious
one—he wrote a scathing and damning epitaph in anticipation
of a friend's death. When reports preserved Shakespeare in
respectable activities, however, they were documented and
credited. Southampton was proven to have munificently rewarded Shakespeare, although the degree of his generosity
needed to be reduced from 1,000 pounds to a more plausible
100, and the purpose must have been not, as the anecdote
specified, to fund a large purchase (of which a record would
have remained) but as a gift in return for dedicating works to
him (of which records did remain in the dedications to Shakespeare's two narrative poems).[16] Nor did Malone question the
accounts illustrating that Shakespeare had 'enjoyed the approbation and favour of two successive monarchs',[17] even
though the only authority for the reports of the King's admiration
was Rowe's assurance that Davenant had communicated it,
and for those of the Queen's attention the prefatory epistle to
John Dennis's 1702 adaptation of *The Merry Wives of Windsor*.
Malone credited another account maintaining that Shakespeare
had based the constable's character in *A Midsummer Night's
Dream* on that of a constable encountered during his regular
trips between London and Stratford; the account was accepted
in part because it featured the dramatist exercising his singular
dramatic gift of observing human nature and in part because
the frequent trips home testified to his affectionate nature
which could not have endured prolonged separation from
friends and family. That the constable appeared in *Much Ado
About Nothing* and not *A Midsummer Night's Dream* did not
'detract in the smallest degree from the credit of the fact
itself'.[18]

Malone's narrative followed Shakespeare along a novelistic
trajectory of increasing prosperity and respectability that could
not accommodate the inculpatory accounts. Yet the earlier

[16] Malone–Boswell, *PPWS*. ii. 480.
[17] Ibid. 478.   [18] Ibid. 490–1.

accounts all shared a structure that made them compatible: whether inculpatory or laudatory, they had in common the theme of requital, in contrast to the biography's theme of gradual attainment and acquisition. Both types of early anecdote represented Shakespeare in commercial, sexual, or verbal exchanges that resulted either in punishment and disapprobation or reward and favour. What characterized these exchanges was not their effect on Shakespeare's moral, professional, social, or economic position, but rather their effect on his relation to others: to neighbours, colleagues, friends, family, nobility, and royalty. The account of Shakespeare's first literary effort, for example, consisted of a series of exchanges: Shakespeare's deer-poaching was followed by the owner's prosecution which prompted Shakespeare to write his first formal work, a vindictive ballad that sparked the plaintiff's redoubled prosecution which the defendant avenged by a satiric reference in *The Merry Wives of Windsor*.[19] An account of what may have stood for Shakespeare's last literary effort also followed a structure of returns. Shakespeare's friend, John Combe, a usurer who by definition takes in more than he gives out, received more than he asked for when in anticipation of the final reckoning he asked Shakespeare to write him an epitaph and received one that left him no hope of atonement and that he could never forgive.[20] In these two accounts, Shakespeare's verse involved him in vindictive rather than productive exchanges that prompted not gratitude or service but punishment and anger. The account of Shakespeare's relation to Ben Jonson followed a similar pattern of exchange, in this case of rejection and acceptance: the unknown Jonson, according to Rowe, offered one of his plays to the Players who would have returned it with 'an ill-natur'd Answer' had not Shakespeare been so impressed that he recommended the author and his work to the public; whether Jonson ever reciprocated in kind remains undetermined at the end of the account —'I don't know whether the other ever made him an equal return'.[21] Even the two theatrical parts that tradition assigned Shakespeare, one comic and the other tragic, cast him in the same retributive configuration. Shakespeare was remembered as having acted Adam in *As You Like It* and the Ghost in

[19] Smith, *Eighteenth Century Essays*, pp. 3, 10.
[20] Ibid. 20.   [21] Ibid. 7.

Hamlet,[22] both old men dramatizing modes of discharging debts to a master, one through antique service, the other through revenge under the old law.[23]

In the traditional accounts, both those accepted and those rejected by Malone, transactions occurred in which Shakespeare's talents were caught up in continuing circuits of exchange that took either the positive form of patronage, in which favour prompted renewed service, or the negative form of revenge, in which offence prompted retaliation. Rather than assessing what Shakespeare accumulated throughout his career, the accounts displayed the various networks of exchange, compensatory and retaliatory, in which his talents engaged him. Thus it was not the inculpatory and the laudatory accounts that were incompatible, but the traditional accounts and the documentary biography. The latter shaped Shakespeare's identity through records of various forms of personal profit and prosperity through which he gradually established himself; the former defined it in terms of his relations to others in systems based on reciprocity and requital. In the factual biography, Shakespeare ended up with his *own* shares, *own* house, *own* coat of arms, *own* monument, and descendants more affluent than his ancestors: a gradual triumph of personal aggrandizement. In the anecdotes, it was his impact on others rather than his own development that mattered: he either compliantly stabilized or defiantly offset diverse transactional relations for which he was publicly answerable. Documentary facts individuated Shakespeare through an inventory of the notice, status, and wealth that he had earned through his own poetic and dramatic genius; anecdotal occasions encoded social, political, and institutional relations that were fractured or ratified by a genius under obligation to render itself into some form of responsible public exchange. Shakespeare's moral conduct is central to both Malone's biographical progress and Rowe's anecdotal transactions: in the former Shakespeare himself embodies uniform virtue that is both confirmed and rewarded by the trajectory

[22] Smith, *Eighteenth Century Essays*, p. 3.

[23] While Rowe recorded Shakespeare's performance as the Ghost, his performance as Adam was first noted by William Oldys, who traced it back to some Restoration actors who had learned it of one of Shakespeare's younger brothers; Capell accepted the account in his notes on *As You Like It*. See Schoenbaum, *Shakespeare's Lives*, pp. 90–1.

of increased prestige and profit structuring his life; in the latter
it is Shakespeare's erratic actions or transactions that are
instructive, demonstrating the uses and abuses of talent as
measured by communal standards.

The anecdotes about Shakespeare provided no dates. Rowe's
life contained only the date of Shakespeare's birth and his age
at death. While his 'Account' was loosely organized around
Shakespeare's early, middle, and late years, no attempt was
made to place the various reports in precise temporal sequence.
Malone's biography, on the other hand, provided the dates of
all the documents from which it was compiled. The chronological
organization of his information was a crucial element in Malone's
attempt to accomplish his aim of weaving 'the whole into one
uniform and connected narrative'. However, he never completed the biography. Having completed his consideration of
the 'scanty information' relating to Shakespeare's roles and
merits as an actor, he broke off just at the point where a
discussion of Shakespeare's dramatic career would have begun.
Boswell picked up the account at the point where that career
had just ended, Shakespeare's retirement to London, regretting
that the task had fallen upon him after Malone's death to
arrange the facts collected from Malone's papers and from the
notes Malone had affixed to Rowe's 'Account' for his 1790
edition. Thus no narrative connected the beginning of his
career with its conclusion, Shakespeare's initial arrival at
London with his final return to Stratford, the very twenty-three
years, by Malone's calculation, during which he wrote the
works that made him deserving of a biography. Instead, a
separate work first published in 1778 and then included in the
1790 edition was inserted to fill the gap: Malone's 'Attempt to
Ascertain the Order in which the Plays of Shakspeare Were
Written'. In the place of information relating to the central
years of Shakespeare's life, the biography supplied a chronology
of all the Folio plays (with the exception of *Titus Andronicus*,
which Malone believed to be only partially by Shakespeare).
No changes were made to fit the chronology into the biographical
narrative that preceded and followed it: except for a few
revisions, it was printed precisely as it had appeared when
published as an independent work. Separate entries for each

play were given indicating how the date for it was determined, from *The First Part of King Henry VI* in 1589 to *The Tempest* in 1612. While Boswell in his preface doubted that Malone had intended the chronology to be inserted into his narrative, he thought 'the life of a writer must be strangely defective which contained no account of his works; and I have, therefore, ventured to give it a place as one of the sections of Mr. Malone's Biography'.[24]

It is not only an 'account of his works' that the biography would have lacked without the chronology, but any kind of account of the years in which Shakespeare wrote the plays which made his life of interest. The documents pertaining to the dates of the plays came to represent the crucial years of his life. Although Boswell considered it a makeshift arrangement, the substitution nevertheless served to forge a continuity based on dates between the biography and the works. The life gave way to the works which passed back into the life, all on a single temporal continuum. In lieu of archival documents, the plays were positioned to serve as the primary sources for information about Shakespeare's life during his years in London. The arrangement itself suggested that only by scrutinizing the plays exhaustively, as if they were archival documents, could Shakespeare's life in its entirety—from the beginning through to the end—be known.

In attempting to determine the dates of the plays, Malone relied primarily on entries in the Stationers' Register and allusions in contemporary publications. Yet he also inspected the plays as if they too were archival repositories, culling them for references that could be matched up with datable events or situations. Regardless of the time in which they had been set, the plays contained 'frequent allusions to the circumstances of the day'. The Porter's references to 'a farmer', that hang'd himself 'on the expectation of plenty' when matched with the College of Eton's audit-book, suggested the date of 1606: the records revealed that the price of wheat, 'the great criterion of plenty or scarcity', was unprecedentedly low that year. Such research was seen to provide not only the date in which a given play was written but also the content of Shakespeare's mind at the time

---

[24] Malone–Boswell, *PPWS*, 1. xx.

of that play's writing. If the Nurse's reference, 'now since the earthquake eleven years', referred to the earthquake recorded as having occurred on 6 April 1580, it would then refer to Shakespeare's memory of 'an earthquake which had been *felt*'in his youth' (emphasis added). At the point where Henry IV assures his brothers that 'This is the English, not the Turkish court, | Not Amurath Amurath succeeds, | But Harry Harry,' Shakespeare 'probably had here *in contemplation* the cruelty practised by the Turkish emperor Mahomet, who after the death of his father, Amurath the Third, in Feb. 1596, invited his unsuspecting brothers to a feast, and caused them all to be strangled'. Sir Andrew's unwillingness to give 'my part for a pension of thousands to be paid by the Sophy', revealed that Shakespeare 'was perhaps *thinking* of Sir Robert Shirley' whose service to the Sophy of Persia was well known in England in 1607, as could be established by a contemporary play and also by later documents. The identification of topical references in dating the plays disclosed the particulars presumed to exist in Shakespeare's mind at the time of their writing. The plays thus functioned as repositories of Shakespeare's thoughts and feelings as stimulated by contemporary events.[25]

Another type of datable event served Malone in devising his chronology: the registration and publication of books. By looking at the dates on title-pages or in the Stationers' entries for works he found echoed in the plays, he obtained further evidence for his determinations. This procedure opened up a new realm of Shakespeare's supposed experience, revealing what he was encountering in his reading as well as in natural and historical occurrences. Because there are two allusions to 'Hero and Leander' in *The Two Gentlemen of Verona*, Malone conjectured that Shakespeare had in 1591 recently read Marlowe's poem— in manuscript, since no copy of the poem was known to exist before 1598 and the Stationer's entry was 1593; similarly, he assumed that it was around 1591 that Shakespeare had read the translation of Plautus's *Menaechmi* on which *The Comedy of Errors'* plot was based, again in manuscript before its publication in 1595.[26] From several passages in Act V of *Romeo and Juliet*, 'it is manifest, I think, that Shakspeare had recently read, and

[25] Ibid. ii. 384, 407, 349, 359, 444.
[26] Ibid. 320, 322, 348, 452.

remembered, some of the lines in Daniel's Complaint of Rosa-mund,' for which there was an entry in 1591–2. Malone's dating of *Cymbeline* rested on his assumption that before writing both *King Lear* and *Cymbeline* Shakespeare had been reading Sidney's *Arcadia* which provided both the model for Edgar and the name for Leonatus: 'Shakspeare having occasion to turn to that book while he was writing King Lear, the name of Leonatus adhered to his memory, and he has made it the name of one of his characters in Cymbeline.' Another book supported this conjecture: 'The story of Lear lies near to that of Cymbeline in Holinshed's Chronicle,' and the fact that Duncan and Macbeth are mentioned on a nearby page draws that play into the same approximate period of Shakespeare's consciousness. The possib-ility that Shakespeare might have read the text in question many years after its publication or many years before in manuscript, gave rise to areas of uncertainty in the dating project; so too did the possibility that particular topical refer-ences might have been added after the original writing of the play. What is important for our purposes, however, is not the validity of Malone's inferences, but rather that in the process of dating the plays, Shakespeare's experience was postulated: what he had observed and what he had read.

The nature and range of the impressions Malone could claim to have been made on Shakespeare was necessarily limited to the kind of public and historical events that had been in Shakespeare's time deemed suitable for documentation. Fur-thermore, the thoughts Malone assigned to Shakespeare, how-ever specific, hardly individuated him from any other person who experienced the same phenomena. Slurs against Puritans in *The Winter's Tale*, for example, were not peculiar to Shake-speare, as Malone allowed in noting that both King James and the theatrical population at large shared his 'hearty detestation'.[27] Nor were the impressions left by the earthquakes, plagues, wars, and coronations to which Malone found allusions in the plays. Because it drew its content from shared perceptions of commonly experienced phenomena, Shakespeare's inner life as represented in these comments could not vary significantly from those of his contemporaries. Nor could his reading of

---

[27] Malone–Boswell, *PPWS*, i. 463.

available manuscripts and printed texts distinguish him from other readers of the same materials. Yet once all the plays were arranged by date, a new possibility for differentiating Shakespeare emerged, for this arrangement formed a discrete serial unit of its own that began to look self-determined and self-contained. Possessing its own complete and integral design, the sequence could be detached from the ties to history by which it had initially been formed. The chronology provided more than a way of identifying isolated memories, feelings, and thoughts; it provided a temporal structure by which to organize not only the plays but the lifetime in which they had been written.

Once arranged in time, the plays charted out a progression that enabled the reader 'to mark the gradations by which [Shakespeare] rose from mediocrity to the summit of excellence; from artless and sometimes uninteresting dialogues, to those unparalleled compositions . . .'.[28] The chronological arrangement called into being a new mode of viewing the works: as development. Although doubting that the chronology demonstrated any 'regular scale of gradual improvement', Malone in dating the plays nevertheless established several scales on which the poet's development might be traced. Because the early works demonstrated an 'addiction to rhyming' that gradually weakened as Shakespeare either tired of 'the bondage of rhyme' or became convinced of its impropriety in the drama, Malone assumed the plays with the most rhymes to be Shakespeare's earliest. Wordplay was also judged to diminish as Shakespeare continued to develop. And characters became more finely delineated and discriminated as 'the elegant and pastoral simplicity' of his early effusions yielded to 'that moral and judicious reflection that accompanies an advanced period of life'.[29] In both style and tone, the plays followed a generally steady and self-generated progression, independent of any contemporaneous historical events.

As Malone noted, Shakespeare's first editors had paid no attention to chronological arrangement; nor had subsequent editors, for until his own effort, 'no attempt has been made to trace the progress and order of his plays'. When first published in 1778, his chronology was a 'new and curious inquiry'

---

[28] Ibid. 290–1.
[29] Ibid. 327, 318, 406.

requiring justification.[30] His eighteenth-century predecessors had done little more than contemplate the desirability of devising one. Rowe in 1709 believed 'it would be without doubt a pleasure to any Man, curious in Things of this Kind, to see and know what was the first Essay of a Fancy like *Shakespear's*'.[31] He doubted, however, that it would reveal any correlation between early and inferior plays; because Shakespeare's genius was, by a tradition tracing back to the 1623 Folio, the result of Nature and not Art, his youngest works might well have been the most excellent, 'the most vigorous', having 'the most fire and strength of Imagination in 'em'. Pope in his 1725 preface also considered the possibility of dating the plays, but disagreed on the relation to be discovered between the time of their writing and their quality. For him, however, the improvement that a chronology might mark would reveal not Shakespeare's spontaneous growth but rather his response to the increased sophistication and support of his audience: 'The Dates of his plays sufficiently evidence that his productions improved, in proportion to the respect he had for his auditors';[32] 'When the encouragement of the Court had succeeded to that of the Town, the works of his riper years are manifestly raised above those of his former.' When for his 1765 edition Johnson turned to the problem of 'by what gradations of improvement [Shakespeare] proceeded', he joined Pope in countering Rowe's opinion by maintaining that, 'however favored by nature', Shakespeare's art perforce improved in time by a steady and arduous 'gradual acquisition', the result of study and experience.[33] Each of these pre-Malonean editors, even Rowe, considered whether chronology would be useful in revealing the relative worth of the various plays; had one been available, it would have served the editor in the evaluative criticism which until the latter part of the century was deemed one of the editor's primary functions. A chronology would have provided a system of ranking the plays that could be used to support the critic's own Judgement or Taste in measuring the Beauties and Defects of a given play.

Edward Capell recognized the importance of the plays' chronology, to the extent of providing, in his *Notes and Various Readings*, an undated chronological list, a 'Scheme of their

[30] Malone–Boswell, *PPWS*, i. 290, 292.
[31] Smith, *Eighteenth Century Essays*, p. 4.   [32] Ibid. 4.   [33] Ibid. 128.

Succession', he too believing that it would be of interest to critics in 'weighing their Author's pieces, and adjusting the comparative merits of them'.[34] In the introduction to the edition itself, he adapted this 'Scheme' to further purpose, defending a number of plays whose attribution to Shakespeare had been challenged by Pope and Theobald—the *Henry VI* trilogy, *Love's Labour's Lost*, *The Taming of the Shrew*, and *Titus Andronicus*—by identifying them as early works rather than works by a lesser playwright.[35] According to Capell, the younger Shakespeare had catered to the taste of 'the people who govern theatres . . . the middle and lower orders of the world' by producing the excessive rhymes and atrocious effects that later came to offend more discerning sensibilities. Taking into account 'the Writer's childhood' at the time of their writing, he pronounced them 'his true off-spring', despite their apparent inferiority, and therefore determined to 'replace [them] amongst [their] brethren'.[36] A play's inferiority to the rest of the plays signalled not un-Shakespearean authorship but rather Shakespearean authorship at an earlier, less practiced stage. Thus it was in order to insist upon the common parentage of the Folio plays that Capell made use of chronology, thereby introducing a new mode of affiliating the plays never considered by the gatherers of the 1623 Folio plays discussed in Chapter 1.[37] While Shakespeare's friends and colleagues can be presumed to have had much readier and fuller access to the information required to date the plays, organizing a collection of plays in relation to a consideration as tendentious to their production as an author's career was apparently unthinkable to them.

When Malone finally devised and published his chronology, he apologized for what he assumed would appear to some a tedious and fruitless inquiry. Yet he did not defend it as a system either of evaluating the relative merits of the plays or of establishing their authorship; its importance lay rather in its demonstration of how Shakespeare's art developed—'how the genius of the great poet gradually expanded itself, till, like his

[34] *Notes and Various Readings to Shakespeare*, ii. 186.
[35] Capell, *MWSHCHT*, i. 44, 43.
[36] Ibid. 40.
[37] See the extensive discussion of chronology in *William Shakespeare: A Textual Companion*, eds. Stanley Wells and Gary Taylor (Oxford, 1987) that faults Heminge and Condell for their generic organization of the Folio (p. 36).

own Ariel, *it flamed amazement* in every quarter'.[38] This was an internally impelled expansion rather than, as held by Pope, Johnson, and Capell, a response to external factors such as the changing status of his audience, his ever-increasing exposure to books and experience, his concessions to popular taste. His talent unfolded spontaneously without influence from the out-side—tentative at first, then becoming bolder and more in-novative, 'advancing in his progress to excellence' during the fervidly inspired middle period of his life, waning somewhat towards the end.[39] The charting of such a development would provide a complete way of looking at all of Shakespeare's work, a totality with a beginning, a middle, and an end that accom-modated variations of style and quality without relinquishing continuity and coherence.

The 1821 edition gave physical reality to this postulated continuity and coherence. Boswell recorded that Malone left specific instructions that the works should appear in this edition in the order in which Shakespeare had, by his deter-minations, written them: 'The plan laid down by Mr. Malone, was to exhibit all his dramas in what he considered to be, from the best judgment he could form, their chronological order, that the reader might be thus enabled to trace the progress of the author's powers.[40] Malone had specified that even the history plays should follow the chronology of Shakespeare's biography rather than that of England's history, thereby breaking with a tradition extending back to the 1623 Folio. On this point, however, Boswell demurred, fearing that the substitution of the 'progress of the author's powers' for the succession of British monarchs would be 'universally objected to'.[41]

The 1623 Folio had established the traditional ordering of the plays that continued to be respected by the editors of subsequent seventeenth-century Folios as well as, in the main,

[38] Malone–Boswell, *PPWS*, ii. 468.
[39] Ibid. ii. xvii–xviii.
[40] Ibid. i. xvii.
[41] Ibid. The recent Oxford editors, however, have not found it objectionable and have printed the histories in the order they believe Shakespeare wrote them. For them, the Folio's ordering of the histories by reign is 'an accident of juxtaposition which continued to inhibit a proper sensitivity to the individuality of the eight plays huddled in this anachronistic chronological ghetto'; Wells and Taylor, *Companion*, p. 38.

by all the eighteenth-century editors.[42] Yet as Malone regretted, 'the Folio editors manifestly paid no attention to chronological arrangement', being in this respect not unlike the anachronistic Shakespeare: 'there is nothing in which he is less accurate, than the computation of time'.[43] The Folio contained no dates at all for the individual plays, neither for the eighteen plays that had previously been published in quarto nor for the eighteen plays that were being published for the first time. The only date it recorded had nothing to do with the time of Shakespeare's writing: 1623, the year of the volume's publication. If dates besides those of publication had been affixed to the plays, they would have been those of their first performance, as in Ben Jonson's 1616 Folio, rather than of their writing. Indifferent to the dates of the plays, the First Folio grouped them into three kinds: comedies, histories, and tragedies. The comedies and tragedies followed no temporal order at all, while the histories, as we have seen, were arranged to reflect England's chronicle history. Nor does the only other early listing of the plays follow Shakespeare's 'progress': Francis Meres's 1598 *Palladis Tamia: Wits Treasury* named twelve of Shakespeare's plays, thereby providing the important information that these twelve were all written by 1598, but the list euphuistically balanced six comedies against six tragedies, just as the Folio respected generic divisions but with no attention to the order in which the plays were written.[44] The plays published in quarto were of course dated,

---

[42] Rowe follows the Folio ordering of the plays; Pope, however, divides its three classifications into four in his 1725 editions: Comedies, Historical Plays, Tragedies from History, and Tragedies from Fable; he also rearranges the order of the Comedies somewhat. Although they do not adapt his nomenclature, subsequent editors more or less follow his precedent, apparently in the attempt to define the genres more strictly. Pope, Theobald, Warburton, and Hanmer classify *Lear* as a History; Capell, Johnson, Steevens, and Malone (1790) classify it as a Tragedy but place *Macbeth* with the Histories. *Cymbeline* remains classified with the Tragedies throughout the century. The Cambridge edition (1863–6) is the first to return to the Folio order and the Globe (1866) makes it standard until the end of the century and beyond. No edition follows the 1821 chronological arrangement, though the Comedy, History, Tragedy, Romance progression formulated by Edward Dowden enables the generic and chronological to be fused. See Ch. 1, n. 37. On the novelty and fluidity of the Folio's generic terms, see Stephen Orgel, 'Shakespeare and the Kinds of Drama', *Critical Inquiry*, 6 (1979), 1, 107–23.

[43] Malone–Boswell, *PPWS*, ii. 451, 351.

[44] 'As *Plautus* and *Seneca* are accounted the best for Comedy and Tragedy among the Latines: so *Shakespeare* among the English is the most excellent in both kinds for the stage; for Comedy, witness his *Gentlemen of Verona*, his *Errors*, his *Loue labors lost*, his *Loue*

though the date was, as with the Folio, that of publication rather than composition; in some cases the date or occasion of its performance is also given. The registers of the Stationers' Company also assigned dates to plays for the purposes of recording when the right to print and sell a play was secured. The significant dates in Shakespeare's period, then, were those specifying not when a play was written, but when it was made public, either in print or in performance. As we have seen, even as late as 1778 Malone felt he had to justify attempting the 'new and curious inquiry' that would ascertain the order in which Shakespeare wrote his plays. Yet once that order was determined, the works became fastened to Shakespeare's sequence of writing, following an arrangement that reflected his and only his contribution to the making of the plays.

The printing of the plays according to the order of composition encouraged the reader to encounter them in that same order. The reader was invited to follow the complete 'progress of Shakespeare's powers', experiencing each successive play as a step in the development of the author's art. Because that creative process possessed its own inherent purpose and design, it no longer needed to depend on the outside world of history for its significance. Self-referential and self-perpetuating, it 'gradually expanded itself', spontaneously unfurling over the years. The organization of the plays along a temporal spectrum provided the mechanism for releasing them from the history that had supplied the very co-ordinates by which that spectrum had been constructed in the first place. It also entirely eclipsed the arrangement of the original 1623 Folio, which grouped the plays into three dramatic kinds and printed them within those groups in accordance with printing-house practices, priorities, and constraints that still remain to be determined.[45] By supplanting that arrangement, the chronology obscured its reference

labours wonne, his *Midsummers night dreame*, & his *Merchant of Venice*: for Tragedy his *Richard the 2. Richard the 3. Henry the 4. King Iohn, Titus Andronicus* and his *Romeo* and *Iuliet*.' *Palladis Tamia* (1598) with intro. by Don Cameron Allen (New York, 1938), pp. 281–2. Quoted by Chambers, *William Shakespeare*, ii. 194, who suggests that Meres may have omitted the *Henry VI* plays in order to retain the balance: i. 208.

[45] On the types of printing-house considerations that might have determined the Folio's arrangement of the plays, see W. W. Greg, *The Shakespeare First Folio: Its Bibliographical and Textual History* (Oxford, 1955), pp. 80–1; Wells and Taylor, *Companion*, p. 38.

to the wide array of productive activities we saw to be diversely represented in the Folio preliminaries. The chronological schema committed the plays to a history of individual and finite creation rather than one of collective and indefinite production on state and in print. Needless to say, the chronological structure could not possibly accommodate the non-authorial contributions of collaborators, book-keepers, adapters, copyists, censors, compositors, and correctors; nor could it allow that a play, constantly subject to modification in the process of being performed and printed, might not at any point possess a finalized state, at least not one of the author's prescribing. The chronology both assumed and determined that Shakespeare, alone, finished a play once and for all in a specified year.

Malone's biography differentiated Shakespeare by accumulating all available factual information and organizing it in a dated temporal sequence; his chronology, by situating the plays on the same temporal continuum, made it possible to extend that biography into the works. Both the documents and the plays provided specifics characterizing Shakespeare's outer life and their postulated inward correlatives. Even specifics concerning his private life appeared to emerge as a result of conjoining the two types of materials. Biographical documents determined that Shakespeare's twelve-year-old son Hamnet died in 1596; believing *King John* to have been written in the same year, Malone inferred that Constance's lament at Arthur's death expressed Shakespeare's own grief at the loss of his son, which in turn gave his dating probability.[46] Documents recorded that Shakespeare's wife was seven and a half years older than he; believing that *A Midsummer Night's Dream* was written thirteen years after his marriage and *Twelfth Night* eleven years after that, he speculated that the former's reference to love 'misgrafted in respect of years' and the latter's injunction that 'the woman take | An elder than herself' expressed Shakespeare's own marital unhappiness, the predictable consequence of 'disproportion of age'.[47] The circularity of the first example and the improbability of the second both betray the degree of Malone's determination to find materials not just about Shakespeare, like the documents, or by Shakespeare, like the plays:

---

[46] Malone–Boswell, *PPWS*, ii. 353.
[47] Ibid. 112–13.

but both about him and by him. The same desire impelled his eager search for the 'unquestionably voluminous' correspondence he believed Shakespeare in London must have sent regularly to family and friends in Stratford.[48] It was writing in the first person, writing that gave unmediated access to Shakespeare's inner self, that the documents and dramatic works lacked. And it was precisely that kind of self-expressive writing that the Sonnets of the 1609 quarto appeared to offer. Written in Shakespeare's own person, the Sonnets ostensibly possessed the subjectivity that could only sporadically and conjecturally be inferred from Malone's objective inquiries.

Malone was the first editor of Shakespeare to publish the 1609 Sonnets in an edition of the works, first in 1780 as a supplement to the Johnson–Steevens 1778 edition and then in the final volume of his own 1790 edition.[49] He was also the first to situate them in a full textual apparatus, one that proved instrumental in establishing their relation to their author. The apparatus opened up a new dimension to Shakespeare's identity that would subsequently be taken for granted in his other works. The identification of the first person in the Sonnets with Shakespeare authorized the practice we have already observed in Malone's dating of the plays: circumstances in the Sonnets were matched up with those in Shakespeare's biography; and beneath those biographical circumstances a correspondent interiority began to be posited. Like the factual particulars that prompted them, these inner feelings or experiences further sequestered Shakespeare from the reader, ensconcing him in an introspective space of his own.

The explicit task of the apparatus was to establish the authenticity of the 1609 *Sonnets*. The first collection of Shakespeare's works, the 1623 Folio, had included only his dramatic works. In the eighteenth century, when the narrative poems *Venus and Adonis* and *The Rape of Lucrece* were added to Rowe's 1709 edition in a supplementary volume, the Sonnets were still omitted—at least as they had appeared in the 1609 quarto, the only edition published in Shakespeare's lifetime.[50] The sup-

---

[48] Malone–Boswell, *PPWS*, ii. 486.   [49] Malone, *Supplement*, i. 579–706; *PPWS*, x.
[50] For the history of the 1609 *Sonnets* and Benson's *Poems*, see Hyder Edward Rollins, *A New Variorum Edition of Shakespeare: The Sonnets* (Philadelphia, 1944), ii. 1–52.

plement, edited by Charles Gildon, reproduced instead a 1640 publication entitled *Poems: Written by Wil. Shake-speare. Gent.* that varied quite flagrantly from the 1609 quarto; and it was only in this form, until Malone, that Shakespeare's sonnets appeared in eighteenth-century editions.[51] Because of its history of exclusion and supersession, the authenticity of the 1609 quarto needed to be established in order to justify first appending it to the Johnson–Steevens 1778 edition and then incorporating it into Malone's 1790 edition. Of all the doubtful works, it was the only one Malone believed to be entirely and unquestionably Shakespeare's. To establish its authenticity, his apparatus adopted a system of cross-references connecting the Sonnets to Shakespeare's other works. The majority of his notes identified verbal parallels between the plays and the sonnets, thereby 'furnishing a very strong proof of their authenticity'. The frequent similarities between expressions in the plays and in the Sonnets were taken as proof of their common authorship by Shakespeare and left 'not the smallest doubt of their authenticity':[52] 'Many of the thoughts that occur in his dramatick productions are found here likewise; as may appear from the numerous parallels that have been cited from his dramas, chiefly for the purpose of authenticating these poems.' By identifying the particular phrases, rhymes, definitions, and images that appeared in the Sonnets with those of Shakespeare's uncontested works, the footnotes drew the Sonnets into the corpus: 'The numerous passages in them which remind us of the author's plays, leave not the smallest doubt of their authenticity.'[53] The system of cross-references worked both ways, the notes tying the plays to the Sonnets as well as the Sonnets to the plays. The stylistic features they shared—word choices, preferred phrases, favoured senses, coinages—proved them definitively Shakespeare's.

In addition to authenticating the Sonnets, parallels from the plays were used to gloss their obscurities: 'Many passages in these poems being obscure, they have been illustrated with notes, in which all such parallel expressions as have been discovered in our author's dramatick performances are quoted'.[54] Rather than providing a definition or paraphrase for a difficult

---

[51] See Ch. 2, n. 1.   [52] Malone, *PPWS*, x. 217.
[53] Malone–Boswell, *PPWS*, xx. 360.   [54] Ibid.

word or locution, comparable citations from several of Shakespearc's plays were given. Passages from Shakespeare clarified other passages from Shakespeare, giving the impression that his work possessed a morphology of its own. By labelling the form and sense of their language 'Shakespeare's', the apparatus qualified the 1609 *Sonnets* for admission into the works, first as a supplement, then as an integral part of the edition, intertwined with the other works by footnotes that glossed the plays with citations from the Sonnets and glossed the Sonnets with citations from the plays. The title of the 1790 edition reflected their new status; while previous editors had called their editions either *The Works* or *The Plays*, Malone entitled his edition *The Plays and Poems*.

While this system of cross-references interwove the non-dramatic and the dramatic, in one salient respect the Sonnets remained distinct from the other poems as well as the plays. They were written in the first person. So consistent were Malone's identifications of the first person with Shakespeare that by the time of the 1821 edition, Boswell recorded that 'it seems to be generally admitted that the poet speaks in his own person'.[55] Malone's apparatus prepared the way for this identification, suggesting the interchangeability of the name to which the work was attributed on the title-page and on the running title of every page (in the 1609 quarto, 'Shake-speares Sonnets') with the first person pronoun appearing in the poems themselves. The identity was assumed, for example, in dating the Sonnets. References in the sonnets to 'my pupil pen' (16) and 'this growing age' (32) were taken to refer to Shakespeare's early poetic career; 'As an unperfect actor on the stage | Who with his fear is put besides his part' (23) was associated with Shakespeare's introduction to the London stage. These internal references suggested that the earliest possible date for the Sonnets was 1592, the year Malone believed Shakespeare had begun his theatrical career. An external reference in Francis Meres's 1598 *Palladis Tamia* to the circulation of Shakespeare's 'sugred Sonnets among his priuate friends' provided the latest possible date, on Malone's assumption that the 'sugred sonnets' were identical with those of the 1609 quarto.

[55] Malone–Boswell, *PPWS*, xx. 219.

Having identified the title-page attribution of the Sonnets with the 'I' within them, the apparatus continued to fuse internal references with external documentation. In the attempt to name the young man to whom some of the sonnets are addressed, it matched up the initials 'Mr. W. H.' on the prefatory dedication with the wordplay in sonnet 20 ('A man in hue all hues in his controlling') in order to arrive at the name W. Hughes. The name on the title-page—William Shakespeare—similarly found its way into sonnet 135 which was 'formed entirely on our author's Christian name'. So, too, documents were used to determine the identity of the rival poet in sonnets 78–80, 'the better spirit' (80). The poet who was in the early 1590s 'at the zenith of his reputation' while Shakespeare's 'name was but little known' was, Malone concluded, Spenser.[56] In all three instances, antecedents for the pronouns within the sonnets were found in documentary materials, the same kind of 'originall and authentick documents' from which Shakespeare's life had been compiled. It should be mentioned that the assignment of antecedents depended on another editorial prescript: the division which Malone's preliminary comments introduced after sonnet 126 ('To this person [W. H.], whoever he was, one hundred and twenty-six of the following poems are addressed. The remaining twenty-eight are addressed to a lady') and repeated before sonnet 127 ('All the remaining Sonnets are addressed to a female'). Without such a dictum, the number of antecedents would have remained unspecified. Nothing in the 1609 quarto limited the reference of the second- or third-person pronouns to two individuals.[57] The dating of the Sonnets, the attempt to assign proper names to their pronouns, and their

[56] Malone, *PPWS*, x. 193, 258.

[57] Until Malone, there appears to be no reason to assume that the first 126 sonnets were read as being uniformly addressed to a man and the following 28 to a woman. Benson obviously assumed that the beloved was a woman, unless a man was specified. So too did the first eighteenth-century editors of the *Poems*. Charles Gildon referred to the 'Poems being most to his Mistress' ('Remarks', Rowe, *WWS*, vii); George Sewell assumed the poems to have been inspired by 'a real, or an imaginary Lady', 'a Mistress to play off the beginnings of Fancy' ('Preface', Pope, *WS*, x. 447). Even in Bernard Lintott's edition of the 1609 quarto, the Sonnets were described as 'One Hundred and Fifty Four Sonnets all of them in Praise of his Mistress, *A Collection of Poems in Two Volumes . . . Being all the Miscellanies of Mr. William Shakespeare, which were Publish'd by himself in the Year 1609, and now correctly Printed from those Editions* (1711). The antiquarian William Oldys made the same assumption, according to Malone, and thought that a woman, Shakespeare's wife, was the subject of sonnet 93 (Malone, *PPWS*, xx. 265 n. 4).

division at 126 all increased their applicability to Shakespeare's own life. As the cross-references made the style his, so these specifications designated the content his.

The footnotes extended Shakespeare's involvement in the Sonnets by the repeated evocations of his name, whether to associate or dissociate him from the circumstances implied by the poems. In some instances, it is not clear whether the abundant references throughout the notes to 'poet' and 'authour' were intended to denote the writer named on the title-page or the writer designated by the sonnets' first person: 'Shakspeare' or 'I'. For example, in the note on the paradox in sonnet 75, 'And for the peace of you I hold such strife', the use of 'poet' is ambiguous: 'The conflicting passions described by the poet were not produced by a regard to the ease or quiet of his friend, but by the high value he set on his esteem'.[58] Yet at other points, the notes quite explicitly intended Shakespeare: 'We learn from the 122d Sonnet that Shakspeare received a table-book from his friend',[59] apparently in exchange for one given to this friend in sonnet 77. So, too, when sonnet 80 admits, 'O, how I faint when I of you do write, | Knowing a better spirit doth use your name,' the reader was to wonder what poet might have intimidated Shakespeare: 'curiosity will naturally endeavour to find out who this *better spirit* was, to whom even Shakspeare acknowledges himself inferior'.[60] When details could not properly be ascribed to Shakespeare, they were glossed as metaphorical: while sonnet 89 instructs, 'Speak of my lameness, and I straight will halt', and sonnet 37 concedes, 'So I, made lame by fortune's dearest spite,' the note maintained that, as in *Coriolanus* and *As You Like It*, 'the expression appears to have been only figurative'.[61] 'If the words are to be understood literally', then line 9 of the same sonnet ('So then I am not lame, poor, nor despis'd') would have to be understood to mean 'that our admired poet was also poor and despised, for neither of which suppositions there is the smallest ground'.[62] Nor need such references to Mr. W. H. as 'the master-mistress of my passion' (20) or to himself after death as 'the deceased lover' of the same Mr. W. H. conflict with the one irrefutable 'fact' which, as we have seen, unified the factual biography. Boswell

[58] Malone, *PPWS*, x. 254.   [59] Ibid. 256.
[60] Ibid. 257–8.   [61] Ibid. 225.   [62] Ibid.

evoked it in his continuation of Malone's preliminary remarks to the Sonnets: 'We may lament that we know so little of [Shakespeare's] history; but this, at least, may be asserted with confidence, that at no time was the slightest imputation cast upon his moral character.'[63] For as the apparatus insisted in commenting on both sonnet 20's 'master-mistress' and sonnet 32's 'deceased lover', 'Such addresses to men, however indelicate, were customary in our author's time, and neither imparted criminality, nor were esteemed indecorous.'[64] Like the First Folio's solecisms, the Sonnets' imputations had to be considered in the context of obsolete uses and customs. The same appeal to conventions and customs of the period that we saw Malone use to justify Shakespeare's grammatical and lexical irregularities also served to allow his apparent moral deviations.

The identification between the Sonnets' poetic 'I' and the title-page's documentary 'Shake-speare' was pushed further when allusions in the Sonnets were found to match events or circumstances in Shakespeare's life. Once an historical determination had been made, a subjective response could be inferred. Two references to the stage registered not only Shakespeare's documented involvement with the theatre, but his undocumented feelings about it. An allusion to fortune's having provided no better 'Than publick means, which publick manners breed' (111) was taken as Shakespeare's own lament for 'being reduced to the necessity of appearing on the stage, or writing for the theatre'.[65] On the basis of sonnet 23's simile, 'As an unperfect actor on the stage, | Who with his fear is put besides his part,' Malone conjectured that the lines were written upon Shakespeare's arrival in London and that 'he had perhaps himself experienced what he here describes'. When George Steevens, who contributed notes to Malone's edition, took issue on this point, arguing that Shakespeare no doubt had seen plays in Stratford before he came to London, Malone emphasized the epistemological distinction between observation and experience. While Shakespeare may have *seen* plays before coming to London, he could not until he was a player in London have

[63] Malone–Boswell, *PPWS*, xx. 220.
[64] Malone, *PPWS*, x. 207.
[65] Ibid. 281.

been 'acquainted with the *feelings* of a timid actor on the stage'.[66]

The same distinction between observing and feeling was debated in the longest note of the edition: an essay-length note stretching across five pages glossing the simile of sonnet 93's opening lines, 'So shall I live, supposing thou art true, | Like a deceived husband'. The combined strength of documents, anecdotes, and four plays established the relevance of this phrase to Shakespeare himself. The terms of Shakespeare's will, which Malone had carefully perused, suggested that he was 'not very strongly attached' to his wife, for he had made his daughter his executor and had bequeathed his wife 'only an old piece of furniture' and even that as an afterthought, '*the clause relating to her being an interlineation*'.[67] The well-known story of Shakespeare's infatuation with the Oxford vintner's wife, William Davenant's mother, lent additional support to this interpretation, as did Malone's observation 'that jealousy is the principal hinge of four of his plays' and that Shakespeare appeared 'to have written more immediately *from the heart* on the subject of jealousy, than on any other'. The combined evidence from these diverse sources gave Malone firm ground for suspecting 'that the author, at some period of his life, had himself been *perplexed* with doubts, though not perhaps *in the extreme*'.

Steevens rejected this hypothesis too, first by finding legal, personal, and medical reasons to explain away the peculiarities of Shakespeare's will and then by challenging the claim that Shakespeare had himself felt jealousy. He maintained that Shakespeare had expressed with equal vigour other states— Timon's cynicism or Shylock's vindictive cruelty, for example —that he could not be supposed to have experienced. If Shakespeare's writing was most intense in *Othello*, it was because jealousy was 'a commotion of mind the most vehement of all others', as well as being one with which 'every man who loves is in some degree acquainted'. Shakespeare's success in portraying it argued not a special familiarity with the passion, but rather a distance from it: 'accuracy of description can be expected only from a mind at rest'. Malone concluded the debate by again emphasizing the distinction between what

---

[66] Malone–Boswell, *PPWS*, xx. 245.   [67] Malone, *PPWS*, x. 266.

Shakespeare felt or experienced and what he observed: '*experience will give a warmth to his colouring, that mere observation may not supply*' (emphasis added).[68] Though Boswell in commenting on the Sonnets for the 1821 edition disputed his mentor's 'uncomfortable conjecture' about Shakespeare's first-hand familiarity with jealousy,[69] the question of Shakespeare's 'personal' involvement in these poems had been raised irrepressibly. The Sonnets had begun to palpitate.

Disagreement between editors was frequently registered in the footnotes, over a proposed emendation of a word, for example, or an elucidation of an obscure phrase. The conflict recorded in the note on sonnet 93, however, was over an entirely different kind of issue: Shakespeare's relation to the circumstances represented in the text. And Malone's pursuit from the externally observed to the inwardly felt or experienced marked more than a new type of consideration: it signalled an important shift in how Shakespeare was read. Shakespeare was now cast not as the detached dramatist who observed human nature but as the engaged poet who observed himself. His dramatization of jealousy was not that felt by any man in love, but the passion as he himself knew it and expressed it. This consideration, even when qualified as conjecture, marked a crucial redefinition of his relation to his works. It drew Shakespeare, who had formerly been distinguished for his accurate observation of others, into his works, casting him as the subject of his own writing, reflecting on his own psychological condition.[70] When the subject of his observation shifted, so too did the content of his verse. His singular experience, rather than the experience of all men, became the content of his sonnets.

---

[68] Ibid. 267, 268.

[69] Malone–Boswell, *PPWS*, xx. 309.

[70] As early as the Restoration, Shakespeare was singled out for his intuitions into character that freed him from dependency on traditional models; see Margaret Cavendish in *Sociable Letters* (1662) and John Dryden in *An Essay of Dramatick Poesie* (1668), both included in *Shakespeare: The Critical Heritage*, ed. Brian Vickers (London, 1974–81), i. 42, 138. See also Pope's evaluation in the preface to his 1725 edition: 'His *Characters* are so much Nature her self, that 'tis a sort of injury to call them by so distant a name as Copies of her. Those of other Poets have constant resemblance, which shews that they receiv'd them from one another, and were but multiplyers of the same image: each picture like a mock-rainbow is but the reflexion of a reflexion. But every single character in Shakespear is as much an Individual as those in Life itself.' (Smith, *Eighteenth Century Essays*, p. 45).

Yet the verbal surface enveloping the content was not exactly correspondent to its personalized interior. As the massive note on 'Like a deceived husband' indicated, the truth within could only be approached by departing from the statement as it appeared without. The phrase could not, as the note began by insisting, refer to the jealousy aroused by the infidelity of Shakespeare's wife, for according to Malone's own editorial edict, it occurred in a sonnet addressed to the man Malone identified as Mr. W. H. All the same, it led readers 'to suspect that the author, at some period in his life, had himself been *perplexed* with doubts'. The logic by which Malone arrived at that suspicion was purely circular: the documents on which the biography was based were glossed by the works (dramatic and non-dramatic) in order to divulge his experience of jealousy; and the works were glossed by the biographical documents to reveal the same experience. The objective biographical facts and the subjective responses to them interpenetrated collusively in order to intimate, though never fully disclose, the private truths underlying both.

The apparatus encouraged readers to pry inward by repeatedly substituting Shakespeare for the first person pronoun, in part to strengthen their readings' claim to authenticity, in part to 'eke out the scanty memorials, which have come down to us, of the incidents of his life'.[71] The notes inserted Shakespeare into what they then came to imply was a biographical narrative, making him ubiquitously present in both the style (parallel passages) and the content (outer and corresponding inner experience) of the verses. Yet at the same time as they implanted Shakespeare there, they also rendered him inaccessible or only guessingly discernible. Once saturated with Shakespeare, the text receded from the reader into an interiorized realm that had at best a tangential relation to the surface of the poem. The poem then had to be sounded, penetrated, and decoded in order to yield what had become its unique mystery, secret, or meaning. The more private it was—the more exclusively Shakespeare's—the more it eluded comprehension.

Malone's footnotes did not typically illuminate the words Shakespeare used; instead, they attempted to cast light on what

---

[71] Malone–Boswell, *PPWS*, xx. 219.

Shakespeare meant or had in mind when he used them. Sometimes the notes appeared definitive in delivering or translating
Shakespeare's thoughts: 'Shakspeare considers the propagations
of the species as *the world's due*'; 'Then do I expect, says
Shakspeare, that death *should fill up the measure* of my days.'[72] In
general, however, the notes qualified themselves as speculation:
'By a *summer's story*, Shakspeare *seems* to have meant some gay
fiction'; '*Perhaps* the poet means, that however slandered his
friend may be at present, his *worth* shall be celebrated in future
time';[73] 'Shakspeare *seems* here to have the burial service in his
thoughts'; 'The poet . . . *seems* to allude to the operation of
spinning' (emphases added). The editor's task up until Malone
had been to illuminate syntactic complexity, lexical obscurity,
and topical allusions; but the 1780 notes continually worked to
clarify not so much the sense of the words as Shakespeare's
sense of the words. Meanings and allusions took on a subjective
cast that required a speculative tone of the notes, a limitation to
the realm of 'seems'. When meaning originated in private
renderings of unique experience, editorial elucidation and
evaluation perforce gave way to conjectural interpretation, a
belated hermeneutic analogue to the 'conjectural' or 'intuitive'
textual criticism from which earlier editors had dissociated
themselves.[74]

Thus the particular experiences that gave Shakespeare definition simultaneously rendered him inscrutable by prompting
singular and singularly expressed responses that could not be
understood through appeals to general human nature or consensual meaning. While the Sonnets could by corresponding
with external fact yield biographical details, true identity—
feelings, thoughts, and meanings—remained deeply embedded
within the verse. This simultaneous revealing and obscuring
occurred on another level as well. Repeatedly in his edition,
Malone invoked his own copy of the 1609 quarto, the 'old copy',
in order to authenticate its own readings. As Shakespeare's
presence in the Sonnets was attended by his inaccessibility, so
too the existence of the authentic quarto was haunted by a sense
of the irretrievability of the truly authentic text—Shakespeare's
own manuscript. As Malone speculated on what Shakespeare

---

[72] Malone, *PPWS*, x. 194, 210.
[73] Ibid. 272, 250.   [74] See Ch. 2 above.

had meant, so too he guessed at what he had actually penned. The printed words on the page were thrown into question as well as the intentions behind them. The notes thus strained to make Shakespeare's physical manuscript imaginable. Although the quarto read '*chrusht*', 'I suspect that our author wrote *frush'd*'; 'I once thought that the poet wrote—*sleepy* night, instead of *steepy* night'; 'Perhaps the poet wrote "the *lives* of life" rather than "the *lines* of life"'; 'Shakspeare, I believe, wrote with *his* rage' not '*this* rage'; 'I once thought Shakspeare might have written—from time's *quest*' rather than '*chest*'; 'Perhaps Shakspeare wrote—*These* vacant leaves' instead of '*The*'.[75] Occasionally the discrepancy between the imagined manuscript and the existent printed quarto could be assumed the result of the compositor's error: 'The compositor might have caught the word *see* from the end of the line'; 'the letters that compose the word *due* were probably transposed at the press, and the U inverted'; 'I suspect the compositor caught the word from a subsequent part of the line'.[76] Yet however concretely imagined, the manuscript could not be definitively reconstructed any more than Shakespeare's own thoughts and feelings could be positively ascertained.

Malone's attention both to the 'old copy' and to the hypothetical Shakespearean manuscript from which it was printed were unprecedented. As we have seen, until Malone not even the printed text of the 1609 *Sonnets* itself had received much attention. The quarto was never reprinted in the seventeenth century; in the eighteenth century it appeared in 1711 in an edition that apparently did not sell, was published in a 1766 collection of twenty Shakespearean quartos with the purely antiquarian intent of preserving the remaining quarto 'pamphlets' in durable book form, and was edited but never printed in 1768.[77] Not until nearly two centuries after their first publication was their position within the Shakespeare corpus secured. Once situated within Malone's apparatus, they were proven more thoroughly Shakespeare's than any of his other works. That the Sonnets were written by Shakespeare became evident

---

[75] Malone. *PPWS*, x. 243, 244, 204, 246, 255.   [76] Ibid. 230, 249, 272.

[77] Bernard Lintott, *A Collection of Poems in Two Volumes* (London, 1711). Edward Capell's edited copy of Lintott is in Trinity College; George Steevens's edition of the 1609 *Sonnets* is in *TPS*, iv.

from their style: the abundant words, phrases, and images that paralleled those in the other works. But it also became evident from their content: Shakespeare's thoughts and observations, reflecting the outside world but above all his own internal feelings and experiences.

Although the identification of 'Shake-speare' with the 'I' in the Sonnets may seem unexceptional now, it would have been virtually impossible to make in the edition which circulated before Malone: John Benson's 1640 *Poems: Written by Wil. Shakespeare. Gent.* Despite the title's blanket attribution, it is clear that the volume did not intend to claim Shakespearean authorship for all of its contents, for it included three initialled elegies to Shakespeare as well as an appendix with a separate title-page labelled 'An Addition of some Excellent poems . . . by other Gentlemen'.[78] Even with the poems presented as Shakespeare's, Benson's arrangement and apparatus prevented them from representing circumstances and experiences as if they were singularly Shakespeare's. The 1609 sonnets were interspersed with twenty-nine poems from another miscellany, the 1612 *The Passionate Pilgrim or Certain Amorous Sonnets betweene Venus and Adonis*, written primarily in the third person rather than the first. The poems in the collection, only five of which have since been attributed to Shakespeare, ranged in length from ten to a thousand lines, the longest ones being nine Ovidian epistles by Thomas Heywood. Most of the 1609 sonnets lost their distinctive form in Benson's edition: while it printed 146 of the 154 sonnets, it regrouped them into units of from one to five sonnets to form seventy-two poems and assigned each a title—'Unkinde Abuse', 'Loath to Depart', 'Immoderate Passion'—that abstracted and universalized its content. The pronouns used in the titles to refer both to the lover and to the beloved are consistently in the third person, as in 'In prayse of her beautie though black' and 'His heart wounded by her eye'; without antecedents, they suggest a representative rather than an individuated subject and object. Nor, unsurprisingly, did Benson assume Malone's partition between a group of sonnets addressed to W. H. and to a group addressed to 'a female'; the sonnet that Malone saw as marking the break, sonnet 126, was

---

[78] 'Finis' appears at the end of the *Poems*, followed by three elegies to Shakespeare and 'An Addition . . . by other Gentlemen'.

not even included. As his titles indicate, when a sonnet did not specify the gender of its addressee, he assumed it to be feminine. For example, he grouped three such sonnets which Malone subsequently directed to Mr. W. H. (113, 114, 115) under the rubric 'Self-flattery of her Beauty' and entitled sonnet 122 'Upon the receit of a Table Booke from his Mistriss'.

As its intermixing of poems from other publications as well as its regrouping, reordering, and titling of the 1609 sonnets demonstrated, the 1640 edition had no interest in publishing what Malone struggled to imagine and reproduce: the text Shakespeare had originally written. By assigning generic titles to the contents of both the 1609 and 1612 publications, Benson blocked the identification of the first person with Shakespeare, just as it blocked all forms of historically specific identification. According to Benson's titles, the 'unperfect actor' was not Shakespeare (as in Malone's apparatus) but 'A bashfull Lover'; the 'man in hue' was not Mr. W. H. but the sexually variable partner of 'The Exchange'; the jealousy of a 'deceived husband' was not provoked by Shakespeare's wife but symptomatic of 'A lovers affection though his Love prove unconstant'; the 'better spirit' was not Spenser intimidating Shakespeare with his poetic superiority, but a rival making the lover 'Love-Sicke'. Yet the edition's purpose in avoiding topicality was not, as has been assumed, to shield Shakespeare from the 'harmful deeds' and 'vulgar scandal' the sonnets reveal, for that concern subtended Malone's identification. It fell upon his immediate successor Boswell to resist the identification by maintaining, as we saw Malone's biography to have done, that 'at no time was the slightest imputation cast upon his moral character'.[79] The identification would have been incompatible with the 1640 edition's presentation of its contents as typical and representative amorous circumstances. It is possible that readers could not recognize the sonnets as such when they were combined to form longer poetic units, shuffled among poems of varying lengths and assigned titles. Indeed, there is no mention of the form 'sonnet' in either Benson's original edition or its eighteenth-century reprints. Retitled *Mr. Shakespear's Miscellany Poems* and *Poems on Seueral Occasions*, reprints of the 1640 *Poems* refer to their

---

[79] Malone–Boswell, *PPWS*, xx. 220.

contents as 'epigrams', that is, short poems distinguished by acumen and wit rather than first-person lyrics generally treating of love.[80]

In addition to the numerous editions of Benson that were printed either independently or as supplements to the collected plays, there is evidence that Theobald and Warburton intended to prepare the 1640 *Poems* rather than the 1609 *Sonnets* for their editions of Shakespeare, and that Capell worked on both collections for his edition.[81] The reason for this preference could not have been that the 1609 *Sonnets* was unavailable, for it was twice reprinted during this period, in 1711 and 1766. It was rather that authenticity and first-person writing were not of paramount importance before Malone. There was no commitment in 1640 to precisely what Shakespeare had penned and to exactly what Shakespeare in his own words had done and felt, no preoccupation with either textual authenticity or personal sincerity. This did not mean, however, that the edition was fraudulent and irresponsible, as Malone assumed in describing its contents as 'spurious performances' which upset the original order and imposed 'fantastick titles'.[82] While all of the poems were not 'Written by Wil. Shake-speare', all of them in the body of the collection had been at some previous point ascribed to him in print. His name had appeared on the title-page of *The Passionate Pilgrim* in a 1599 edition as well as on that of the augmented 1612 edition, the edition which Benson used. Benson had taken two poems ascribed respectively to Marlowe and Raleigh from *England's Helicon*, but shorter versions of both

[80] In Charles Gildon's preface printed in editions of the *Poems* to supplement the 1710, 1714, 1725, and 1728 *Works*, the majority of the poems are classified as epigrams: 'All that I have to say of the Miscellaneous Poems is that they are generally Epigrams, perfect in their kind according to the best Rules that have been drawn from the Practice of the *Ancients* . . .'. Shakespeare 'has something Pastoral in some, Elegiac in others, Lyric in others, and Epigrammatic in most': 'Remarks', Rowe, *WWS*, vii. 458. Capell also appears to have associated sonnets with epigrams, describing them as each containing 'a single thought'; see Vickers, *Critical Heritage*, vi. 76, n. 97.

[81] On Theobald's and Warburton's intention of editing the 1640 *Poems*, see Rollins, *Sonnets*, ii. 30, 334, 605 and *Poems*, pp. 461. In 1775 a volume containing the 1640 collection appeared, printed in the same style as Capell's 1767–8 edition of the plays which it was intended to supplement. William Jaggard records that Capell himself may have edited the supplement: *Shakespeare Bibliography* (New York, 1959).

[82] Malone, *PPWS*, x. 193. See Josephine Waters Bennett, 'Benson's Alleged Piracy of *Shake-speares Sonnets* and of Some of Jonson's Works', *Studies in Bibliography*, 21 (1968), 235–48.

poems had been published as Shakespeare's in the 1612 edition.[83] Similarly, he included a song from Beaumont and Fletcher's *Bloody Brother* which had appeared in a shorter version in *Measure for Measure*; like the song from *As You Like It*, it could have been found in the 1623 Shakespeare Folio. 'The Phoenix and the Turtle' had been attributed to Shakespeare in the collection of 'Poeticall Essaies' appended to Thomas Chester's *Love's Martyr or Rosalind's Complaint*. If 'ascription to Shakespeare in print' was the criterion for Benson's selection, the poems from all four publications—the 1601 *Love's Martyr*, the 1609 *Sonnets*, the 1612 *The Passionate Pilgrim*, the 1623 *Shakespeares Comedies, Histories, & Tragedies*—qualified equally for acceptance.

Benson's publication constituted a fairly full and representative collection of Shakespeare's poetry. Its only notable omissions were substantial, certainly, but perfectly explicable: *Venus and Adonis* and *The Rape of Lucrece*, unlike the 1609 and 1612 publictions, had been regularly reprinted from the time of their first appearance.[84] No claim to Shakespeare's authorship could possibly have been intended by the three elegies to him at the end of the *Poems* (two signed by I.M. and W.B. and one anonymous), and the appended final collection was separated by a new heading identifying its contents as 'Additional Poems . . . by other Gentlemen'. Thus all the poems Benson included possessed some relation to Shakespeare: they were either by him, at some point attributed to him in print, in his memory, or (the poems by other gentlemen) in his style as broadly defined by the collection itself.

Another rationale for the collection was announced by its physical format. Benson's 1640 octavo was modelled on Heminge and Condell's 1623 Folio, the second edition of which had been printed in 1632 by the same Thomas Cotes who printed Benson's octavo. The 1640 octavo and the 1632 Folio

---

[83] *The Passionate Pilgrim* was attributed to Shakespeare on the title-pages of the 1599 edition and of one of the two 1612 editions. For a facsimile of the 1599 edition, see the edition with introduction by Joseph Quincy Adams (New York, 1939); for the 1612 edition, see the edition with introduction by Hyder Edward Rollins (New York and London, 1940).

[84] Unlike the collections of poems Benson drew from, *Venus and Adonis* and *The Rape of Lucrece* had never gone out of print and could therefore not be appropriated. By 1640, *Venus and Adonis* had been reprinted fourteen times and *The Rape of Lucrece* eight. See Rollins, *Poems*, pp. 374–9 and 406–13.

shared more than a printer: both opened with an engraved portrait, an address to the reader, and commendatory verses by some of the same poets.[85] William Marshall's engraving in the octavo (Pl. 4) was clearly taken from Droeshout's in the Folio (Pl. 1); six of the eight lines of the inscription underneath the engraving were taken from Jonson's encomium in the Folio. Benson's address to the reader, like that of Heminge and Condell, attempted to establish both the authority of the edition's copies and the integrity of its publishers. Both publications claimed to have respected the author's wishes: the poems 'appear of the same purity, the Author himself then living avouched'; the plays are printed 'as he conceiued them' by colleagues and friends who wished 'the Author himself had liu'd to haue set forth, and ouerseen his owne writings'.[86] Both collections stated that their purpose was to perpetuate Shakespeare's glory: Benson's apology—'I have been somewhat solicitous to bring this forth to perfect view of all men and in so doing, glad to be seruiceable for the continuance of the glory to the deserued Authour in these poems'—amplified Heminge and Condell's insistence that their undertaking was 'without ambition either of self-profit or fame: onely to keep the memory of so worthy a friend, & Fellow alive, as was our Shakespeare'. The 1640 *Poems*' adaptation of the Folio format declared its own design: as the Folio collected Shakespeare's dramatic works, so the *Poems* gathered his non-dramatic works, with the notable exception of the unprocurable *Venus and Adonis* and *The Rape of Lucrece*. Further, by adapting the Folio's apparatus it appropriated something of its authority, despite its modest octavo dimensions. With the 1623 First Folio and the 1599 and 1612 editions of *The Passionate Pilgrim*, William Jaggard had printed the first collections of both Shakespeare's plays and his poems. With the 1632 Second Folio and the 1640 *Poems*, Thomas Cotes printed the second such pair. In 1710 the third appeared, consisting of Rowe's edition of the 1685 Fourth Folio and Gildon's edition of the 1640 *Poems*, as well as the two previously

---

[85] Leonard Digges's 'To the Memorie of the deceased Authour Maister W. Shakespeare' was printed in the 1623 Folio and reprinted, in a longer version, in the 1640 *Poems*. Both versions are published in Chambers, *William Shakespeare*, ii. 231–2. See also John Freehafer, 'Leonard Digges, Ben Jonson, and the Beginning of Shakespeare Idolatry', *Shakespeare Quarterly*, 21 (1970), 63–75.

[86] All citations from the 1623 Folio are from Hinman, *TNF*.

unobtainable Ovidian poems.[87] For almost 150 years, the matching formats coupled together the folio and octavo volumes, the drama and the poetry, to comprise Shakespeare's complete works.

Because of the liberties it took with the attribution and arrangement of its contents, the 1640 collection has since Malone been dismissed as spurious. It has generally been assumed that the edition was intended to hoodwink stationers and readers alike by passing itself off as a new collection by Shakespeare.[88] Yet it has recently been convincingly argued that there was nothing transgressive about the publication.[89] Benson appears to have been a respectable publisher who obtained and published the contents of the *Poems* without violating the regulations then governing book production; his printer, Thomas Cotes, was the established printer of the 1632 Second Folio. That no entry appeared in the Stationers' Register for Benson's publication was not unusual: *The Passionate Pilgrim* had never been entered and the entry for the 1609 *Sonnets* had expired, and the copyright to both would therefore have reverted to the Stationers' Company. Benson did register 'An Addition . . . by other Gentlemen' in an entry that made it clear that he was also printing Shakespeare's poems: 'John Benson. Entred for his Copie under the hands of Dr. Wykes and Master ffetherston warden. An Addicion of some excellent Poems to Shakespeares Poems by other gentlemen . . .'.[90] It appears doubtful that the wardens would have allowed the publication if they had deemed it illegal, especially if it violated their own claim.

As I shall explain in the next chapter, no modern under-standing of literary property is adequate to account for the regulation of book production and circulation in the sixteenth

---

[87] In 1710, E. Curll published a spurious volume 7 to Tonson's six-volume edition of Shakespeare edited by Rowe; see n. 80. Edited by Charles Gildon, it was published by Tonson with the *Works* themselves in 1714.

[88] Malone's censure of the 1640 *Poems* remains traditional: 'nobody who studies Benson's *Poems* without preconceived opinions can fail to see that it was an illegal publication . . . a deliberate and evidently successful attempt to deceive readers and hide the theft': Rollins, *Sonnets*, ii. 22. Compare Stephen Booth's more qualified explanation: 'he presumably did so for the simple commercial purpose of disguising a pirated reprint as something new': *Shakespeare's Sonnets* (New Haven, Conn., 1977), p. 545.

[89] See Bennett, 'Benson's Alleged Piracy', pp. 235–48, and Hallett Smith, *The Tension of the Lyre: Poetry in Shakespeare's Sonnets* (San Marino, Ca., 1981), pp. 140–44.

[90] Quoted by Bennett, 'Benson's Alleged Piracy', p. 237.

and seventeenth centuries. The Benson addition is instructive precisely because of what appears, from a post-Malonean perspective, to be its open disregard for authenticity—for what poems Shakespeare actually wrote and how he intended them to be arranged—as well as for the autobiographical potential of the poems as first-person lyrics. The assumption that the publication was at least unscrupulous if not illegal stems from a later preoccupation with what Shakespeare originally wrote and meant. With Malone, Shakespeare simultaneously became the principal producer of the text and the primary source and referent of its meaning. Benson, however, appears not to have distinguished between what Shakespeare had written and what had been ascribed to him or associated with him in print; nor was he interested in singling out Shakespeare's experience from commonplace occasions and conventional Ovidian encounters.

It may be helpful to think of Benson's mode of attribution in the context of manuscript collections in which ascriptions could indicate roles as various as the author of the poem, the poet in whose style the poem was written, a member of the poet's circle, a reviser or transcriber, and a composer who set the poem to music.[91] Authorship was only one of the functions contributing to a poem's production that included its writing, adaptation, transmission, circulation, and preservation; the author's name, therefore, was only one among several that might be chosen to identify that poem. The ascription worked synecdochally to refer to a poem's production and reproduction, the stages of its materialization being less than entirely distinct when the making of a poem was often a remaking of or response to a prior composition and when the duplication of a poem often modified and adapted the form it copied. Circumstances were different, of course, for a manuscript and for a printed book, for a manuscript's circulation was confined at least initially to a familiar and informed circle that must have known how poetic

[91] Peter Beal, the compiler of the *Index of English Literary Manuscripts* (London, 1980), in his response to the attribution to Shakespeare of 'Shall I Die?', explains the various ways attribution can function in manuscripts: 'Names became associated with poems in these miscellanies for a variety of reasons besides simple authorship. A man's name might become linked with a poem in the course of manuscript transmission because he was the copyist, or because it was written by someone in his circle, or because he added his own stanzas to it, or wrote a reply to it, or set it to music, and so on,' *Times Literary Supplement*, 3 Jan. 1986, p. 13.

labours were divided.[92] Yet the printed anthologies which took
their materials from manuscript collections must also have
adopted their synecdochic mode of attribution, even when
what the Folio addressed as 'the great Variety of Readers'
could no longer be expected to substitute the productive whole
for the signifying part. The materials Benson collected as
Shakespeare's *Poems* issued not from Shakespeare's pen but
rather from earlier publications bearing his name or associated
with his works.

This is not to exclude the possibility that Benson and his
publisher intended to increase profits by fleshing out *The
Passionate Pilgrim* with the 1609 *Sonnets*, poems from *Love's
Martyr*, and verses 'by other Gentlemen'; it was, after all, 'the
laudable custom of the Trade, to swell the Volume and the
Price', to make it more copious by copying, another instance of
how the *copia*/copy cognate proposed in Chapter 2 might take
material form.[93] In 1640, after the second edition of the Folio,
fifteen editions of *Venus and Adonis*, and eight of *Rape of Lucrece*,
the name 'Shakespeare' may have been even more 'sufficient to
vent his worke' than it was said to have been in the 1622
stationer's address to the quarto of *Othello*.[94] Nevertheless, that
the edition's promiscuous content and presumptive attribution
were, if not typical, certainly permissible, reflects not lax
regulations or unethical policies but rather a more pliable
concept of book and author. Until the very notions that are the
subject of this present study were fixed and legally codified,
authorship—especially when posthumously assigned—was a
more flexible and variable ascription having more to do than
has been generally allowed with a sprawling nexus of stationers'
practices and printed materials than with a direct line to the
author and his holograph. The engraved portrait of Shakespeare

[92] For the various modes in which printed texts appropriated the practices of
manuscripts, see J. W. Saunders, 'From Manuscript to Print: A Note on the circulation
of poetic MSS. in the sixteenth century', *Proceedings of the Leeds Philosophical and Literary
Society*, vi. 8, 1951, 508–28. I wish to thank Arthur Marotti for permitting me to read his
major essay, 'Shakespeare's *Sonnets* as Literary Property', which inaugurates an
important discussion of the differences between manuscript circulation and book
publication: in *Soliciting Interpretation: Literary Theory and Seventeenth-Century English
Poetry*, eds. Katherine Maus and Elizabeth Harvey (Chicago, 1990).

[93] Gildon, 'Remarks', p. ii.

[94] 'The Stationer to the Reader', in the 1622 quarto of *Othello*, quoted by Chambers,
William Shakespeare, ii. 227–8.

on the title-page of the 1640 *Poems* recalled not the individual
Shakespeare but rather the Folio title-page from which it was
taken and to which it was also connected by its publishing
history and printed format. Even that portrait in the 1623 Folio
might have had a more important relation to another printed
volume, Jonson's 1616 folio, than to the once flesh-and-blood
Shakespeare; it may have been more germane to distinguish
Martin Droeshout's engraved, unadorned portrait (Pl. 1) from
William Hole's ornate architectonics (Pl. 2) than to provide
a likeness faithful to Shakespeare. As Marshall duplicated
Droeshout's model to associate the modest poetic octavo with the
authoritative dramatic Folio, so Droeshout may have eschewed
Hole's precedent in order to assert a different claim to the same
folio status, based on propagative, vulgarizing Nature rather
than monumental, classicizing Art. In addition, the 1640 *Poems*
may have possessed a relation to another publication besides
the 1623 Folio: *Benjamin Jonson's Q. Horatius Flacuus: His Art of
Poetry Englished By Ben: Jonson. With other Workes of the Author.*[95]
Published in the same year and by the same publisher in the
same octavo format, also claiming its contents had never been
published before, this edition featured on the frontispiece an
engraving of the poet by the same William Marshall (Pl. 6), in
the form of a classicized or 'artful' bust rather than a natural
countenance. Benson's 1640 octavo could then have fulfilled a
double function: pairing with the Folio to comprise Shakespeare's dramatic and poetic works and pairing with Jonson's
octavo to provide the poems of the two most acclaimed poets in
the language.[96]

Benson's edition reflected a fidelity to a bibliographical
rather than a personal entity during a time when the Stationers'
Company regulations protected the bookseller's interests rather
than the author's. His collection was not designed to preserve
the author's poetic output; rather, it established a classification
of printed materials according to their status among stationers
and readers. The contingencies and pressures of publication
affected ascription to a greater degree than the identity of

---

[95] *Benjamin Jonson's Q. Horatius Flacuus: His Art of Poetry Englished By Ben: Jonson. With
other Workes of the Author* (London, 1640).

[96] Peter Blayney has suggested in conversation that this type of 'printing-house
logic' would not have been unusual.

an author who, once dead, existed in the printing house primarily as a bibliographic function. To suggest that dead authors in the seventeenth century possessed a bibliographic rather than a personal identity is not to deny that live authors were not concerned with correct attribution. Shakespeare himself has been thought to have objected to *The Passionate Pilgrim*'s attribution to him of verses written by Heywood, an attribution Heywood indignantly contested in print.[97] To authors, there must have been a distinct difference between what they had written and what others had written; nothing less than their reputations, advancement, and patronage depended upon it. Their concerns, however, as we shall see, were not primary to the Stationers' Company, which regulated the printing and selling of books according to their own priorities and to the exclusion of the interests of all but their own members.

When his plays and poems were printed in the seventeenth century, Shakespeare in the printing house was a name in the Stationer's Register and on title-pages rather than a man with a personal identity. Accounts of his life that assigned to him incidents and attributes, like Thomas Fuller's *Worthies of England* (1662) and John Aubrey's *Brief Lives* (1681), circulated in separate compendia in the context of other lives rather than in conjunction with Shakespeare's works. Rowe was the first to bring the two together by prefacing his 1709 *Works* with 'Some Account of the Life . . .'. Yet even when physically juxtaposed, the edition provided no way of interconnecting the two. Though the 'Account' might satisfy the reader's curiosity, it accompanied the works without relating to them: 'And tho' the Works of Mr. *Shakespear* may seem to many not to want a Comment, yet I fancy some little Account of the Man himself may not be thought improper to go along with them'.[98] It was Malone who converted that 'little Account of the Man himself' into a voluminous biography with a fundamental relation to the works. He provided the mechanism for interrelating the two by inserting the chronology of the plays into the biography and by

---

[97] In an epistle to the printer appended to *An Apology for Actors*, Thomas Heywood objected to Jaggard's having added his heroical epistles, translations from Ovid, from *Troia Brittanica* (1609) to the 1612 *The Passionate Pilgrim* and alluded to Shakespeare's offence at the misattribution. See Rollins's speculations on Shakespeare's reaction: *The Passionate Pilgrim*, p. xx.

[98] Smith, *Eighteenth Century Essays*, p. 1.

arranging the plays in biographical order; only then did the works and life come into contact with one another in a reciprocal relation by which the life illuminated the works and the works eked out the life. Malone's apparatus conferred upon Shakespeare a personal identity that both informed the works and issued from them. It is no wonder, then, that Benson's edition appeared to Malone 'spurious', for clearly Shakespeare was by the end of the eighteenth century much more than a name on title-pages and in register entries, much more than a subject of conversation and reports. Situated within an historical period, differentiated by a factual biography, personalized by outer and inner experiences, Shakespeare had within Malone's apparatus become an 'individual' divisible from the productive network he represented. That autonomy gave new definition and urgency to the categories of both 'authentic' and 'spurious'.

Malone's supplementary notes of 1780, published with the full edition of the works in 1790, conclusively ousted the 1640 *Poems* and instated the 1609 *Sonnets*. Its apparatus simultaneously drew the Sonnets into the corpus and fastened them to Shakespeare and only Shakespeare. The procedures by which it authenticated them extended Shakespeare's relation to the Sonnets to include not simply style but also content, and not simply what all men experienced, but what Shakespeare uniquely experienced, not only in the public world of observable events and available publications but also in the private world of hidden feeling. Yet the earlier 1640 form in which the Sonnets had previously been circulating was indifferent to both that authenticity and that privacy. It contained verses *associated with* Shakespeare through various publications rather than *belonging to* him in deed or by right. These verses were assigned titles that denoted them as applicable to the experience of all men rather than emanating from the exclusive experience of the author alone. It was Malone's apparatus that made the Sonnets *Shakespeare's*, both by situating them in the context of his works, themselves enmeshed with the life, and by drawing out allusions that made them singularly and uniquely his.

As we move back in time from Malone, Shakespeare's relation to the Sonnets becomes increasingly attenuated. Just prior to Malone, Steevens in 1766 had based his acceptance of the 1609

Sonnets as Shakespeare's on the information provided by the quarto title-page: 'That they were published in 1609, by G. Eld, one of the printers of [Shakespeare's] plays . . . added to the consideration that they made their appearance with his name, and in his lifetime, seems to be no slender proof of their authenticity.'[99] In Gildon's edition of Benson that supplemented Rowe's 1709 edition, the style of each poem or epigram bore the 'Author's Mark and Stamp upon it' in the form of 'the frequent *Catachreses*, his Starts aside in Allegories, and in short his Versification, which is very unequal; sometimes flowing smoothly but gravely like the Thames, at other times down right Prose'. Gildon allowed, however, that the content, unlike the style, was less clearly personalized: 'it is but too visible, that Petrarch had a little infected his way of thinking on their subject'—'Love and its Effects'.[100] The generic nature of the content was stressed still more, as we have seen, by the labels Benson assigned the verses in his 1640 edition. Finally, according to the very first recorded allusion to the Sonnets in Francis Meres's *Palladis Tamia* of 1598, what distinguished the style of the verses as well as their content was their relation not to Shakespeare but to Ovid: 'As the soule of *Euphorbus* was thought to liue in *Pythagoras*: so the sweete wittie soul of Ouid liues in mellifluous & hony-tongued *Shakespeare*. Witness his *Venus* and *Adonis*, his *Lucrece*, his sugred Sonnets among his priuate friends, & c.'[101] The 'sugred Sonnets' no less than the two narrative poems derived their 'sweetness' from Shakespeare's 'mellifluous and hony-tongued' style; but that style expressed not Shakespeare, but rather 'the sweete wittie soul of Ouid'. It was Ovid's soul that was transmitted into Shakespeare's verse, as Shakespeare's well-versed circle of 'priuate friends' would no doubt have recognized.[102] In the sentence describing this trans-

[99] Steevens. *TPS*, iv. preface.   [100] 'Remarks'. Rowe, *WS*, vii. 445, 446, 450.

[101] Meres, *Palladis Tamia*, p. 281ᵛ–2ʳ. Thomas Tyrwhitt first brought this source to light in 1766; see Schoenbaum, *Shakespeare's Lives*, p. 167.

[102] For speculations on the taste of Southampton's circle and Shakespeare's 'priuate friends', see C. H. Hobday, 'Shakespeare's Venus and Adonis Sonnets', *Shakespeare Survey*, 26 (1973), 103–9, Arthur Marotti, ' "Love is not love": Elizabethan Sonnet Sequences and the Social Order', *English Literary History*, 49 (1982), 410–12, and Marion Trousdale, *Shakespeare's Poetry*, forthcoming. The 1612 edition of *The Passionate Pilgrim* bore witness both to the popularity of Ovidian poems and to their association with Shakespeare when it expanded its title to *The Passionate Pilgrim Or Certaine Amorous Sonnets Between Venus and Adonis*.

migrational metamorphosis, Meres himself tapped the same sweet and witty Ovidian fountainhead, as is evidenced by the wordplay on 'wittie' and 'witness', the strain of savoury adjectives ('sweete', 'mellifluous', 'sugred') and their erotic undertones, which Ovid's very name was capable of conjuring up within social and literary circles like those of Shakespeare's 'priuate friends'. Also animated by Ovid, Meres proved himself privy to the very artifice he applauded, at the same time illustrating with his own euphuistic prose how English could rival its ancient models, the argument of the discourse containing this reference.

Francis Meres's *Palladis Tamia* provided the most consequential contemporary reference to Shakespeare. Brought to light in 1766, this work proved crucial to Malone's major projects as defined in Chapters 1–3: in confirming the authenticity of the plays published before 1598 without Shakespeare's name on the title-page, in providing dates for his characterization of Shakespeare's period by yielding information about some 125 Elizabethan writers, painters, and musicians, and, above all, in grounding the chronology of the works by giving *termini ad quem* for eleven plays as well as the Sonnets. The materials relevant to authenticity and the chronology were derived from two sentences; the materials contributing to the construction of an historical period were based on the ten-page 'A comparatiue discourse of our English Poets with the Greeke, Latine, and Italian Poets' consisting of long heterogeneous inventories of classical authors and their British counterparts, many of whom have since been forgotten, as the list of English tragedians demonstrates: 'the Lorde *Buckhurst,* Doctor *Leg* of Cambridge, Doctor *Edes of Oxforde,* maister *Edward Ferris,* the Authour of *the Mirrour for Magistrates, Marlow, Peele, Watson, Kid, Shakespeare, Drayton, Chapman, Decker,* and *Beniamin Johnson'*.[103] The rest of Meres's 333-page commonplace book consisted of sententious and poetic passages freely transcribed not from authentic sources, but from quotation books, epithet books, and compendia of universal knowledge. His critical comments were lifted from other writers without acknowledgement; some of his historical details concerning British authors had no

---

[103] Meres, *Palladis Tamia,* p. 283^r.

factual basis whatsoever, having been lifted from classical accounts; not a single date was given.[104]

There is more than irony in the observation that the late-sixteenth-century source on which Malone depended respected none of the late-eighteenth-century premises he assumed and secured—not even (as the inclusion of Shakespeare's name in several of those undiscriminating lists indicates) Shakespeare's pre-eminence. There is illustration of the radical incompatibility between the textual imperatives and desiderata that instructed reading and understanding at these two historical junctures.

---

[104] D. C. Allen, in his critical edition of *Francis Meres' Treatise 'Poetrie'*, establishes that Meres borrowed both the form and content of this tribute from the 1520 *Officina* by Ravisius Textor and merely inserted the English names (Urbana, Ill., 1933), p. 35. The title-page of the 1634 edition of *Palladis Tamia* subtitles it *A Treasury of Divine, Moral, and Philosophical Similes and Sentences, Generally Useful.*

5

Shakespeare's Entitlement:
Literary Property and Discursive Enclosure

COPLEY's painting has served to illustrate how Malone's apparatus enclosed Shakespeare in a discrete period and a singular identity both derived from and sustained by authentic documents. Both the painting and the apparatus scrupulously attend to historical facts and individuated subjects, as if the one entailed the other. A unique event (Charles's entry) in precisely specified space and time (the House of Commons on 4 January 1642) involves participants differentiated by proper names and unique identities: Charles I, Prince Rupert, Lenthall, Walsingham, Faulkland, and the fifty-three other participants enrolled in the brochure available at the painting's first showing in 1793.[1] As if to authenticate the work's minutiae, their primary source, the assistant clerk John Rushworth, is depicted at the far right taking minutes, documenting the event as it occurs.[2]

Yet it may be more than the style of Copley's painting—its meticulous focus on particulars (including, as one contemporary viewer sniped, even 'buttonholes')—that affiliates it with Malone's Shakespeare apparatus.[3] As Malone pointed out, in addition to representing Charles's climactic entry, it 'cannot but be also a very flattering exhibition to every Englishman, an arbitrary monarch attempting the grossest violation of the privilege of Parliament and foiled in the attempt'.[4] To the glory of all Englishmen, the painting exhibited the preservation of

[1] The portraits are identified in Julius David Prown, *John Singleton Copley in England 1774–1815* (Cambridge, Mass., 1966), fig. 600.

[2] Although Rushworth's minutes were the primary source, Malone also drew from several of the members' diaries. Roy Strong lists the first-hand accounts Malone recommended to Copley in '*And When Did You Last See Your Father?*' *The Victorian Painter and British History* (London, 1978), p. 28.

[3] Prown, *John Singleton Copley*, p. 348.

[4] Malone's letter to Copley of 4 January 1782 is discussed by Strong, *The Victorian Painter*, p. 28 and Prown, *John Singleton Copley*, pp. 343–50; it is reprinted in Martha Babcock Armory, *The Domestic and Artistic Life of John Singleton Copley, R.A.* (Boston, 1882), pp. 450–53.

Parliamentary privilege: the King violated it by entering the
House; the Speaker maintained it by refusing the King's demand
for the impeached members. As Malone specified, faithfully
following Rushworth's first-hand account, 'privilege' is the
very word that the members shout at the conclusion of the
King's speech, in unanimous support of the Speaker's more
circuitous and polite reply: 'May it please your majesty; I have
neither eyes to see nor tongue to speak in this place, but as the
house is pleased to direct me, whose servant I am here; and
humbly beg your majesty's pardon, that I cannot give any
other answer than this to what your majesty is pleased to
demand of me'.[5] The painting defends Parliament's privilege to
convene and discuss (the privilege implicit in its very name)
without sovereign intervention, a claim to autonomy from the
sovereign exercised in its resolute refusal of his demand. Parliament's privilege to say or gainsay presupposes an identity
separate from the monarch's, an identity derived from its
constituency and embodied in its propertied members.

Yet in Copley's painting, each of its members possesses an
identity every bit as distinct as that of the King and Prince that
complicates the corporate univocality expressed in its unanimous
choric cry, 'Privilege'. The painting's historical subject cele-
brates a privilege jointly possessed, while its authentic style
clamours for rights severally held. The distinct features, position,
and reaction differentiating each individual may require a
more precisely articulated franchise: individual rights rather
than corporate privilege, something closer to the right to vote
than the right to be represented. By setting Carolean parliamentary privilege in a scene defined by late-eighteenth-century
discriminations, the painting's style inauthentically or ana-
chronistically anticipates its professed subject, celebrating
collective privilege with the punctilious refinements of a later
political vocabulary, exhibiting political representation at the
demise of Charles I in a style of pictorial representation contemporary with the reign of George III.

[5] John Rushworth, *Historical Collections . . . Containing the Principal Matters Which
Happened from the Meeting of the Parliament . . . 1640–42* (London, 1721), iv. 477–8.
Accounts by four other members present at the event were also consulted: Edward
Hyde Clarendon, *The History of the Rebellion and Civil Wars*; Thomas Frankland, *The
Annals of King James I and Charles I*; Philip Warwick, *Memoirs of the Reigne of Charles I*; and
Bulstrode Whitelocke, *Memorials of English Affairs*.

Once again, it is possible to substitute the subject of Malone's apparatus for that of Copley's painting. The privilege the painting assigns specifically to Parliament and by extension to the individual English subject is grounded in and dependent on the kind of historical and personal autonomy we have seen the apparatus confer upon Shakespeare. Shakespeare's historical and personal identity entitles him to his works just as those of the members of Parliament entitles them to a voice. A distinct position in time co-ordinated with a correspondingly distinct consciousness serve as prerequisites for possession, of immaterial rights as well as material property. Malone's apparatus establishes Shakespeare's qualifications as proprietor of his works; his edition variously encodes a relation of ownership into editorial practices that insist on the exclusivity of both Shakespeare's words and their meaning. At the same time, this proprietary relation is being inscribed in other areas that come into contact with Malone's edition: in the debates over literary property leading to a modern concept of copyright, in the publication of a spate of variorum editions that demarcate and assign the various comments on Shakespeare to their proper owners, and in the systematic use of quotation marks to signal words belonging to another.

This discussion of modes of discursive appropriation must begin with John Locke, whose defence of private property figured prominently in the debates over literary property which, as we shall see, variously involved all the major eighteenth-century Shakespeare editions until Malone. In his 'Second Treatise of Government', written sometime around 1688, Locke made the concept of private property fundamental to civil society and government: 'The great and chief end, therefore of mens uniting into Commonwealths, and putting themselves under Governments, is the Preservation of their Property.'[6] His justification of property reappears in William Blackstone's magisterial 1766 *Commentaries on the Laws of England* and

---

[6] John Locke, 'The Second Treatise of Government', in *Two Treatises of Government*, 2nd edn., ed. Peter Laslett (Cambridge, 1967). On the difficulty of dating the 'Second Treatise', see Laslett's 'Two Treatises of Government and the Revolution of 1688' in the same edition, pp. 45–66.

repeatedly in the debates over literary property that attempted to influence opinion and legislation governing the book trade.

In describing how what at first was given in common to all men came subsequently to be owned by separate individuals, Locke maintained that the right to self-preservation made it necessary for man to take possession of the food and subsequently the land that he needed to sustain himself. It was the exclusive property each individual had in himself that authorized the takeover: 'Man (by being Master of himself, and Proprietor of his own Person, and the Actions or Labour of it) has still in himself the great Foundation of Property.'[7] Possessing himself (self-mastered), he also possessed his abilities and therefore the product of those abilities: 'Though the Earth and all inferior Creatures be common to all Men, yet every Man has a Property in his own Person. This no Body has any Right to but himself. The Labour of his Body, and the Work of his Hands, we may say, are properly his.'[8] By virtue of being proprietor over himself and his own labour, the individual was justified in seizing for himself as much land or goods as he worked and could use without waste or injury to others. 'Labour was to be his title to it.'[9] By merely apprehending an object, by gathering acorns or apples for example, a man became their proprietor, for expropriation led to appropriation; it is 'the taking any part of what is common, and removing it out of the state Nature leaves it in which begins *the Property*'.[10]

Locke's grounding of the right to property in man's inherent and natural possession of himself precluded obligations to others.[11] It was because he was quite literally 'a person in his own right', owing no one for his abilities, that his appropriation of property was justified. The earlier theories on the origin of property discussed by Locke had implied some type of obligation to others. For Filmer, property originated in God's bequest to Adam and was subsequently transferred by genealogical succession: 'at the creation one man alone was made, to whom the dominion of all things was given, and from whom all men

---

[7] Locke, 'Treatise', ii. 44.
[8] Ibid. v. 28.   [9] Ibid. 34.
[10] Ibid. 28.
[11] On the relation of individualism to possession of property, I am indebted to C. B. Macpherson, *The Political Theory of Possessive Individualism: Hobbes to Locke* (Oxford, 1962), esp. ch. 5, pp. 194–262.

derive their title'.[12] For Grotius and Pufendorf, the world originally belonged to no one and was open to all, until to avoid war men assigned it by common consent and contract: 'the Grant of Almighty God . . . was not the immediate Cause of Dominion . . . Dominion necessarily presupposeth some human Act, and some Covenant, either tacit or express.'[13]

Locke's basis of ownership on man's inborn relation to himself pre-empted the need for any genealogical or contractual relations. The duties and obligations required by the earlier formulations were superseded by self-ownership: a man's proper identity (his mastery over himself and proprietorship of his own person) justified his occupation or taking possession of things. A definition of the individual as one with no relations of dependency authorized the private possession of property to the exclusion of others; it also reinforced that independence, especially after the introduction of money enabled unrestricted personal acquisition. Autonomy entitled a person to property; property in turn bore witness to autonomy.

While Locke's defence pertained specifically to private property, he used the term 'property' or 'propriety' to cover immaterial as well as material possessions: 'Lives, Liberties and Estates . . . I call by the general Name, Property.'[14] Immaterial rights and material possessions were both categories of the *suum* that included rights to life, limb, and liberty as well as lands, houses, goods, and chattels. The painting displays the interdependence of proper selfhood (expressed through unique physical properties) and the right to property (in the form of real estate or political privilege).

In his *Commentaries on the Laws of England*, William Blackstone, a friend of Malone's who supplied him with notes on Shakespeare, extended Locke's defence to cover a type of property Locke had never considered: literary property.[15] The second book of the

---

[12] Quoted by James Tully, *A Discourse on Property: John Locke and His Adversaries* (Cambridge, 1980), p. 56. For Filmer's, Grotius's, and Pufendorf's theories of property in relation to Locke, see ibid., ch. 3, pp. 53–79.

[13] Tully, *Discourse*, p. 75.

[14] On Locke's use of 'property' and 'propriety' to cover both material and immaterial possessions, see Karl Olivecrona, 'Locke on Origin of Property', *Journal of the History of Ideas*, 35 (1974), pp. 219–20.

[15] Malone acknowledges Blackstone's contributions in the Advertisement to his *Supplement to the Edition of Shakespeare's Plays Published in 1778* (London, 1780), p. iii,

work, entitled 'Of the Rights of Things', opened with a definition of 'the right of property' that forcefully emphasized its exclusive nature: 'that sole and despotic dominion which one man claims and exercises over the external things of the world, in total exclusion of the right of any other individual in the universe'.[16] As Blackstone repeatedly urged, occupancy, 'the taking possession of those things, which before belonged to nobody', was 'the true ground and foundation of all property'.[17] In a subsection of the chapter 'Of Title to Things Personal by Occupancy', Blackstone extended Locke's theory to cover the occupancy of letters: 'the right, which an author may be supposed to have in his own original literary compositions'.[18] In the same way that a person, through self-ownership, was entitled to the products of his physical labour, so too he was entitled to the 'exertion of his rational powers':

> The right of occupancy itself is assumed by Mr. Locke, and many others, to be founded on the personal labour of the occupant. And this is the right which no other may be supposed to have in his own literary compositions: so that no other person without his leave may publish or make profit of the copies. When a man by the exertion of his rational powers has produced an original work, he has clearly a right to depose of that identical work as he pleases, and any attempt to take it from him, or vary the disposition he has made of it, is an invasion of his right of property.[19]

The product of mental rather than physical work, a literary composition belonged as much to the man who wrote it as a cultivated field belonged to the man who cultivated it. By the same right that a man made as much land as he prepared into his property, so too he could make as much language as he fashioned his own. In both cases, a person by admixing his efforts with the original material effectively staked out and closed off from common use stretches of land or language respectively. Locke's most graphic analogy for occupancy lent itself readily to the new application. Repeated several times, the analogy derives from agrarian enclosure, the parcelling out

published the year of Blackstone's death. In the *Supplement*, his notes are assigned to E ('in conformity to [Blackstone's] own desire [to] have no other distinction than the final letter of his name'), but they are assigned to him in all of Malone's later editions.

[16] William Blackstone, *Commentaries on the Laws of England*, (London, 1766), ii. i.
[17] Ibid. ii. ch. 16, p. 258.   [18] Ibid. ch. 26, p. 405.   [19] Ibid.

of the common lands of the traditional manor as private property: '[the occupant] by his Labour does, as it were, inclose it from the Common.'[20] Once verbal territory has been roped off and annexed to the author by his intellectual 'exertion', public access is prohibited and incursions constitute verbal trespass or plagiarism, 'invasions of [the author's] right of property'. Words previously 'belonging to nobody' are then, through the construction of unique combinations, removed from the common domain and converted into private possessions.

Blackstone noted that except for Roman law, which assigned whatever was written on a piece of paper or parchment to the owner of the material, there was 'no other mention in the civil law of any property in the works of the understanding'. Nor had any mention been made in common law, though Blackstone cited the frequent injunctions in the Court of Chancery that had protected literary property.[21] All of these injunctions were secured by prominent London booksellers against lesser ones (mainly from Scotland, Ireland, and the provinces) who had reprinted and undersold their publications. As Blackstone's discussion makes clear, and as the pamphlet debate generating from the litigation attests, it was the conflict arising from the reproduction of a literary composition that threw its status into question.[22]

Now the identity of a literary composition consists entirely in the sentiment and the language; the same conception, cloathed in the same words, must necessarily be the same composition: and whatever method be taken of conveying that composition to the ear or eye of another, by recital, by writing, or by painting—it is always the identical work of the author which is so conveyed.[23]

If a composition was identical in its language and sentiment before and after reproduction, it remained the property of the author; only a change of its identity would justify a change of

---

[20] For Locke's repeated use of this analogy, see Laslett's notes to v. 28, ll. 16–26, 306–7.

[21] Blackstone, *Commentaries*, ii. ch. 26, p. 407.

[22] For a discussion of the legal issues that stimulated the debates, see Gwyn Walter, 'The Booksellers in 1750 and 1774: The Battle for Literary Property,' *The Library*, 5th ser., 29 (1974), 287–311. Facsimile reprints of the pamphlets printed during the literary property debate have been published in seven volumes of *The English Book Trade 1660–1853*, 42 vols., ed. Stephen Parks (New York, 1974), ix, xii, xiii, xv, xvi, xix, xx.

[23] Blackstone, *Commentaries*, ii. ch. 6, p. 406.

ownership. Because it remained identical to itself after publication, 'no other person without [the author's] leave may publish
or make profit of the copies.'[24] Yet the purpose of such arguments was not to privilege the author but rather to secure and
extend the bookseller's right to copy an author's works: to
copyright, as it was just at the time of Blackstone coming to be
called.[25] If the author could be legally entitled to his works,
then he could consign that ownership to the bookseller perma-
nently, like any part of his estate. Blackstone himself sold his
Commentaries to the booksellers for a sizeable sum and assigned
it to them, their heirs, and assigns for ever; he also defended
their claims to literary property in court.[26]

Before the booksellers defended their holdings by appeals to
common law, they had enjoyed the protection of what is
considered the first copyright statute in not only England, but
any state: the Statute of Anne entitled 'An Act for the Encouragement of Learning, by vesting the Copies of printed
Books, in the Authors or Purchasers of such Copies, during the
times therein mentioned'.[27] The Act was prompted by the

---

[24] Blackstone, *Commentaries*, ii. ch. 6. p. 405.

[25] 'Copyright in the modern sense of the word as implying the rights of an author in
his own work was unknown in the sixteenth and seventeenth centuries and indeed the
word itself is not met with till after 1700': W. W. Greg, *The Shakespeare First Folio: Its
Bibliographical and Textual History* (Oxford, 1955), p. 28. While the *OED* gives Blackstone's
Commentaries (ii. ch. 26, p. 407) as the first use of the term, Giles E. Dawson locates an
earlier one in a 1734 quarto edition of *Merry Wives*: 'The Copyright of Shakespeare's
Dramatic Works', *Studies in Honor of A. H. R. Fairchild*, ed. Charles T. Prouty, The
University of Missouri Studies, xxi (Columbia, Mo., 1956), p. 11.

[26] On Blackstone's negotiation with the booksellers, see Augustine Birrell, *Seven
Lectures on the Law and History of Copyright in Books* (New York, 1899), p. 131 and n. 1.

[27] The standard account of copyright in the eighteenth century is A. S. Collins,
'Some Aspects of Copyright from 1700 to 1780', *The Library*, 4th ser., 7 (1927), 67–81,
the basis for the account in his *Authorship in the Days of Johnson* (London, 1927), pp. 53–113.
See also Birrell, *Seven Lectures*, esp. chs. 4 and 5, pp. 99–166, and Lyman Ray Patterson,
Copyright in Historical Perspective (Nashville, 1968), esp. chs. 7–8, pp. 143–79. John
Feather notes that 'a new study of copyright from 1710 to the end of the century is a
major desideratum', and in the interim offers a clear and succinct summary in 'The
English Book Trade and the Law 1695–1799', *Publishing History*, 12 (1982), 63–6 and a
scrupulous account of the 1710 Statute in 'The Book Trade in Politics: The Making of
the Copyright Act of 1710', *Publishing History*, 7 (1980), 19–44. For the significance of
these legal issues to larger questions of authorship, creativity, and subjectivity, see
Martha Woodmansee, 'The Genius and the Copyright: Economic and Legal Conditions
of the Emergence of the "Author"', *Eighteenth-Century Studies*, 17 (1984), 425–48 and

booksellers' petitions for statutory intervention after the juris-
diction of the Stationers' Company formerly regulating the
book trade had by the end of the seventeenth century effectively
lapsed, leaving no legal basis for registration of copy. The Act
responded to their appeals by granting 'the Authors or Proprietors' sole rights over their copies, but it thwarted their
designs by limiting the duration of that protection: to fourteen
years for new publications (renewable for another fourteen
years) and for twenty-one years for those already in print. It
was in order to circumvent this restriction and yet retain
protection for their monopolies that booksellers evoked the
concept of literary property. If their right to copy works were a
property right, then it would be protected by common law,
which superseded civil law statutes and prescribed no temporal
limitation. Like Blackstone (whom they often cited), proponents
of literary property or perpetual copyright used Locke's defence to
formulate their own claim: the author was entitled to his
compositions as the product of his own resources, and this title
was transmissable to his heirs and assigns for ever. Since the
composition was generally of no value to the author until it was
published, and since the booksellers were reluctant to publish
or promote works they did not themselves own, the booksellers
were invariably the proprietors—by their argument, in
perpetuity.[28]

Opposing the common law or perpetual copyright claim of
the dominant London booksellers were the lesser booksellers
from Scotland, Ireland, and the provinces. They regarded
literary property as a euphemism for monopoly, an exclusive
privilege assumed over goods which should be circulated as
widely and inexpensively as possible. In their view, the concept
of literary property was viable only before a work was published.
An author might by common law own his work in manuscript,
but once it was reproduced in print he forfeited that right,
except in so far as it might be extended by statute. Thus, from
the position of the defendants, once the statutory limitation had

---

Mark Rose, 'The Author as Proprietor: *Donaldson* v. *Becket* and the Genealogy of
Modern Authorship', *Representations*, 23 (1988), 51–85, to be expanded in his forthcoming *The Author as Proprietor*.

[28] On the impractibility of the author's retaining his copyright rather than selling it
to the booksellers even after 1774, see Collins, 'Some Aspects of Copyright', p. 79.

expired on a given work, anyone was free to publish it. That vested interests motivated both positions is unquestionable: the big booksellers (or 'monopolists') argued in favour of literary property and against the statute in order to hold on to the coveted copies indefinitely; the small booksellers (or 'pirates') argued against literary property and for the statute in the hopes of acquiring the right to publish the most vendible books. Both sides also argued from more altruistic motives, in the interests of the 'commonwealth' and for the 'encouragement of learning': the large booksellers on behalf of the authors who would be discouraged from writing if they could not be assured of the proper remuneration only unlimited ownership of their works could confer; the lesser, on behalf of the public which would not be able to purchase books unless they were more cheaply available. Boswell quoted Johnson caught in the dilemma, shifting from one extreme to the other on the subject, first defending the author's inalienable property right and then releasing it to the public:

> He descanted on the subject of Literary Property. 'There seems, (said he,) to be in authours a stronger right of property than that by occupancy; a metaphysical right, a right as it were of creation, which should from its nature be perpetual; but the consent of nations is against it, and indeed Reason and the interests of learning are against it . . . . For the general good of the world, therefore, whatever valuable work has once been created by an authour, and issued out by him, should be understood as no longer in his power, but as belonging to the publick.'[29]

After the term of the statute's protection expired for the two categories of books (1731 for old, 1738 for new), the 'monopolists' began to secure injunctions against the 'pirates' who had encroached upon what they, despite the 1710 statute, maintained was their perpetual property. Each case prompted a battery of pamphlets for and against literary property; the court consistently ruled in its favour, thereby overruling the Statute. Not until 1774 did the court reverse these decisions in a

---

[29] *Boswell's Life of Johnson, together with Boswell's Journal of a tour to the Hebrides,* ed. George Birkbeck Hill, rev. and enl. by L. F. Powell (Oxford, 1934–50), ii. 259. See Alvin Kernan's gloss on this passage, as well as his discussion of 'Copyright and the Writer's Identity', *Printing Technology, Letters & Samuel Johnson* (Princeton, NJ, 1987), pp. 97–102.

ruling against the London booksellers and in favour of a printer who had published a copy of one of their publications after its statutory limitation had run out. This ruling definitively abolished perpetual copyright, enforced the statutory limitation, and released a work into the common domain after its expiration.

Although the 1774 ruling destroyed common law or perpetual copyright, the claims on which it had been based proved longer-lasting. The most influential argument issued from the booksellers' claim, also cited by Johnson, that the author had more than a common law right to his compositions:

> By composing and writing a literary work, the author *necessarily* is the *first possessor* of it; and it being the produce of his own labor, and in fact a *creation* of his own, he has, if possible, a *stronger* title, than the *usual* kind of *occupancy* gives; because in the *latter* the subject has its existence *antecedently* to, and *independently* of, the person from whom the *act* of *occupancy* proceeds.[30]

Literary property was unlike any other kind of property because it was the result, not of the worker's intermixing his abilities with something that previously existed, as in Locke, but rather of his having created or brought into existence something that never had existed before. Because the author was a creator, he possessed what Johnson termed 'a metaphysical right'. Yet that right could not pertain to the verbal surface of a work which could only too readily be lifted from him through reproduction. The entitlement pertained instead to the inalienable and inaccessible meaning behind the words and within the work. Thus while the eighteenth-century literary property debate rarely involved authors in litigation (the authors of the contested works, primarily classics, were generally dead) or prompted them to contribute to the array of pamphlets and petitions, it posited a determining relation of ownership between the author and his work.[31] In the early part of the nineteenth century, when motions were again made to extend copyright protection, authors like Southey and Wordsworth were involved, and invoked the metaphysical claims that the booksellers had

---

[30] Francis Hargrave, *An Argument in Defence of Literary Property* (1774), in Parks, *The English Book Trade*, 20, pp. 35–6.
[31] Mark Rose discusses both Pope's and Catharine Macaulay's involvement in copyright litigation in *The Author as Proprietor*, forthcoming.

previously devised to protect their own interests.[32] When Coleridge was charged with having plagiarized from Schlegel, the principles of literary ownership and its infringements had moved into another realm entirely: from that of production and reproduction to that of creation.[33]

The history of the eighteenth-century copyright is generally traced back to the two sixteenth-century procedures for protecting the copy of a work: the granting of patents or privileges by the Crown and the licensing procedures of the Stationers' Company, a collective monopoly of printing and publishing founded by a Royal Charter in 1557 to regulate and control the printing and publishing of books.[34] Both practices for regulating print encouraged the identification of the right to copy with the right of property. The issuing of patents was a form of granting monopolies that conferred exclusive ownership over goods, whether linen or playing cards or, in this instance, the printing of a given book or type of book. An examination of the Stationers' Registers' prescriptions suggests how readily the right to copy translated into a property right: infringements were penalized and the copy was assigned, sold, settled, given in trust, like any type of freehold.

Yet accounts which draw copyright out of these earlier practices of patents and registration cannot sufficiently stress the novelty of the concept on which it depends. In neither case was ownership the natural or innate right of the author, as it came to be after Locke when a man's 'Property in his own Person' entitled him to possession of other goods. It could only

[32] On Wordsworth's and Southey's pleas for extending authorial copyright, see Ian Parson, 'Copyright and Society', in *Essays in the History of Publishing in Celebration of the 250th Anniversary of the House of Longman 1724–1974*, ed. Asa Briggs (London, 1974), pp. 42–3. On the central role German authors and philosophers played in defining literary property at this time, see Martha Woodmansee, 'The Genius and the Copyright', 425–48.

[33] On Coleridge's 'plagiarism' or 'naturalization' of Schlegel, see Thomas G. Sauer, *A. W. Schlegel's Shakespearean Criticism in England 1811–1846* (Bonn, 1981), pp. 80–100.

[34] On the establishing of ownership through the Stationers' Company and through royal patent, see W. W. Greg, *Some Aspects and Problems of London Publishing Between 1550 and 1650* (Oxford, 1956), esp. ch. 4, pp. 63–81 and ch. 5, pp. 89–102. For a more exacting account of what procedures secure ownership within the Company, see C. J. Sisson, 'The Law of Elizabethan Copyright: the Stationers' View', *The Library*, 5th ser., 15 (1960), 8–20; and for a further refinement, see Peter Blayney, 'Shakespeare's Fight With What Pirates?' *Shakespeare Quarterly*, forthcoming.

be conferred upon him from the outside; by the power invested in the Crown or by a licence granted by the Stationers' Company. Not only was the right not an inherent right, it could not be the possession of the author, except under exceptional circumstances. Patents, like those granted to Richard Totell to print law books, or to Thomas Bright to print all works in shorthand, or to William Eres to print primers and books of private prayers were made to printers, and only rarely to authors.[35] In those rare instances, conflict and protest ensued within the company in which absolute power over printing and publication had been invested. The possibility of an author establishing ownership through the Stationers' Company was even more remote, for the most important provision of its Charter limited ownership to members of the Company. Although authors complained about the liberties that were taken with their works, there was no way they could obtain legal ownership of their work or take legal action against appropriation of their work. Nor was there anything illegal or even seriously reprehensible about publishing without authorial consent.

The only point at which a work might be said to have belonged to an author without Royal privilege was before it was made public; it would then have been considered a freehold property like any other type of good. Once it was handed over to be made public, in Shakespeare's case to the players or printers, it was legally (and physically) out of the author's hands. Even before such a transfer, a work might be 'taken' from its author; when circulating in manuscript form, it was copied into commonplace books, with or without proper assignment, and subsequently appropriated for the uses of other readers, as indeed were Shakespeare's sonnets when circulating among his private friends.[36] The only respect in which Shakespeare could legally have owned his plays was not in his own right as author, but as a member of one of those two corporations: the acting company or the Stationers' Company: as a shareholding member of the former, he did have some title to his

---

[35] On the nature of these patents and the disturbance they caused within the Stationers' Company, see Greg, *Some Aspects*, pp. 89–102.

[36] Arthur Marotti raises the important distinction between ownership before and after publication in his forthcoming essay 'Shakespeare's *Sonnets* as Literary Property', in *Soliciting Interpretation: Literary Theory and Seventeenth-Century English Poetry*, eds. Katherine Maus and Elizabeth Harvey (Chicago, 1990).

plays as well as those of other playwrights purchased by the company.

As owners of what was reproduced, the Stationers, no less than the acting companies, were liable for their offences. Stationers—whether printers, publishers, or even binders—who issued or 'uttered' a treasonable, seditious, or heretical book were punished, not infrequently by having the instruments by which they multiplied and distributed the offensive book (presses, materials, the books themselves) seized and defaced.[37] Offending authors also were sometimes punished. In the famous case of John Stubbes's pamphlet opposing negotiations for Queen Elizabeth's marriage to the Duke of Anjou, its publisher, printer, and author were all three tried and sentenced to have their right hands cut off. In another publicized case, William Prynne had his ears removed for libel and sedition; he was subsequently imprisoned without pen and ink.[38] These examples suggest that authors were publicly deformed and defaced in their capacity as instruments of reproduction. As books were burned and printing presses smashed, authors were mutilated; they were thereby rendered disfunctional, disabled from participating in the circulation of information. When an author was held responsible for his work, it may have been more for his function within a circuit of reproduction and distribution than as its creator and originator.

Just as a work could not under normal circumstances by law belong to the author, so too it could not by law belong to the common domain. If the owner of a copy died intestate, his copy would be considered derelict and revert to the Stationers' Company, from which it would have to be purchased in order to be reprinted. Because a work could be assigned only to a member or 'brother'—by sale, trade, or bequest—ownership remained within the company to the exclusion of all non-

---

[37] The frequency with which the presses were damaged for offences can be gauged by looking at the index listing for 'Printing-presses seized for disorderly printing', in *Records of the Court of the Stationers' Company 1576–1602*, eds. W. W. Greg and E. Boswell (London, 1930) and also for 'Press(es)', in *Records 1602–1640*, ed. William A. Jackson (London, 1957).

[38] For the symbolic import of the mutilations of both Stubbes and Prynne, see Annabel Patterson, *Censorship and Interpretation: The Conditions of Writing and Reading in Early Modern England* (Madison, Wis., 1987) ch. 3, pp. 44–119.

members or 'foreigners' and 'strangers'.[39] If the widow of a deceased member were to carry a non-member, her bequest would transfer to the Company. The concepts of private owner-ship and common domain crucial to the modern definition of copyright simply do not apply to the regulations governing printed materials before the eighteenth century. They were introduced, though in practice still ignored, by the 1710 statute which, unlike the Stationers' monopoly, recognized the author as a possible proprietor and required a work to fall into the common domain after its limited sanctions had lapsed.

Before Jaggard and Blount published Shakespeare's plays in 1623, it is assumed that they purchased sixteen of them from the King's Men and negotiated with the owners of the remaining twenty who had registered titles; the inclusion in the colophon of two former owners suggests that they joined Jaggard and Blount as undertakers of the publication. Thus four different stationers owned four unequal shares of the First Folio, sub-sequently assigned to different syndicates with each of the three subsequent folio reprintings. By 1709, Jacob Tonson had pur-chased from the latest owners twenty-five of the Folio plays; he appears to have subsequently added more plays, the poems, and apocryphal plays.[40] Although his ownership of the plays was not complete, it was sufficient to constitute a claim to all of Shakespeare and to bequeath it to his nephew Jacob Tonson who in turn shared it with his son the third Jacob Tonson.[41]

[39] Greg notes the use of these terms within the Company records; for 'brothers as members' see Jackson, *Records*, lviii; for 'foreigners' as non-members, see ibid. lviii, lvi.

[40] On the original rights to copy the plays of the 1623 Folio, see Greg, *The Shakespeare First Folio*, pp. 76–9, 443, 445; Dawson traces its transfer through the seventeenth century: 'The Copyright', pp. 12–27; and Terry Belanger extends it to 1767, 'Tonson, Wellington and the Shakespeare Copyrights', *in Studies in the Book Trade in Honour of Graham Pollard* (Oxford, 1975), pp. xviii, 195–209. For the copyright to the apocryphal plays and *Pericles*, first published in the Third Folio, see Harry M. Geduld, *Prince of Publishers: A Study of the Work and Career of Jacob Tonson* (Bloomington, Ind., 1969), pp. 199–200; for Tonson's obtaining of the rights to the Poems which had been spuriously appended to Rowe's 1709 *Works*, see Kathleen M. Lynch, *Jacob Tonson Kit-Cat Publisher* (Knoxville, Tenn., 1971), pp. 131–2.

[41] Jacob Tonson I (1656?–1736) began the business in 1677 and was joined by his nephew Jacob II, to whom he passed his business in 1720. When Jacob II died in 1735, he left the business to his son Jacob III. Both Jacob I and Jacob III had brothers named Richard; Richard I opened a shop of his own in 1676, and Richard III played a minor role in Tonson publications from 1740 (*DNB*). The death of Jacob III in 1767 'put an end to what had for long been the leading firm of publishers in London'; Dawson, 'The Copyright', p. 24 n. 36.

Along with other works of proven duration—those of Milton, Dryden, Locke, and Newton, for example—Shakespeare's writings needed to be protected from cheaper reprints.

For three generations, the Tonson house extended and defended its claim to Shakespeare in and out of the courts. The first Tonson edition—indeed, the first Shakespeare edition with a named editor—appeared in the same year that the copyright statute was being enacted. The timing was no coincidence: as a recent Shakespearean has noted, the publication was calculated 'to call attention to possession of new rights'.[42] The statute protecting those rights, however, did so only until its expiration in 1731. From then on, the Tonson claim was periodically challenged and defended, not directly by court action but by manipulation of the book trade.[43] When Robert Walker felt free in 1734 to begin printing cheap quarto editions of the single plays, Jacob Tonson III contrived both to anticipate each of Walker's printings and to undersell them, thereby effectively cutting into Walker's sales. When Edward Cave issued proposals in 1745 for a new edition of Shakespeare to be edited by Samuel Johnson, Tonson appears to have frightened him off by threatening legal action, and eventually himself hired Johnson for an edition. Once only was the Tonson ownership successfully challenged. In 1744, an edition by Thomas Hanmer was brought out by a publisher too formidable to oppose: Oxford University. All the same, Tonson retaliated by publishing a cheap octavo edition of the Oxford edition in which Hanmer's tacit appropriations of notes by Tonson's editors were denounced and their contributions reclaimed by the insertion of carets (ˆ) in the text; the next two Tonson editions continued to berate Hanmer for having 'appropriated the labour of his predecessors'.[44] When John Osborn in 1747

[42] Ronald B. McKerrow, *The Treatment of Shakespeare's Text by his Earlier Editors, 1709–1768* (London, 1933), p. 7.

[43] For Tonson's employment of Theobald for an edition that would reassert his claim after the termination of the statutory protection, see Geduld, *Prince of Publishers*, pp. 143–7. For the various stratagems by which the Tonsons intimidated their rivals, see Dawson, 'The Copyright', pp. 29–34.

[44] Tonson's reprint of the 1744 Hanmer edition (*The Works of Shakespeare*, 6 vols., 1745) contains an 'Advertisement from the Booksellers' that admits that its contents were 'exactly copied' from the Oxford edition except that Hanmer's emendations have been marked with a caret, the readings he discarded returned to the bottom of the page, and the anonymous annotations duly assigned to their owners. Dawson proposes that

published an octodecimo edition of the same Oxford edition, Tonson bought up the copies and inserted cancel title-pages substituting his own name for Osborn's. In 1767, with all three Jacob Tonsons dead and the Tonson publishing house shut down, the copyright to Shakespeare was sold in lots or shares as if the 1710 statute had never existed and Shakespeare were still Tonson property to keep or assign in perpetuity.[45]

The Tonsons had another strategy for securing their perpetual copyright in Shakespeare: successive publication of authoritative editions. They passed the Shakespeare text from one editor to another, establishing a dynastic line that perpetuated its claim to Shakespeare, despite the conflicts among the editors themselves. The successional treatment of the Shakespeare text, life, and likeness both reflected and asserted its publishing pedigree. Having purchased the controlling share to Shakespeare, Tonson announced his claim with the 1709 edition, reasserted it in 1733 after the statute's protection had expired, and continued to assert it with reprints and new editions. Warburton's 1747 Tonson edition, published soon after the Oxford edition, defended the claim, denouncing the prejudice against Shakespeare's 'Proprietors' that denied them 'that security for their Property, which they see the rest of their Fellow-Citizens enjoy [in their own property]'.[46] The sequence of Tonson Shakespeares worked to overcome that prejudice, each edition appearing in a format inherited from its predecessor, passing on to its successors a related text, biography, and likeness, a long line of issues sponsored by a publishing dynasty that with each new Shakespeare ratified its claim to perpetual ownership. The repeated reproduction of the Tonson editions certainly made Shakespeare available in what was thought an increasingly improved state;

Warburton was responsible for identifying the emendations and notes, motivated by his desire to reclaim materials he had shared with Hanmer before commencing his own edition: 'Warburton, Hanmer, and the 1745 Edition of Shakespeare', *Studies in Bibliography*, 2 (1949–50), 35–48.

[45] The prefaces of Rowe, Pope, Theobald, Warburton, and Johnson are quoted from D. Nichol Smith, ed., *Eighteenth Century Essays on Shakespeare*, 2nd end. (Oxford, 1963). Subsequent references to all these editors will be from Smith.

[46] On the eighteenth-century book auctions and the going price for the Tonson shares in Pope, Milton, the *Spectator*, and Shakespeare, see Terry Belanger, 'Booksellers' Trade Sales 1718–1768', *The Library*, 5th ser., 30 (1975), 281–302, esp. pp. 295–6; and 'Publishers and Writers in Eighteenth-Century England', in *Books and Their Readers in Eighteenth-Century England*, ed. Isabel Rivers (New York, 1982), 5–25, esp. pp. 17–18.

'not one,' Johnson maintained, 'has left *Shakespeare* without improvement'.[47] At the same time, the appearance of an edition, both in the eyes of the book trade and in the courts, was a mode of appropriation or occupancy—a Lockean stratagem for seizing and making one's own through the labour of the editor. In the same year that Tonson published his edition, Warburton issued one of the earliest pamphlets defending literary property, in which he argued that moveable property or goods became 'property either by first Occupancy or Improvement'; by improving Shakespeare, an edition established occupancy.[48] Tonson secured his claim at the start by employing Rowe to introduce Shakespeare in a new multi-volumed format, with a 'Life', engravings, dramatis personae for each play, and emendations. The appropriative design behind the publication was duly noted: 'The booksellers . . . from employing Mr. Rowe are henceforth grown to be proprietors.'[49] The whole sequence of Tonson editions after Rowe was similarly implicated:

[A commentator] may lay hold of this property, and transfer it to himself, by only making a few insignificant criticisms, in the form of notes, or perhaps correcting the text, by the addition of some words and commas. *Shakespear's* works have been published by a number of persons in England; by Mr. Rowe, Mr. Pope, Mr. Theobald, Sir Thomas Hanmer, Mr. Samuel Johnson, & c. and if we can believe what these critics say of one another, their alterations are oftener for the worse than the better; yet, bad as they are, they carry along with them a property in the book thus manufactured, and each critic becomes proprietor of a work which he never was capable of writing.[50]

Indeed, similar designs were suspected to lie behind recent editions of all the English classics: 'In this way, not only the works of Shakespeare, but those of Spenser, Ben Jonson, Butler, Milton, & c. have been appropriated by different

[47] Smith, *Eighteenth Century Essays*, p. 134.
[48] *A Letter from an Author to a Member of Parliament concerning Literary Property* (London, 1747) in *The English Book Trade*, 12, p. 6. In 1762, however, Warburton published, also anonymously, a pamphlet against literary property, having found upon investigating its origins that it was a '*chimerical*' rather than '*real*' concept: *An Enquiry into the Nature and Origin of Literary Property* (London, 1762), *The English Book Trade*, 12, p. 2.
[49] Thomas Edwards, *Canons or Rules for Criticism Extracted out of Mr. Warburton's Notes on Shakespeare* (London, 1765), p. 25.
[50] Hay Campbell, *Information for Alexander Donaldson and John Wood*, *The English Book Trade*, 16, pp. 19–20.

commentators.'[51] It was not simply opponents to the powerful publishers that recognized editions as a tactic of appropriation. When Tonson brought suit against a publisher for reprinting *Paradise Lost*, one of his most profitable properties, the court ruled in Tonson's favour even though the statutory limitation had expired, on the grounds that Tonson had encased Milton's text in an apparatus consisting of a life and compiled notes prepared by Thomas Newton.[52] The ruling was perfectly consonant with Blackstone's extension of Locke's defence of property: the editor had made the author's work his own by infusing it with his emendations, illustrations, and evaluations; he then assigned his newly appropriated property to Tonson: for ever, by common law right; until the 21-year limitation lapsed, by statute.

In order to suggest the context in which the Shakespeare editions were reproduced in the eighteenth century, it has been necessary to sketch out the various practices by which the Tonsons secured and retained their proprietorship of his works: by arguments for the common law and therefore inalienable right of literary property, by intimidating trade tactics and legal threats, and by a series of impressive editions. Yet it must also be stressed that the Tonson interest was not solely commercial. From the time of his first acquisitions in the 1680s, the founding Tonson had been interested in establishing and publishing works of English literature, starting with Dryden and Congreve and expanding to include Rochester, Cowley, Beaumont and Fletcher, Otway, Johnson, Milton, Prior, Spenser, Pope, Gay, Addison, and Cibber, providing responsible editions for dead authors and working in collaboration with living ones, conferring a new dignity on national literature by raising the quality of formatting, styling, and scholarship.[53]

---

[51] Ibid.

[52] For the 1752 *Tonson* v. *Walker* case, see Lyman Ray Patterson, *Copyright*, p. 164. Transcripts of the Chancery decisions regarding the case are printed by G. F. Papali, *Jacob Tonson, Publisher: His Life and Work (1656–1736)*, (New Zealand, 1968), appx 3, 215–16.

[53] For an example of Tonson I's impact on contemporary writers, see D. F. McKenzie, 'Typography and Meaning: The Case of William Congreve', in *The Book and the Book Trade in Eighteenth-Century Europe*, Proceedings of the Fifth Wolfenbutteler Symposium, eds. Giles Barber and Bernhard Fabian (Hamburg, 1981), pp. 108–112.

Tonson appears to have recognized from the start how both England's interests and his own would be mutually served by promoting Shakespeare. He relocated his shop just after Rowe's 1709 edition and adapted the Chandos image as his shop sign as well as his trademark; Shakespeare's image appeared sometimes on the title-page and sometimes on the colophon of the various Tonson publications.[54] Like the 1710 statute itself, framed as 'An Act for the Encouragement of Learning', the Tonson ownership of Shakespeare met cultural needs by 'improving' Shakespeare through the periodically renewed efforts of his editors and by protecting the text from the hazards of cheap printing and formatting. In the preface to his 1747 Tonson Shakespeare, Warburton maintained that if 'Shakespear or good Letters have received any advantage, and the Public any benefit, or entertainment, the thanks are due to the Proprietors, who have been at the expence of procuring this Edition'.[55] That Tonson's accomplishments were recognized by the state is indicated by the fact that in 1719–20 he received a grant for himself and nephew to print, bind, and sell the papers of the Post Office, War Office, Office of the Treasurer of the Navy, and Commissioner for Stamp Duties, a grant which his nephew renewed for another forty years.[56] Thus the Tonson publishing house served the state by reproducing and distributing its official documents as well as its cultural legacy.

The Tonson editions served to cultivate Taste and Judgement, to inculcate and gratify in their readers a taste for the aesthetic and moral categories of good and bad, primarily through their determinations of Shakespeare's Beauties and Defects. It was precisely because Shakespeare had traditionally been associated with irregular and artless Nature that he

Tonson also published translations of Ovid, Plutarch, Persius, Horace, Seneca, Juvenal, Virgil, Demosthenes, Cicero, Homer, Manilius, Lucian, Tibullus, and Pythagoras, besides several Greek and Latin originals; see Papali, *Jacob Tonson*, p. 117.

[54] Papali's *Jacob Tonson*, published by the Tonson Publishing House in New Zealand, bears the Tonson imprint.

[55] Smith, *Eighteenth Century Essays*, p. 98.

[56] Edmond Malone, 'Some Account of the Life and Writings of John Dryden', in *Critical and Miscellaneous Works of John Dryden* (London, 1800), pp. 535–6. Though Tonson never published any of Malone's work, most of what is known about Jacob Tonson II is derived from the factual sketch Malone included in his biography of Dryden ('compiled from authentick documents').

served this purpose so well. Rowe and others repeatedly referred to his 'Extravagance' and 'Fancy', Theobald considered no author 'more various from himself', Johnson termed him 'an author not systematick and consequential, but desultory and vagrant'.[57] It was precisely the inconsistent quality of his writing that made him, in Pope's words later repeated by Warburton, 'the fairest and fullest subject for Criticism', affording 'the most numerous as well as most conspicuous instances, both of Beauties and Faults of all sorts'.[58]

As Pope stated in the very first sentence of his preface, the criticism of Shakespeare provided the best occasion to shape both aesthetic and moral sensibility: 'to form the Judgment and Taste of our nation'.[59] His system of evaluation, also adopted by Hanmer and Warburton, consisted of degrading 'suspected passages' (amounting to over 1,500 lines) to the bottom of the page, highlighting 'shining passages' with commas in the margin, and honouring distinguished scenes by prefixing an asterisk.[60] Of course, such a project hardly addressed the whole 'nation'; it was intended for privileged purchasers who mainly embodied that Judgement and Taste and needed no more than a typographical signal to receive what they were prepared by their station to accept. Four hundred and eleven of them had put down a deposit on the edition before publication; 'The Names of the Subscribers' are printed just before the plays, beginning with 'The King' and then following in alphabetical order, according to rank ranging from Duke, Earl, and Lord to esquire, merchant, druggist, and bookseller.[61] Pope's explanation for Shakespeare's Faults encouraged this latter-day form of patronage by implying that if Shakespeare could have enjoyed such backing in his own time, he might have been perfect rather than defective, for his defects were the result of his obligation 'to please the lowest of people, and to keep the worst of company'.[62]

[57] Smith, *Eighteenth Century Essays*, p. 141.
[58] Ibid. 45.   [59] Ibid. 44.
[60] For Pope's 'degradations', see S. Schoenbaum, *Internal Evidence and Elizabethan Dramatic Authorship: An Essay in Literary History and Method* (Evanston, Ill., 1966), pp. 10–11.
[61] On the subscription arrangements for Pope's Shakespeare, in the context of subscriptions for his translations of the *Iliad* and *Odyssey*, as well as for Theobald's and Johnson's Shakespeares, see Pat Rogers, 'Pope and His Subscribers', *Publishing History*, 2 (1978), 7–36, esp. pp. 17–18.
[62] Smith, *Eighteenth Century Essays*, p. 49.

His plays were marred by his having conceded to the vulgar taste of his audiences ('generally composed of the meaner sort of people') and of the players (who 'were led into the Buttery by the Steward, not plac'd at the Lord's table, or Lady's toilette').[63] Pope could refine Shakespeare because the titled or moneyed 'Names' endorsing his edition were themselves more refined than the nameless vulgar 'Populance' or 'Common Sufferage' that had swayed Shakespeare's output.[64] Thus while extenuating Shakespeare's Faults, he simultaneously argued for a system that would release authors from debasing dependencies, linking them instead with the very system represented by the mainly aristocratic subscribers, hierarchically ranked (the highest male title heads every alphabetical column), as were the lists of dramatis personae introduced by Rowe.

Theobald's non-subscription edition, the most frequently reprinted of the Tonson Shakespeares, aimed to cultivate decorous taste and decent manners, as the aesthetic and moral inflections of his judgements reveal: Faults were Depravities, Deformities, and Blemishes. To be a critic for Theobald was to entertain 'Suspicions of Depravity', for 'there are very few Pages in Shakespeare, upon which some Suspicions of Depravity do not reasonably arise'.[65] 'An exact Scrutiny and Examination' of such Depravities resulted 'in discriminating the true from the spurious'.[66] What depraved the text depraved behaviour too, an excess of freedom or licence that characterized all of the following: Shakespeare's barbarous times, his own 'wild extravagant notes' and 'Poetic License',[67] the 'Outrage' of Rymer's 'hypercritical' railing 'beyond all Bound of Decency',[68] Pope's 'splenetick Exaggerations' against Theobald as well as his 'Freedom' toward Shakespeare 'in his Fits of Criticism', and finally, a tendency in the English themselves, encouraged by 'a free Constitution, and a Turn of Mind peculiarly speculative and inquisitive'. When Shakespeare's excesses, the raw material of the critic's Beauties and Faults, were brought under 'the Rule of just Criticism, and an exact Knowledge of human Life,' other excesses were simultaneously brought within 'the Limits of common Decency',[69] to which Theobald confined his own

[63] Smith, *Eighteenth Century Essays*, p. 55.
[64] Ibid. 46.   [65] Ibid. 76.   [66] Ibid. 73.
[67] Ibid. 81.   [68] Ibid. 80.   [69] Ibid. 74.

criticism. Each note, argued Theobald, 'hinders all possible Return to Depravity; and forever secures [Shakespeare] in a State of Purity and Integrity not to be lost or forfeited'. Notes saved the text from 'fall[ing] into the old confusion'[70] that had existed before his restoration of Shakespeare (*Shakespeare Restored* was the title of his attack on Pope's edition); before, too, the political and cultural disarray thought to have preceded the Restoration of the monarchy.[71]

Johnson no less than his editorial predecessors, lighted on Shakespeare's Beauties and Faults, believing that 'SHAKE-SPEARE stands in more need of critical assistance than any other of the English writers.'[72] If he was nevertheless 'one of the original masters of our language',[73] it was because Johnson proferred 'critical assistance', in the Preface, in the 'strictures' appended to the individual plays 'containing a general censure of faults, or praise of excellence',[74] and in the often 'judicial' footnotes themselves. Once again, Shakespeare served as the perfect subject—or, more accurately, object—of criticism. Unlike Pope, Hanmer, and Warburton, Johnson did not privilege and degrade passages and scenes typographically; he did so through critical approbation and disapprobation. His critical task was to identify and determine what deserved to endure and what to perish. What he praised was permanent: essential character, purposeful plot, sound morality, stable diction. What he dispraised was accidental: purposeless deviations, digressions, and distractions. There was no need to mark Shakespeare's text: once Johnson had demonstrated the precepts, the reader could privilege and degrade unassisted: 'I have therefore shewn so much as may enable the candidate of criticism to discover the rest.'[75] By exercising Johnson's precepts on Shakespeare's text, the initiated reader was better qualified to determine what in language and letters possessed the 'stability of truth'. Critical reading, like 'the stream of time', washed over its Shakespearean

---

[70] Ibid. 78.

[71] 'To the other evils of our civil war must be added the interruption of polite literature . . . The utter neglect of ancient English literature . . .': Steevens, 'Advertisement to the Reader', *PWS*, i. E 6ʳ.

[72] 'Proposals for an Edition of Shakespeare' (1756), in Brian Vickers, ed., *Shakespeare: The Critical Heritage* (London, 1974–81), iv. 268.

[73] Smith, *Eighteenth Century Essays*, p. 113.

[74] Ibid. 142.   [75] Ibid.

object, dissolving worthless detritus to reveal the pure 'adamant'.[76]

Pope's investment of culture with the élite, Theobald's curbing of impolite or indecent excess, Johnson's stabilizing of English letters and language were all projects compatible with the Tonsons' commercial aims. In all cases, Shakespeare was used, precisely because of his irregularity, to define and inscribe cultural codes that related to both value and action, style and manner, letters and probity. Shakespeare did not deliver the standards ready-made; they had to be worked into and out of his works by the editor's critical activity, an effort which in turn strengthened the publisher's proprietary claim. In approving Shakespeare's Beauties and reproving his Faults, the editions delivered him from his 'extravagant' and 'wild' genius, simultaneously redeeming England from its past 'barbarism', civilizing the unruliness native to both Shakespeare and the nation. By improving and rectifying Shakespeare, the Tonson editions simultaneously cultivated English taste and manners, thereby creating a cultural need which its own publications could gratify.

The interests of Tonson and of British culture would be difficult to dissociate, just as the names of Tonson and Shakespeare were practically inseparable. With the death of the last Tonson, Steevens acknowledged the interdependency of the latter in an elegy at the end of his 1773 preface: 'Let it not be thought that we disgrace Shakespeare by appending to his Works the name of Tonson.' Indeed, his name had been literally appended to the title-page of enough editions to make the connection inescapable: Rowe's 1709 (2 edns.) and 1714; Pope's 1725 and 1728; Theobald's 1733, 1740, 1752, 1757, and 1762; the 1735 'Tonson' quartos; Hanmer's 1745, 1747 (2 edns.), 1748, 1751, and 1760; Warburton's 1747; Johnson's 1765 (2 edns.) and 1768; Steevens's (*Twenty Quartos*) 1766; and Capell's 1767.[77] Even the one major edition Tonson did not publish, Hanmer's 1744 Oxford edition, was, as we saw, cheaply reprinted in 1745 with his name on the title-page. While the 1773 Johnson–Steevens' edition appeared after the last Tonson's death, it too was associated with him: a public advertisement in

[76] Smith, *Eighteenth Century Essays*, p. 113.
[77] Dawson, 'The Copyright', p. 26, n. 4.

1766 announced that the Tonson mantle would pass from
Johnson to Steevens, whose Tonson edition of the plays in
quarto had already appeared.[78]

'The consequence of [Tonson's] death will perhaps affect not
only the works of Shakespeare, but of many other writers,'
Steevens ventured in his tribute.[79] Malone's 1790 edition is the
first of the major eighteenth-century Shakespeare editions to
which the name Tonson was not appended or associated. The
Tonson house had shut down, its holdings having been auctioned
off in lots. The dynasty of three Jacob Tonsons had ended and
so too had their long line of Shakespeare editions. After Tonson's
death, the imprints of the Johnson–Steevens and Malone
editions bear the names of over thirty different booksellers.
Steevens had good reason to anticipate a change, for the
Tonson proprietorship had established and preserved patterns
of preparing and commenting on Shakespeare for three generations. The tradition of the received text was certainly fortified
by the fact that its ownership passed from one Tonson to
another. We know, in the case of Theobald at least, how the
transferral took place. Tonson gave Theobald an interleaved
copy of Pope, his most recent predecessor; Theobald made his
changes on Pope's copy-text and transferred notes from his own
papers on to the interleaved pages.[80]

We also know from a note by Warburton that upon completion of his labours and payment for them, the editor relin-
quished all rights to his editorial contributions and assigned
them to Tonson and his assigns for ever.[81] In the same way that

[78] Steevens had published a collection of quartos for Tonson, *Twenty of the Plays of Shakespeare in Four Volumes*, in 1766: 'Proposals for a new edition of Shakespeare' (1766), in Vickers, *Critical Heritage*, v. 251.

[79] Steevens, 'Advertisement', E7r.

[80] A major part of Theobald's interleaved copy of Shakespeare has survived. See Richard Corballis, 'Copy-Text for Theobald's "Shakespeare"', *The Library*, 6th ser., 8 (1986), 156–9. Johnson had already heavily annotated his copy of Warburton's 1747 Shakespeare, but he later adapted readings from a new edition of Theobald; see Arthur M. Eastman, 'The Texts from which Johnson Printed his Shakespeare', *Journal of English and Germanic Philology*, 49 (1950), 182–91.

[81] Dawson, 'The Copyright', pp. 33–4, quotes the document now in the Folger Shakespeare Library dated 24 January 1746, by which Warburton transferred his rights to Tonson, in language that makes apparent the status of editorial 'improve-ments' as property: 'I William Warburton . . . for and in consideration of the sum of Five hundred Pounds . . . do hereby confess and acknowledge; Have granted, bargained, sold, assigned, transferred and set over . . . unto the said Jacob Tonson, his

Shakespeare's text, life, and likeness were passed down through the editorial line, so too their ownership was passed down from Tonson to Tonson. The principle of succession thus regulated both the preparation and the ownership of Shakespeare. Securing both lineages was the *de facto* perpetual copyright that by defining Shakespeare's works as literary property made them assignable to Tonson and his heirs or assigns for ever. For the better part of the century, Tonson's Shakespeare was ratified by nature (the three Tonsons), tradition (inherited textual practices), and the law (the decisions supporting perpetual copyright).

With the Tonsons dead and perpetual copyright overruled, the principle of succession itself appears to decline. Malone's commitment to the criterion of authenticity cut him off from the received text, life, and likeness. There is another break, too, that attends the switch from the Tonson perpetual copyright to the statutory stipulations enforced in 1774: the very aspect of editing that promoted the Tonson cultural project disappears. Malone slights the evaluative duty of the editor so central to the tradition from Pope to Johnson. While Defects disappear, Beauties are preserved in another bibliographical format entirely. In the second half of the eighteenth century, anthologies are published which provide another mode of assigning Shakespeare ownership over his words. The selections originate in the indices to Shakespeare's Beauties introduced by Rowe and greatly elaborated and refined in Pope's 'Index of the Characters, Sentiments, Speeches and Descriptions in Shakespeare'.[82] While they begin as collections which exercise the critic's and

Executors, Administrators, and Assigns, all the full and sole right and title of, in, and to the Copy of the Notes, Corrections, emendations, Preface and all additions, which I have made to the plays of the said Shakespeare, and all my Copy-right, interest and Claim, of, in or to the same, and every part thereof, To have and hold the same and every part thereof unto the said Jacob Tonson his Executors, Administrators and Assigns, for the benefit of himself, and the other Proprietors of the Copy-right of the said Shakespeare Plays, as his and their own proper Good and Chattels for ever . . .'.

[82] Rowe's final volume contained 'An Index of the most Beautiful Thoughts, Descriptions, Speeches, &'; *WWS*, vi. Pope's edition ended with a more elaborate index containing: 'I. Characters of Historical Persons, II. Index of Manners, Passions, and their external effects, III. Index of fictitious Persons with the Characters ascrib'd to them, IV. Index of Thoughts, or Sentiments, V. Speeches. A table of the most considerable in Shakespeare, VI. Index of Descriptions or Images': *WS*, vi.

reader's sensibility, they end up as citations belonging to Shakespeare. The first anthology, William Dodd's 1752 *The Beauties of Shakespear*, surrounded each quotation with evaluations, often based on Johnson's authority; but by 1818 the apparatus had been removed, leaving the quotes without a context.[83] The next anthology, by an unnamed compiler but also called *The Beauties of Shakespear*, announced its purpose of 'inculcating the noblest system of morality', maintaining that 'the study of the best Poet in the World, will produce the most beneficial influence in the great interest of Society.'[84] It traced its inspiration to Johnson's pronouncement that a moral system could be collected from Shakespeare, though Johnson had specifically warned against constructing it from 'select quotations'.[85] Furthermore, for Johnson, a moral system could not be constructed without judicious assistance any more than a critical one, especially when materials were to be supplied by an author he censured above all for seeming 'to write without any moral purpose'.[86] Yet the anonymous anthology appeared without instructive commentary, giving the impression that Shakespeare himself was expounding on such issues as 'Infidelity', 'Bastardy', and 'Friendship'. In 1787 yet another anthology appeared, presenting itself even more categorically as Shakespeare's own sentiments and ideas. Entitled *A Concordance to Shakespeare*, it contains passages from Shakespeare on different topics, yet no longer are they to be related to any literary or moral system.[87] 'The intention of the present selection is, to make the poet sometimes speak in maxims or sentences . . . and at other times to give his description of one and the same affection or passion as it is seen in different persons and at

[83] William Dodd, *The Beauties of Shakespear Regularly Selected from Each play with a General Index Digesting them Under Proper Heads* (London, 1752). William Jaggard lists thirty-nine editions of Dodd up to and including 1893: *Shakespeare Bibliography* (New York, 1959), p. 80. For other collections of 'Shakespeare's Beauties' in this period see ibid. 561–3.

[84] *The Beauties of Shakspear Selected from his Works*, a rival to Dodd's *Beauties* that was printed in 1783, 1784, 1790, and 1798.

[85] Smith, *Eighteenth Century Essays*, p. 107.

[86] Ibid. 114; Johnson, *PWS*, viii. 230, 114. Such a compilation was extracted from Johnson's own writings by Hester Lynch (Salusbury) Thrale Piozzi, *The Beauties of Samuel Johnson . . . consisting of Maxims and Observations, Moral, Critical, and Miscellaneous . . .* (London, 1797).

[87] Andrew Beckett, *A Concordance to Shakespeare . . . in which the distinguished and parallel passages in the plays of that justly admired writer are methodologically arranged* (1787), vii.

different seasons . . .'.[88] Like the sonnets in Malone's apparatus, the concordance gave Shakespeare the first-person voice the plays cannot directly admit, quoting passages from the plays as his own words. The difference between the 1752 and 1787 anthologies illustrates the change undergone by the word 'quote' itself: by the end of the century, to quote no longer signified 'to remark' or 'to look' but to cite what someone has said or written. The passages selected in 1787 are selected because they are remarkable, but what makes them remarkable is that they give voice to what Shakespeare thought on a wide range of subjects, not unlike those that were to be pursued in the critical writings of the next century.

Malone's respect for the singularity of Shakespeare's period disallowed the Judgement of his phrases, morality, customs, and manners. Emendation, in theory at least, could no longer be a matter of Taste or Reason, as it was most strikingly in Pope; emendations had to be made either on the basis of the earliest reliable quartos and the First Folio or precedents in Shakespeare's other works. Even more dramatically, illustration or explanation changes. Shakespeare's difficulties are only rarely illuminated by synonyms or paraphrases; they are generally glossed with parallel passages from other works of the period, in the majority of cases from Shakespeare's own works.[89] Because Shakespeare typically, in Malone's words, 'borrows from himself', it is only logical that the meanings of words and locutions be inferred from his own usage; by looking to his other works for clarifying parallels, the editor allows Shakespeare 'to speak for himself'.[90] Thus the text is repaired and its meaning clarified not by outside principles of correctness and Sense, but by possibilities inhering in the works themselves.

By looking to what Shakespeare wrote elsewhere in order to clarify his meaning in a given passage, Malone's apparatus

[88] Andrew Beckett, *A Concordance to Shakespeare . . . in which the distinguished and parallel passages in the plays of that justly admired writer are methodologically arranged* (1787), vii.

[89] Theobald is the first to introduce parallel passages, though for purposes of justifying his emendations rather than explaining Shakespeare's sense: 'wherever our Poet receives an Alteration in his Text from any of my *Corrections* or *Conjectures*, I have throughout endeavour'd to support what I offer by *parallel Passages*, and *Authorities* from himself'. *Shakespeare Restored: or, A Specimen of the Many Errors as well Committed, as Unamended, by Mr. Pope* (London, 1726), viii.

[90] Malone periodically introduces a parallel passage with, 'Let our poet speak for himself': *Othello*, Malone–Boswell, *PPWS*, ix. 373.

suggests that the meaning resides not in language or usage but in Shakespeare's language or usage, and therefore in Shakespeare. Because meaning has its source in him, so too does difficulty. For the earlier editors, Shakespeare's Obscurities were types of defects that had their origin in outside circumstances: in theatrical exigencies, the remoteness of his time, the fluctuating and unformed state of the language. When Obscurities were considered peculiar to Shakespeare, they pertained to his irregularity or Extravagance, his want of artful discipline. Theobald found obscurity 'peculiar to himself' in Shakespeare's vast but cursory knowledge, 'rather That of a Traveller than a Native', that skimmed across subjects without dwelling upon them.[91] Johnson found difficulty in a similar stylistic impetuosity: a tendency to oversupply his phrases ('load his words with more sentiment than they could conveniently convey') and to rush precipitously from thought to thought (hurrying 'to a second thought before he had fully explained the first').[92] With Malone, a new source of difficulty emerged independent of those stemming from theatrical, historical, and philological circumstances and stylistic excess: a difficulty residing in Shakespeare himself. As many of Malone's glosses insinuate, the meaning of words and phrases belongs to Shakespeare; to understand them one must understand him. The text needs to be interpreted by inferring what Shakespeare had in mind rather than explained and evaluated by appealing to assumed standards of intelligibility and correctness.

The Sonnets were among the first of Shakespeare's works edited by Malone. As we have seen, the unique presence of the first-person pronoun in those lyrics encouraged the identification of the events and situations to which they alluded with Shakespeare's own external and internal experience as inferred from those events and situations. Precipitating the conflation of the title-page 'Shakespeare' with the Sonnets' 'I' was the desire to locate 'Shakespeare's own words', both what he had penned and what he had intended. One play, *Hamlet*, particularly lent itself to the same collusion; Malone's notes to this play provide more parallel passages to the Sonnets than any other work, and Malone dates the two works within a year or two of each

---

[91] Smith, *Eighteenth Century Essays*, p. 78.
[92] Johnson, 'Proposals' (1756), in Vickers, *Critical Heritage*, iv. 270.

other.[93] The notes to *Hamlet*, like those to the Sonnets, frequently deliver not what the phrases mean, but what Shakespeare may have intended them to mean. Confusion in a passage, whether logical or textual, drives his notes to probe inwards towards what are imagined as prelinguistic sites of meaning: 'in Shakespeare's mind', 'in Shakespeare's contemplation', 'in his thoughts', 'in his memory'. Apparent inconsistencies are thereby dispelled: Shakespeare does not contradict himself in referring both to a country from which 'no traveller returns' and to a ghostly traveller just returned from that country, for 'Our poet without doubt in the passage before us *intended to say*, that from the unknown regions of the dead no traveller returns with all his corporeal powers.'[94] Similarly, there is no excuse for comparing Hamlet's vows to Ophelia to 'bawds', as Theobald had done, rather than 'bonds': 'The bonds here *in our poets thought* were bonds of love' (emphasis added);[95] parallel passages from one of his sonnets and two of his plays confirm their residence there.

The apparatus thus gives the impression that meaning originates in Shakespeare, that understanding a passage is tantamount to retrieving its sense from Shakespeare's mind. On the rare occasions when Johnson made Shakespeare the subject of his glosses, it was, as might be expected, in his evaluative notes, often to criticize him for some aspect of his irregular style: after attempting to parse out 'Peace should stand a Comma between their amities', Johnson concluded, 'this is not an easy style; but is it not the style of Shakespeare?'[96] Shakespeare was not the subject of Johnson's explanatory notes because, unlike style, meaning was not characteristic: it was consensual. Thus Johnson gave synonyms and paraphrases when explaining a phrase, not because of his ingrained lexical habits, but because it was the meaning of the words rather than Shakespeare's meaning that was at issue. He resisted emendation not because he would preserve what Shakespeare put to paper, but because he would not lose ancient forms of the language. For this reason, he retained the uncouth 'In hugger-mugger to interr him';[97] had

[93] In the revised chronology, Malone gives 1600 as the date for Hamlet: 'An Attempt to Ascertain the Order of his Plays', *PPWS*, ii. 369; while he does not include the Poems in his chronology, he assigns the date 1598 to the *Sonnets* in his preliminary note to them: ibid. xx. 217.
[94] Ibid. vii. 328.   [95] Ibid. 225.
[96] Ibid. 294; Johnson, *PWS*, vii. 294, 209, 230.   [97] Ibid. 430.

he emended it, as had previous editors, to the more polished 'In private to inter him', he would have destroyed a piece of the language's past: 'If phraseology is to be changed as words grow uncouth by disuse, or gross by vulgarity, the history of every language will be lost.'[98] Malone was even more conscientious about preserving Shakespeare's words; he retained, for example, 'To grunt and sweat', a phrase Johnson had emended to 'To groan and sweat', believing 'the true reading' could 'scarcely be born by modern ears'.[99] Yet neither the history of the language nor the cultivation of taste determined Malone's treatment of the text, but rather a mission to 'exhibit what [the] authour wrote'.[100]

Because Johnson looked for the meaning of words rather than Shakespeare's meaning, he rarely had recourse to parallel passages, either from Shakespeare or from other writers. This was no doubt due in part to his experience as compiler of the Dictionary, which provided him with 'more motives to consider the whole extent of our language than any other man from its first formation'.[101] He glossed 'by the card' by giving both its literal and figurative meaning: 'The card is the paper on which the different points of the compass were described. To do anything by the card, is, to do it with nice observation.'[102] Malone, however, after citing Johnson and giving both Ritson's and his own rendition of it, supports or proves the gloss with exact references to three late-sixteenth-century sources,[103] giving author, title, date, and page number to enable them to be verified. Malone's supply of parallel passages, whether from Shakespeare or his contemporaries, is as crucial as the facts in his biography of Shakespeare or his history of the theatre. These references, like facts, even when apparently inconsequential, provide the objective stimulus for his insights into Shakespeare's subjectivity. As in the biography and chronology, an overwhelming accumulation of documented details tapers into inferences about Shakespeare's singular person. As those facts called Shakespeare into biographical being, so too

[98] Ibid. 26.
[99] Malone–Boswell, *PPWS*, viii. 209.
[100] Ibid. 327.
[101] Johnson, 'Proposals' (1756), in Vickers, *Critical Heritage*, iv. 272.
[102] Johnson, *PWS*, vii. 284.   [103] Malone–Boswell, *PPWS*, vii. 471–2.

these primary literary sources help articulate his exclusive meaning.

Malone's psychologizing notes serve to personalize the text, affixing Shakespeare's signature to the work, literally subscribing it beneath the page as the ubiquitous subject of the notes, and then underwriting it with his own name, as if to make proper assignation doubly sure. The Obscurities in the text are no longer so much historical, philological, or stylistic as hermeneutic: arising from within Shakespeare rather than without. They issue not from temporal change but from the singularity of the experience and consciousness that the biography also strives to discover. As Steevens predicted, Tonson's passing away did affect Shakespeare. Once Shakespeare fell into the public domain and became more commonly available for both publication and purchase, the author's 'metaphysical right' came to be asserted through his claim on meaning. Once Shakespeare's works had no legal proprietors, Shakespeare himself became their hermeneutic proprietor. Unlike the Tonson editions from Rowe to Johnson, Malone's does not appropriate Shakespeare for the purpose of processing cultural value. His apparatus omits the Evaluation and Judgement by which its predecessors encoded aesthetic and moral value through their comments on Shakespeare's Beauties and Defects. In Malone, Shakespeare's history and subjectivity protect him from modern censure, making him accountable only to criteria emerging from his own chronological progression. The various Tonson apparatuses secured the Tonson ownership; Malone's secures Shakespeare's self-ownership, not legally as copy but hermeneutically as original meaning. The function of the title-page changes when the site of ownership is relocated. Ownership belongs not to the thirty-three names typed in minuscule letters on the imprint, but to the name engrossed in the title: *William Shakspeare's Plays and Poems*. The title lays claim not to the superficial and reproducible properties of the text but to its profound and inalienable ones. The two works which begin to receive attention in this period, and which will hold it throughout the next century, are the Sonnets and *Hamlet*. They are also the two works that most invite probing: in the former by the presence of the first person; in the latter by the main character's inscrutability.

Amid so many types of textual or bibliographic annexation, variorum editions of Shakespeare began to merge, containing notes from various commentators and editors (*cum notis variorum*), sorted out and assigned. Although Theobald and Warburton had included the contributions of earlier editors, sometimes acknowledging their origins, Johnson in his 1756 Proposals was the first to propose an edition structured on the classical variorum model: 'All that is valuable will be adopted from every commentator, that posterity may consider it as including all the rest, and exhibiting whatever is hitherto known of the great father of the English drama.'[104] The project was realized in his 1765 variorum, which announced, in language echoing the literary property debates, a new respect for the editorial and critical claims of others:

Whatever I have *taken* from [others] it was my intention to refer to its original authour, and it is certain, that what I have not *given* to another, I believed when I wrote it to be my *own*. In some perhaps I have been anticipated; but if I am ever found to *encroach* upon the remarks of any other commentator, I am willing that the honour, be it more or less, should be *transferred* to the first *claimant*, for his *right*, and his alone, stands above *dispute*. . . . (emphasis added)[105]

In the same way that he was careful to distinguish the words of others, so too he came to distinguish his own words or emendations from those of Shakespeare's text, resolving to insert none of his own readings into the text, confining them instead to the 'dominion' at the bottom margin.[106] Johnson's 1765 edition initiated a whole series of variorum editions (1773, 1778, 1790, 1803, and 1813), culminating in Malone's variorum, completed by Boswell.[107] In the later variorums, that 'dominion', at one

---

[104] Johnson, 'Proposals', in Vickers, *Critical Heritage*, iv. 273. On the late seventeenth- and early eighteenth-century proliferation of classical variorums, see John Edwin Sandys, *A History of Classical Scholarship*, (Cambridge, 1908), ii. 445. On Johnson's acknowledgements, see Arthur Sherbo, *Samuel Johnson, Editor of Shakespeare* (Urbana, Ill., 1956), ch. 3, pp. 218–45.

[105] Smith, *Eighteenth Century Essays*. p. 139.   [106] Ibid. 145.

[107] Scholarship is divided on exactly what constitutes a Shakespeare variorum: 'Under one convention, the editions of 1773, 1778, and 1785 are referred to as Variorum; but under another, slightly more appropriate, Reed's editions of 1803 and 1813 are called the First and Second Variorum, and [Malone] Boswell's the Third', J. Philip Brockbank, 'Shakespearean Scholarship: From Rowe to the Present', in *William Shakespeare His World, His Work, His Influence*, ed. John F. Andrews (New York, 1985), iii. 723. I have used the term variorum to cover any edition that systematically quotes and

time limited to the bottom reaches of the page, sprawls out into a discursive space of its own, threatening to overtake the entire page, occasionally leaving room for no more than a single line belonging to Shakespeare.

The marginal space was completely unoccupied in the seventeenth-century folios. Their 'superintendors' did not set off their own corrections from Shakespeare's text: they 'corrected' the text without notice as if revising something of their own, not claiming the changes they introduced, much less acknowledging those by others. So, too, Rowe and Pope did not distinguish what they inserted from what Shakespeare wrote: in his second edition, Pope tacitly slipped in the better part of Theobald's published corrections to his first edition; though he admitted to having introduced only twenty-five of them, he blended many more in with his own emendations, which were also indistinguishable from Shakespeare's text.[108] Theobald and Hanmer appear to have done the same thing with Warburton's unpublished notes. Hanmer consistently, in Johnson's words, 'appropriated the labour of his predecessors',[109] digesting their contributions in his own notes as well as their emendations in Shakespeare's texts.[110] Theobald began his career by dissociating his own work from Pope's in his published excoriations of Pope's first edition, though he appears to have fused his own with Shakespeare's, not in his edition, but in passing off his own composition as a newly discovered play by Shakespeare, obtaining a Royal privilege which protected it as his own.[111] Capell, in the preface

names other commentators; thus Johnson's 1765 (repr. 1768) *The Plays of William Shakespeare . . . with the Corrections and Illustrations of Various Commentators* and Malone's 1790 *The Plays and Poems of William Shakspeare, collated verbatim with the most authentick copies, and revised with the Corrections and Illustrations of the Various Commentators* also qualify as variorum.

[108] On Pope's tacit incorporation in the 1728 edition of Theobald's emendations from his *Shakespeare Restored*, see Thomas R. Lounsbury, *The Text of Shakespeare: Its History from the Publication of the Quartos and Folios Down to and Including the Publication of the Editions of Pope and Theobald* (New York, 1970), pp. 215–320 (first published 1906).

[109] Smith, *Eighteenth Century Essays*, p. 136.

[110] See A. W. Evans, *Warburton and the Warburtonians: A Study in Some Eighteenth-Century Controversies* (Oxford, 1932). Vickers discusses the proprietary disputes between Theobald and Warburton (*Critical Heritage*, ii. 17–18) and Hanmer and Warburton (ibid. iii. 15–16); see also Smith, *Eighteenth Century Essays*, pp. xli–l.

[111] By claiming in 1727 that *Double Falsehood* was a play by Shakespeare, Theobald obtained a fourteen-year privilege from George II; see Greg, *The Shakespeare First Folio*, note C, p. 70.

to his 1768 edition, informed readers that he assigned initials to the 'proper owners' of emendations in his own manuscript notes, yet 'suppressed [them] from print', preferring to omit 'unsightly' ciphers from the page, especially when his sole object was to do Shakespeare service;[112] he also cleared the page of all notes, publishing them later in three separate volumes, here too 'suppressing' the names of the contributors.[113] His failure to acknowledge the words of others forfeited his right to his own, so that Steevens and Malone were uncharacteristically casual in adapting them without acknowledgement, though Steevens insisted that any duplication of Capell's material is 'accidental coincidence of opinion', not 'plagiarism'.[114]

In the context of this free-for-all, the variorum edition looks like a welcome territorial settlement. The format provides a region in which the multiple and even conflicting claims could be numbered, registered, and accredited. Yet at the same time that it settles disputes, it sets Shakespeare up as a territory to be disputed. By 1765, the Shakespeare text is no longer the massive solitary unit occupying the double columns of the vast seventeenth-century folio page. Even after the size of the page had contracted into the eighteenth-century octavo multiple volumes, the autonomy of the text remained intact. Rowe's tacit changes and Pope's quiet signals left its spatial dominion undisturbed. With Theobald, it becomes necessary to reserve a liminal space at the lowly bottom of the page in order to avoid intrusions upon Shakespeare's text. It is that area, what Johnson referred to as the 'dominion' of the margin, that is contested in the editorial rivalries recorded above and settled by the variorum dispensation. No longer inserted in the text proper, the notes do all the same proclaim the need for insertion. What must be stressed is that respect for the impermeable boundaries of Shakespeare's text was attended by a formation of independent auxiliary texts. It is not only Shakespeare who occupies the page, but the commentators as well, and that occupancy entails a repartitioning of the space of the page, a remapping of typography to represent a coalition of minor texts. All the

---

[112] Capell, *MWSHCHT*, i. 23–5, n. 10.
[113] *Notes and Various Readings to Shakespeare* (New York, 1970), p. xxiii (first published in 1779–83).
[114] Steevens, 'Advertisement', *PWS*, E7ᵛ.

eighteenth-century editions give Shakespeare the full width of
the page, but the variorums reserve a section of its length for
other occupants. Their presence there is clearly subordinate:
the typeface is smaller and they are beneath the text. At the
same time, however, that this space expands, its two columns of
print increasingly appear to support the text as they perceptibly
stand under it and ostensibly make it understandable.

Though first to reproduce Shakespeare in a variorum edition,
Johnson expressed reservations about the format. The proliferation of notes vying with the text for the reader's attention
interrupted the reading process: 'The mind is refrigerated by
interruption; the thoughts are diverted from the principal
subject'.[115] In comparison to those of its successors, the interruptions in the 1765 format are relatively restrained, limited by
their purpose. Johnson only included the notes of other commentators when he believed that they had either conclusively
settled a difficulty or else come up with the best temporary
solution; when he 'borrowed' an explanation from another, 'I
suppose it to be commonly right'.[116] Malone and the others,
however, record contributions that repeat, contradict, and
refute one another without settling the difficulty in question.
Volleys like the one set off between Steevens and Malone by
Sonnet 93's 'Like a deceived husband' (see Chapter 4, pp. 158–9)
are not unusual in the notes to the plays; marginal dialogues
involving two or more commentators periodically occur beneath the dramatic exchanges prefixed to the names above. It
was, in fact, a dispute over who would have the final word in
Malone's 1790 edition that triggered the antagonism between
Steevens and Malone.[117] The later variorums consequently can
appear to be more concerned with giving commentators their
presumptive say than clearing difficulties in the text.

Other differences separate the 1765 variorum from its successors. While Johnson subscribed the names of the other
contributors, he omitted his own. Although the editor's name
appears among all the rest in the later variorums, Johnson's
comments were unsigned. His emendations, synonyms, and
paraphrases possessed a transitional status, neither quite Shake-

[115] Smith, *Eighteenth Century Essays*, p. 148.   [116] Ibid. 140.
[117] See Boswell's account of their falling out based on Malone's correspondence, 'A
Biographical Memoir of Edmond Malone, Esq.', Malone–Boswell, *PPWS*, i. lvii–lviii.

speare's nor quite his own. His practice of citing other commentators demonstrated a similar resistance to the variorum's
allocations. He used no quotation marks.or italics when reproducing the comments of others; his reprinting of their comments
was more loose paraphrase than exact borrowing. The later
variorums, however, do set off the various comments typographically, displaying their status as individuated property;
and the transcriptions are largely accurate, a measure of their
respect for what belongs to another. By the end of the century,
the variorum apparatus came to look like a format for attribution,
registering critical as opposed to literary property, accurately
drawing the lines between the various shares. And just as
forgeries and counterfeits trail authentic documents and paintings, and plagiarism follows authorial ownership, so too bogus
attributions slip into the accurate record of acknowledgements.[118]

The late-eighteenth- and early-nineteenth-century variorums
are the consummate productions of a new preoccupation with
identifying and acknowledging the words of others, with marking them off in quotations and properly subscribing them. The
meum and *suum* of the various commentators are settled in the
process of fixing Shakespeare's text. In demarcating Shakespeare, the variorum inscribes a system of demarcations: distinguishing Shakespeare's works from the works of others (the
apocryphal plays), Shakespeare's works from their sources,
what Shakespeare wrote in one play from what he wrote in
another (parallel passages), what Shakespeare wrote and what
the editions—even the earliest ones—printed, what Shakespeare
wrote from what his contemporaries wrote, and finally, what
Shakespeare wrote from what editors inserted. At the same
time as it surveys Shakespeare's property according to all those
possible delineations, it stakes out the comments of the various
contributors, not only those of previous editors but those of
other Shakespearean scholars, some previously in print and
others in manuscript, as well as those from other readers who
responded to personal or public solicitations for information,
some with distinguished names (like Blackstone, Reynolds,

---

[118] Steevens 'fathered' obscene and disreputable notes on two acquaintances who
had offended him, Richard Amner and John Collins; see Arthur Sherbo, *The Birth of
Shakespeare Studies: Commentators from Rowe (1709) to Boswell–Malone (1821)*, Studies in
Literature 1500–1700 (East Lansing, Mich., 1986), pp. 56–63, 67–71.

and Hume) and others quite unknown.[119] The variorum thus instates a complex system of attributions that draws typographical boundaries around the *notis variorum*, staking out critical property at the same time as establishing what properly and authentically belongs to Shakespeare. The proprietary relation assigned to Shakespeare is thereby reproduced in the territorializing of the critical field.

It is not only the voices of Shakespeare and his commentators that come to be marked off at the end of the eighteenth century. It is then that quotation marks start being used systematically to mark off the words belonging to another. The discursive partitioning we have observed in eighteenth-century legal debates, book trade, and editions and anthologies of Shakespeare applies to all forms of transcription and inscription. Quotation marks are small-scale copyrights, labelling word combinations the property of their originators and protecting them by making acknowledgement the condition for their general use. Like copyright, they enclose discursive regions: the effort of composing a phrase or a book justifies appropriation so that the composer, like Locke's original occupant, 'by his Labour does, as it were, inclose it from the Common.' The reiteration of the words of another, like the reproduction of larger compositions, needs to be sanctioned by special prescriptions permitting or licensing duplication. Only at the end of the century do grammar books make quotation marks mandatory.[120] It is then, too, that novels begin uniformly to distinguish one character's words from another's, as well as from the narrator's, by bracketing them in quotes.[121]

The format for play texts, unlike that for novels, isolates one speaker's words from another's spatially. The need to insert quotes occurs, however, when one speaker repeats the words of another. Commonly no typographic distinction differentiated

---

[119] For an account of the variety of scholiasts who submitted comments for the variorum editions, see Sherbo, *The Birth of Shakespeare Studies*, pp. x–xi.

[120] Ronald B. McKerrow, *An Introduction to Bibliography for Literary Students* (Oxford, 1928), pp. 316–17 and C. J. Mitchell, 'Quotation Marks, Compositorial Habits, and False Imprints', *The Library*, 6 ser., 6 (1983), 359–84. Mitchell lists four late eighteenth-century grammars that prescribe quotation marks: p. 377, n. 50.

[121] Vivienne Mylne, 'The Punctuation of Dialogue in Eighteenth Century French and English Fiction', *The Library*, 6 (1979), 43–61.

'original' from 'borrowed' locutions in the quartos and folios; occasionally a colon or comma will separate the two, though more to introduce a rhetorical pause than to set off words lifted from another context.[122] It was not words specific to a single speaker that were cordoned off in the early printings of the plays, but words properly belonging to all speakers. What we call quotation marks were used to signal *sententiae*, sayings that were proper for any speaker to say. Although the *sententiae* often had an identifiable authoritative source, Aristotle or Horace for example, quotation marks were used for purposes not of assignation but of emphasis. They set off what deserved to be remembered. 'Gnomic pointing', as it has recently been termed, drew attention to the messages it highlighted because of their exceptional importance.[123] Their claim on the reader's attention was even more obvious when they appeared, as they frequently did, in the white of the margin; the printing-house instruments designed to measure the marginal space between *sententiae* were therefore called 'quotation quadrants'.[124] Even when included in the text itself, they were generally flagged by single or double quotation marks in the left-hand margin, so that according to the seventeenth-century dictionaries to quote meant 'to mark in the margin' and therefore simply 'to observe'.[125] When a quotation appeared within the text itself, a mark generally appeared only at its beginning, so that no typographical boundary prevented the end of the quote from running into the beginning of the text proper. Quotations were distinguished from the rest of the discourse, whether set off by their position in the margins or by quotations marks or by both, not because they originally belonged somewhere else, but rather because they belonged everywhere: they were commonplaces rather than private discursive units.

It was no doubt because quotation marks were used to draw attention to remarkable sayings that Pope adapted the same sign for distinguishing the 'shining' passages in Shakespeare, a

---

[122] Percy Simpson, *Shakespearean Punctuation* (Oxford, 1911), pp. 100–1.

[123] G. K. Hunter, 'The Marking of *Sententiae* in Elizabethan Plays, Poems, and Romances', *The Library*, 5th ser., 6 (1951), pp. 171–88.

[124] Joseph Moxon, *Mechanick Exercises on the Whole Art of Printing (1663–4)*, eds. Herbert Davis and Harry Carter (London, 1958), p. 349.

[125] 'To quote, or marke in the margent, to note by the way': Randle Cotgrave, *A Dictionarie of the French and English Tongues* (Menston, 1968; first published 1611).

precedent followed by both Hanmer and Warburton. The
'quoted' passages were those which merited special notice;
indeed, they often themselves qualified as *sententiae*. Pope found
only two shining passages in all of *Hamlet*: Polonius's advice to
his departing son, consisting of precepts to be charactered in
Laertes's memory, and Claudius's attempted prayer, also
abounding in prescriptive axioms.[126] Capell idiosyncratically
adapts the same mark for a new purpose announced in his 1760
Prolusions and introduced in his 1768 edition of Shakespeare: to
'constantly denote in this work that the words they are prefix'd
to are spoke or apart or aside and have no other significations
whatsoever'.[127] In editing the plays, Rowe and Pope followed
the folios in not typographically distinguishing quotations.
Theobald was the first editor to punctuate them, though commonly signalling only the start of the quote rather than bracketing
the entire unit. Warburton, Johnson, and Capell used italic
type to distinguish them.

Yet even when isolated in italics, it was still not clear that
quotes were signalling borrowed passages as opposed to memor-
able ones. Lines worth repeating or reciting in the plays, like
sententiae, were invariably of dramatic import: they called back
to mind what needed to be remembered. Feste quoted, though
not verbatim, Malvolio's three offensive sentences that are the
pretext for time's whirligig of revenges ('Why some are borne
great, some atchieue greatnesse, and some haue greatnesse
throwne upon them. . . By the Lotd Foole, I am not mad . . .
Madam, why laugh you at such a barren rascall. . . .' 2541–6);
Exton twice repeated, approximately, the anguished wish he
overheard Henry IV himself twice urge that resulted in the
murder of a Richard ('Haue I no friend will rid me of this liuing
feare?' 2655); Macbeth loosely recalled the witches' two equi-
vocal pronouncements that made his fatally resolute ('Feare
not Macbeth, no man that's borne of woman, Shall ere haue
power upon thee' and 'Feare not, till Byrnane Wood | Do come

---

[126] For Pope's penchant for Shakespeare's sententious passages, see John Butt,
Pope's Taste in Shakespeare (London, 1936).

[127] Capell in his introduction announces that he has introduced 'new pointings' in
his edition (*MWSHCHT*, i. 28–9, n. 12) and for an explanation of his system refers the
reader to *Prolusions: or Select Pieces of Ancient Poetry*, (London, 1760), i. vi.

to Dunsinane,' 2220–1, 2368–9).[128] These restatements have the dramatic significance of letters which the Folio italicized with relative consistency; Macbeth's letter to Lady Macbeth, the Oracle's message to Leontes, Malvolio's petition to Olivia for example, were reiterated utterances, occurring at the implied site of writing as well as the enacted site of recitation. Repetitions activated memory, the faculty that also retained *sententiae*. Re-marking words (putting marks on them again after they had already been marked in characters) implied that they were worth remarking for purposes of remembering. That italics and quotation marks were used interchangeably in this period suggests that citation and emphasis were not distinct: what was worth repeating was worth stressing and remembering.

By the end of the eighteenth century, 'gnomic pointing' appears to have ceased; Malone himself is confused by its use and assumes that what is printed in quotation marks in Shakespeare's period has a specific source rather than proverbial use; he therefore commits himself to the futile course of tracking down the source of maxims.[129] His confusion is understandable, for the function of quotation marks had completely reversed itself by the end of the eighteenth century. What formerly marked the universal and true (and therefore public) had come to designate the unique and exclusive (and therefore private). The sign once distinguishing the commonplace sets the bounds for private enclosure.

After the eighteenth century, the omission of quotation marks is an ethical offence as well as a grammatical solecism; it violates the rights of another as well as the rules of grammar. To quote without acknowledgement, as to print without copyright, is a form of theft, an encroachment on private property. Once a writer or speaker is entitled to his words, any unlicensed repetition constitutes an invasion of his property. So too does a misrepetition or misquotation of his words. To return to Blackstone, if 'the composition is varied', 'an invasion of [the writer's] right of property' occurs. The obligation to repeat accurately presupposes the recognition of the original utterance as a

---

[128] The quotations from the plays are from the *TNF*: TLN 2541–6; 1655; 2220–1; 2368–9.

[129] Hunter notes Malone's confusion at the practice of putting *sententiae* in quotes: 'The Marking of *Sententiae*', p. 171 n. 2.

separate and inviolable entity, a linguistic lot roped off by quotation marks and tethered to its source. Johnson in his 1755 Dictionary defined quoting as 'to adduce by way of authority or illustration the words of another'; as *sententiae* gave weight to a writer's claims, so too the passages Johnson quoted (without quotation marks) in his lexical entries authorized and illustrated his definitions. Yet his Dictionary quotations, like those in his edition of Shakespeare, tended to be paraphrastic rather than exact; 'hasty detruncations', he admitted, which might have changed not only the phrasing, but even 'the general tendency of the sentence'.[130] Not until language has been demarcated as property and removed from the free flow of discourse, could a quotation be committed to a verbatim rendition. The original utterance—whether issuing from Shakespeare, an editor, or any other user of the language—had to be objectified as something unto itself and apart from the medium of its transmission before its reproduction could be held to accuracy.

The earliest anthology to contain quotations or remarkable passages from Shakespeare was *Englands Parnassus* (1600), a compendium of 'choysest Flowers' illustrating that 'Moderne' English contained the makings of an elegant and copious vernacular.[131] Almost 10 per cent of its selections were either misascribed or unsigned; quotations from Shakespeare's *Richard II*, for example, were assigned to Daniel, Spenser, and 'M.Dr'.[132] Nor was much attention given to reproducing the quotations accurately: the selections from *Richard II* contain as many as six variants, and in the cases when quotations are repeated, changes are commonly introduced.[133] Yet at the time of its publication the anthology was perfectly adequate to its task of making the best examples of English usage available to its readers. The collection was not concerned with preserving the expressions of its authors as they had penned them; it worked instead to make them commonplaces, the stuff of English itself, all to the end of enriching the vernacular. The malleability of the selections

---

[130] *Dictionary* (1755) (New York, 1967), preface, b4.

[131] *Englands Parnassus, Compiled by Robert Allott, 1600*, ed. Charles Crawford (Oxford, 1913), pp. xliii, xxv.

[132] Ibid. p. 380.

[133] Of the thirty-one cases in which a passage is repeated, twenty-two are altered. Ibid. xxxix.

made for easier assimilation into the reader's spoken and written utterances.

The compendium's method comes to appear lax and irresponsible only after Malone, as the labours of a mid-nineteenth-century Shakespearean illustrate. This scholar spent fifty years trying to trace the quotations from *Englands Parnassus* so that they could be both correctly ascribed and correctly reproduced: 'I have done my best to restore the property, as well as the language of . . . the authors.'[134] The scholar's name was John Payne Collier, remembered less for his research than for his forgery, including that of the documents on which both his edition and his life of Shakespeare were based.[135] We see here embodied in one individual the complementary obsessions illustrated in the previous century by two contemporaries: the researcher Malone and the forger Ireland. In the case of Collier as well as in that of Malone and Ireland it is clear that accurate reproduction is indispensable to both authenticity and forgery. (And at both historical junctures new technologies made possible higher degrees of accuracy: first type facsimile and then photo-lithography.) What is also apparent is its importance to the discursive allotment that has been the subject of this chapter. If reproduction alters an author's phrasing, that text ceases to be identifiable as his property.

In this chapter I have discussed various modes of allocating discourse within Shakespeare editions (in anthologies, annotations, and variorums) and without (in discussions of literary property, copyright, and quotation marks). I have argued that these allocations are grounded in a notion of entitlement or proprietorship that derives from Locke's defence of private property. In the same way as a worker's labour entitled him to the product of that labour, so too a writer's (or speaker's)

[134] *Seven English Poetical Miscellanies reproduced under the care of J. Payne Collier* (London, 1867), iv. xvi. For the numerous instances of Collier's own inaccuracy and misascription, see Crawford, *Englands Parnassus*, p. 383.

[135] Collier's edition based on forged documentation—*The Works of William Shakespeare . . . . To which are added glossarial and other notes by Knight, Dyce, Collier, Halliwell, Hunter and Richardson* (New York, 1866)—was published in the same year as *A Reproduction in Exact Facsimile of the Famous First Folio, 1623, by the newly discovered process of photo-lithography, executed by R. W. Preston under the superintendence of Howard Staunton* (London, 1866).

labour entitled him to his own composition (or utterance). Both forms of occupancy presuppose a person who has ownership of himself, for it is that autonomy that justifies his appropriation of the products of his industry. Malone's apparatus confers upon Shakespeare the historical and personal autonomy that qualified him to own his work. At the same time, it reproduces what it represents as Shakespeare's proprietorship through the variorum's format of attributions. The introduction of quotation marks to identify and acknowledge borrowings indicates that this form of discursive entitlement is not peculiar to Shakespeare and his commentators. What the apparatus made unique to Shakespeare could, by right, be extended to any individual.

Yet this apparatus is an historical phenomenon, not an inevitable truth finally understood, codified, and instituted— as one last look at Copley's Malonean painting will illustrate. Despite the painting's exacting fidelity to the authentic particulars of 4 January 1642, it betrays its subject in a fundamental way. It bases its portrayal on first-hand accounts, on the secretary's minutes and on the diaries of several Members of Parliament, in order to depict the event exactly as it occurred. Copley's brush rivals the secretary Rushworth's pen in providing on-the-spot coverage of Charles I's entry. Yet in 1642, there were sanctions against publishing any record taken during Parliament's proceedings. The King himself was not entitled to a copy; upon command, Rushworth provided Charles I with a transcript of his own speech, but not of what the other Members had spoken.[136] While accounts constructed from memory were permissible, the sanctions against eye-witness reporting were not lifted until the 1780s, when they were seen to violate constitutional liberties.[137] Boswell, father of Malone's successor, himself a renowned reporter as well as a lawyer who participated

---

[136] In the preface to his eight-volume history, Rushworth qualifies his 'report to Posterity' by establishing himself as Parliament's reporter: 'I began early to take in Characters, Speeches and Passages of Conferences in Parliament, and from the King's own Mouth . . . and have been upon the Stage continually and an Eye and Ear-witness of the greatest Transactions . . .': *Historical Collections of Private Passages of State, Weighty Matters in Law, Remarkable Proceedings in Five Parliaments*, (London, 1721), i. b3ʳ. Rushworth records that he was summoned by the King and asked for a transcript of his speech to the House: iv. 479.

[137] Alan Downie, 'The Growth of Government Tolerance of the Press to 1790', in *Development of the English Book Trade, 1700–1899*, eds. Robin Myers and Michael Harris (Oxford, 1981), pp. 58–61.

in the literary property debates, was surprised that these restrictions should have so recently existed, believing Englishmen entitled to 'a fair, open, and exact report of the actual proceedings of their representatives and legislators'.[138] This entitlement to an 'exact report', however, was as novel as Malone's determination to have a *Life* that was documented and *Plays and Poems* that were 'collated *verbatim* with the most authentick copies'. The scrupulous authenticity of Copley's painting thus proves profoundly inauthentic and ahistorical in opening to full public view the documentary account that at the time would have remained behind Parliament's closed doors, thereby divulging the time-bound dependencies of its authentic style and of its historicized, personalized, and entitled subjects.

[138] Hill, *The Life of Samuel Johnson*, i. 116.

Afterword
The Enlightenment Reproduction

In retrospect, what appears most admirable about Malone is his attempt to reproduce Shakespeare in his own terms—without 'admixtures', without 'sophistications'. Throughout his long career, his Shakespearean projects were all directed towards stepping past traditional treatments and returning directly to Shakespeare. As his editions demonstrate, his practices were literally conservative: his volumes provided the storage for the texts from the earliest quartos and Folio as well as for documents from archives and registers. Justifying this conservative policy was what might be termed an historical relativism that, without unsettling his own absolutes, allowed for cultural differences as variants of the 'customary'. At the end of the eighteenth century, facsimile reproduction became available, making it possible to reproduce materials without the mediations that he found so corrupting. Providing a seemingly exact duplicate of the original, facsimiles were the mechanical corollary to Malone's conservative practices and historicism.

As Malone himself discovered, Shakespeare had not shared his commitment to accurate reproduction, not even of his own text. With predictable indignation, Malone observed that when even a written document—a letter or proclamation, for example —was read at one point in a play and then again at some later point, 'inaccuracies' were introduced: 'When [Shakespeare] had occasion to quote the same paper twice (not from memory, but *verbatim*) from negligence he does not always attend to the words of the paper which he has occasion to quote, but makes one of the persons of the drama recite them with variations, though he holds the very papers before his eyes.'[1] In a scene from *Henry VI Part II*, for example, the same articles of peace between France and England are twice read aloud, first by the Bishop who reads 'dutchy of Anjou and the county of Maine'

---

[1] Malone, *PPWS*, vi. 416.

and then by the Duke who read 'the dutchies of Anjou and of Maine'. That the words on the page (of a legal instrument, no less) appeared to have been transformed from one reading to the next must have seemed something of a nightmare to the editor who advertised his edition as 'collated *verbatim* with the most authentick copies', who punctiliously transcribed wills and accounts, and who published some of the first facsimiles. How could a text be faithfully reproduced unless fastened and secure to begin with, locked into place by the author? An exact reproduction presupposed the stability of the original: 'Words cannot change their form.' Yet the nightmare of a shifting text may not have been so very far from the physicality of Shakespeare's pages, where any word could take varying forms and yet remain the same word.

For Malone, these deviations within the text were symptomatic not of the medium's instability, but rather of Shakespeare's 'negligence'. Indeed, he found them so characteristic in the contested works that he considered them conclusive proof of Shakespeare's authorship. At this point, we can see how the notion of a single authorial consciousness (with its occasional lapses into unconsciousness) serves a regulatory function, converting what we have called the 'copiousness' of both mechanical and rhetorical 'copy' into personal idiosyncrasy. Verbatim repetition requires a language in standardized stasis, put under the mastery of precisely the historicized, individuated, and entitled subject Malone both presupposed and projected in his 1790 Shakespeare.

No less than the 1623 Folio's organization of the disparate and dispersed quarto pieces into the consanguineous Folio corpus, no less than the earlier eighteenth century's rectifications of Shakespeare's unruly 'Extravagance', Malone's apparatus worked to control the erratic fecundity of Shakespeare's texts. The apparatus made the text accountable to the vast parameters of Shakespeare's consciousness. The more fissured and differentiated the apparatus, the better it was able to accommodate the intricacies of textual overflow. Historical events registered as unique experiences, further particularized when extended across a personalized chronological trajectory. As if to make the dependency indissoluble, a relation of ownership was inscribed that assigned the texts to Shakespeare both stylistically and hermeneutically. Yet however capacious and reticulated the author, the text invariably exceeded his limits, transgressing the bounds of coherent (logical) and decent (moral) personal identity. The critical history of *Hamlet*, like that of the Sonnets, begins with a recognition of this incommensurability: Hamlet's words could not be aligned with the character assumed behind them. While earlier critics, Johnson above all, found Hamlet's behaviour incoherent and unconscionable (even unspeakable), later critics, including Malone and Boswell, found a way of preserving both Hamlet's integrity and his presence in language.[2] In order to retain, for example, the connections between a conscionable Hamlet and his unconscionable refusal to kill the King at prayer, interpretation delved below, mining the text for a justification concealed from and mystified by its surface. Inaudible and imperceptible, the essential meaning of his words was stifled within the postulated inner regions of his psyche or soul. While his words expressed the desire not only to kill Claudius but to damn him, their real meaning lay in Hamlet's proto-Coleridgean (or proto-Schlegelian) 'gentleness'.[3] Their viciousness betrayed that gentleness, deceiving not only others, but Hamlet himself. By locating meaning in psychological immanence, self-deception provided the mechanism for releasing Hamlet from responsibility for his words. Shakespeare's own meaning in this play similarly receded from voice or print, present only vestigially in a solitary phrase expressing at the last moment his own none the less abiding understanding of Hamlet, 'Now cracks a noble heart.'[4] Shakespeare unlocked his heart in the Sonnets and in his Hamlet, the words on the surface there opening to yield psychologically resonant voids as rich in content as the musty coffers chock-full with documents.

Thus the recourse to immanent readings emerged as a response to the strain of exclusivity; the intractable deviations

---

[2] Immanent readings of *Hamlet* emerge in essays by Henry Mackenzie, William Richardson, and Thomas Robertson, all in Brian Vickers, ed., *Shakespeare: The Critical Heritage* (London, 1974–81), vi. 272–80, 365–70, 480–99. For Johnson's comment, see Vickers, *Critical Heritage*, v. 159; for Malone and Boswell, see Malone–Boswell, *PPWS*, vii. 533–40. See also Margreta de Grazia, 'The Motive for Interiority: Shakespeare's *Sonnets* and *Hamlet*', *Style*, 23, 3 (Fall 1989).

[3] Richardson, in Vickers, *Critical Heritage*, vi. 368.

[4] Robertson, in Vickers, *Critical Heritage*, vi. 481.

of the text were mastered by a retreat into more tractable immanent meaning. This subterfuge had an uncanny counterpart, a shady unacknowledged double like the forgeries linked to authentic materials: an entitled Shakespeare was accompanied by a disentitled Shakespeare. It is at this time, too, that Shakespeare's ownership of the plays was questioned, and by procedures not unlike those followed by Malone. Dissatisfied by the lack of correspondence between literary text and biographical documents, the first anti-Stratfordian looked back to history for a more appropriate author.[5] The text gave traces of nobility, refinement, education, and experience, while Shakespeare's life showed no such signs. Similarly, Shakespeare's life as revealed in Stratford documents was impressed with topical events that left no traces in the plays. The failure to find a close fit between Shakespeare and his works drove the anti-Stratfordian to appoint another more commensurate author, one whose name did not appear on the title-page but which would in time be found encrypted ingeniously within the text. Thus the attempt to make the text compatible with its author draws anti-Stratfordians and post-Maloneans alike into the encoded inner region that bears at most a tendentious relation to the verbal texture; in honouring the proprietary relation between subject and language, it renounces its surface in order to maintain an overstressed and untenable exclusivity.

Authentic materials, the historicized and individuated subject, exclusive ownership, immanent or psychologized texts: all are part of a schema by which textual activity is regulated. This is the legacy of the 1790 apparatus and its enlarged successor of 1821. It is a distinctly Enlightenment construct precisely because its terms appear so incontrovertible, as if, like truth itself, they could not be otherwise. Constructed from authentic materials, based on verifiable facts, avoiding contaminating mediation, the apparatus satisfies all the criteria of objective truth. Like a facsimile, it appears to be reproducing the thing itself—Shakespeare in history. Yet, like the facsimile, it has to

---

[5] For an overview of the anti-Stratfordian controversy, see S. Schoenbaum, *Shakespeare's Lives* (Oxford, 1970), 541–5. Marjorie Garber has noted that the Shakespeare authorship controversy begins in the late eighteenth and early nineteenth centuries, just at the point that Foucault identifies with the emergence of the author function: *Shakespeare's Ghost Writers: Literature as Uncanny Causality* (New York, 1987), p. 4.

suppose that thing defined in order to reproduce it; it has to assume it a distinct object, or, in the case of Malone's *Shakspeare*, into an autonomous and entitled subject—a textual counterpart to the reader.

If the apparatus appears to have done no more than deliver Shakespeare, it is because its terms have been so perfectly in keeping with the reader's sense of the real and the rational. Their transparency derives from their involvement in what a recent critique of the Enlightenment has termed its 'metanarrative', an epistemology that assumes an essential reality outside discourse.[6] The 1790 apparatus, the site of Shakespeare's emergence in his modern aspect, is a striking example of how the Enlightenment represented its constructs as Truth, inscribing factual objects and autonomous subjects (each grounded in the other) in the process of reproducing Shakespeare. Perhaps this explains the astonishing efficacy with which it has performed its preparatory function for the past two centuries. In accordance with an Enlightenment dispensation of factuality and selfhood, of objectivity and subjectivity, it has prepared the text for readers by disciplining it and it has prepared readers for the text by instructing them, meanwhile appearing to have merely reproduced the authentic Shakespeare—verbatim.

[6] Jean-François Lyotard, *The Postmodern Condition: A Report on Knowledge*, trans. Geoff Bennington and Brian Massumi, Theory and History of Literature, 10 (Minneapolis, Minn., 1988).

BIBLIOGRAPHY

ALLEN, MICHAEL J. B. and MUIR, KENNETH, *Shakespeare; Plays in Quarto*, (Berkeley, Ca., 1981).

ALTHUSSER, LOUIS, 'Ideology and Ideological State Apparatuses', in *Lenin and Philosophy and Other Essays*, trans. Ben Brewster (London, 1971),

AMORY, MARTHA BABCOCK, *The Domestic and Artistic Life of John Singleton Copley, R.A.* (Boston, 1882).

ANDREWS, JOHN F. ed., *William Shakespeare: His World, His Work, His Influence* 3 vols. (New York, 1985).

BALIBAR, ÉTIENNE and MACHEREY, PIERRE, 'On Literature as an Ideological Form', in *Untying the Text: A Post-Structuralist Reader*, ed. Robert Young (Boston, 1981).

BALDWIN, T. W., *William Shakspere's Smalle Latine & Lesse Greeke*, 2 vols. (Urbana, Ill., 1944).

—— *On the Literary Genetics of Shakspere's Poems and Sonnets* (Urbana, Ill., 1950).

—— *On Act and Scene Division in the Shakspere First Folio* (Carbondale, Ill. and Edwardsville, 1965).

BARTLETT, HENRIETTA C. and POLLARD, ALFRED W., *A Census of Shakespeare's Plays in Quarto 1594–1709* (New Haven, 1939).

BEAL, PETER, *Index of English Literary Manuscripts* (London, 1980).

BEAUMONT, FRANCIS and FLETCHER, JOHN, *Comedies and Tragedies* (London, 1647).

BECKETT, ANDREW, *Concordance to Shakespeare* (London, 1787).

BELANGER, TERRY, 'Tonson, Wellington and the Shakespeare Copyrights', in *Studies in the Book Trade in Honour of Graham Pollard* The Oxford Bibliographic Society Publications, new ser. 18 (Oxford, 1975).

—— 'Booksellers' Trade Sales 1718–68', *The Library*, 5th ser., 30 (1975).

—— 'Publishers and Writers in Eighteenth-Century England', in *Books and Their Readers in Eighteenth-Century England*, ed. Isabel Rivers, (New York, 1982).

BENSON, JOHN, *Poems: Written by Wil. Shake-speare. Gent.* (London, 1640).

BENJAMIN, WALTER, *Illuminations*, trans. Harry Zohn (New York, 1969).

BENNETT, JOSEPHINE WATERS, 'Benson's Alleged Piracy of *Shakespeare's Sonnets* and of Some of Jonson's Works', *Studies in Bibliography*, 21 (1968).

BENTLEY, GERALD EADES, *Shakespeare and Jonson: Their Reputations in the Seventeenth Century Compared* (Chicago, 1945).

—— *Shakespeare: A Biographical Handbook* (Princeton, 1961).

—— *The Profession of a Dramatist in Shakespeare's Time: 1590–1642* (Princeton, NJ, 1971).

—— 'Shakespeare's Reputation: Then Till Now', in Andrews, *William Shakespeare*, 3.

BERTRAM, PAUL and COSSA, FRANK, ' "Willm Shakespeare 1609": The Flower Portrait Revisited', *Shakespeare Quarterly*, 86 (1985).

BIRRELL, AUGUSTINE, *Seven Lectures on the Law and History of Copyright in Books* (New York, 1899).

BIRRELL, T. A. *English Monarchs and Their Books from Henry VII to Charles II*, The Panizzi Lectures (London, 1987).

—— 'The Influence of Seventeenth-Century Publishers on the Presentation of English Literature', *Historical and Editorial Studies in Medieval and Early Modern English for Johan Gerritsen*, ed. Mary-Jo Arn and Hanneke Wirtjes (Groningen, 1985).

BLACK, M. W. and SHAABER, M. A., *Shakespeare's Seventeenth Century Editors, 1632–1685* (New York, 1937).

BLACKSTONE, WILLIAM, *Commentaries on the Laws of England*, 4 vols. (London, 1766).

BLAYNEY, PETER, *The Texts of 'King Lear' and Their Origins*, i, *Nicholas Okes and the First Quarto* (Cambridge, 1982).

BOADEN, JAMES, *An Inquiry into the Authenticity of Various Pictures and Prints* (London, 1824).

BODLEY, THOMAS, *Letters of Sir Thomas Bodley to Thomas James, First Keeper of the Bodleian Library*, ed. G. W. Wheeler (Oxford, 1926).

BOOTH, *Shakespeare's Sonnets*, ed. Stephen Booth (New Haven, Conn., and London, 1977).

BOSWELL, JAMES, *Letters of James Boswell*, ed. Chauncy Brewster Rinkers, 2 vols. (Oxford, 1924).

—— *Boswell's Life of Johnson, together with Boswell's Journal of a tour to the Hebrides*, ed. George Birkbeck Hill, rev. and enl. by L. F. Powell, 6 vols. (Oxford, 1934–50).

BOWERS, FREDSON, *On Editing Shakespeare and Other Elizabethan Dramatists* (Charlottesville, Va., 1966).

—— 'Authority, Copy, and Transmission in Shakespeare's Texts', in *Shakespeare Study Today*, ed. Georgianna Ziegler (New York, 1986).

BRACKEN, JAMES K., 'William Stansby and Jonson's Folio, 1616', *The Library*, 6th ser., 10 (1988).

BRONSON, BERTRAND H., *Joseph Ritson: Scholar-at-Arms*, 2 vols. (Berkeley, Ca., 1938).

BROWN, ARTHUR, 'Edmond Malone and English Scholarship', an inaugural lecture delivered at University College London, 21 May 1963 (London, 1963).

BRYANT, DONALD CROSS, *Edmund Burke and His Literary Friends* (St Louis, Mo., 1939).

BULLOKAR, JOHN, *An English Expositor* (Menston, Yorks, 1967).

BURKE, EDMUND, *Reflections on the Revolution in France*, ed. A. J. Grieve (London, 1967).

CAMPBELL, HAY, *Information for Alexander Donaldson and John Wood*, in Parks, *The English Book Trade*, 16.

CAPELL, EDWARD, *Prolusions; or Select Pieces of Antient Poetry*, 8 vols. (London, 1760).

—— *Notes and Various Readings to Shakespeare*, 1783, 3 vols. (New York, 1970).

CAVE, TERENCE, *The Cornucopian Text: Problems of Writing in the French Renaissance* (Oxford, 1979).

CAVENDISH, MARGARET, *Sociable Letters*, in Vickers, *Shakespeare: The Critical Heritage*, i.

CHAMBERS, E. K., *The Mediaeval Stage*, 2 vols. (Oxford, 1903).

—— *The Disintegration of Shakespeare's Texts* (London, 1924).

—— *William Shakespeare: A Study of Facts and Problems*, 2 vols. (Oxford, 1930).

COLERIDGE, S. T., *Coleridge on Shakespeare: The Text of the Lectures of 1811-12*, ed. Reginald A. Foakes (Charlottesville, Va., 1971).

CORBALLIS, RICHARD, 'Copy-Text for Theobald's "Shakespeare"', *The Library*, 6th ser., 8 (1986).

CORBETT, MARY and LIGHTBROWN, RONALD, *The Comely Frontispiece: The Emblematic Title-Page in England 1550-1660* (London, 1979).

COLLINS, A. S., 'Some Aspects of Copyright from 1700 to 1780', *The Library*, 4th ser., 7 (1927).

DAWSON, GILES, 'Warburton, Hanmer, and the 1745 Edition of Shakespeare', *Studies in Bibliography*, 2 (1949-50).

—— 'The Copyright of Shakespeare's Dramatic Works', *Studies in Honor of A. H. R. Fairchild*, ed. Charles T. Prouty, The University of Missouri Studies, xxi (Columbia, Mo., 1956).

—— and KENNEDY-SKIPTON, LETITIA, *Elizabethan Handwriting* (New York, 1966).

DE GRAZIA, MARGRETA, 'The Essential Shakespeare and the Material Book', *Textual Practice*, 2 (1988).

—— 'The Motive for Interiority: Shakespeare's *Sonnets* and *Hamlet*', *Style*, 23, 2 (1989).

DODD, WILLIAM, *The Beauties of Shakespear* (London, 1752).

DOWNIE, ALAN, 'The Growth of Government Tolerance of the Press to 1790', in *Development of the English Book Trade, 1700–1899*, eds. Robin Myers and Michael Harris (Oxford, 1981).

DRYDEN, JOHN, 'A Discourse Concerning the Original and Progress of Satire', in *Of Dramatic Poesy and Other Essays*, 2 vols., ed. George Watson (New York, 1962).

—— *An Essay of Dramatick Poesie*, in Vickers, *Shakespeare: The Critical Heritage*, i.

EAGLETON, TERRY, *The Function of Criticism from the Spectator to Post-Structuralism* (London, 1984).

EASTMAN, ARTHUR M., 'The Texts from which Johnson Printed his Shakespeare', *Journal of English and Germanic Philology*, 49 (1950).

EBELING, HERMAN J., 'The Word Anachronism,' *Modern Language Notes*, 52 (1937).

EDWARDS, THOMAS, *The Canons of Criticism and Glossary Being a Supplement to Mr. Warburton's Edition of Shakspear* (London, 1750).

EISENSTEIN, ELIZABETH, *The Printing Press as an Agent of Change* (Cambridge, 1985).

Englands Parnassus, Compiled by Robert Allott, 1600, ed. Charles Crawford (Oxford, 1913).

EVANS, A. W., *Warburton and the Warburtonians: A Study in Some Eighteenth-Century Controversies* (London, 1932).

EVANS, G. BLAKEMORE, 'Shakespeare's Text: Approaches and Problems', in *A New Companion to Shakespeare Studies*, ed. Kenneth Muir (Cambridge, 1971).

FEATHER, JOHN, 'The Book Trade in Politics: The Making of the Copyright Act of 1710', *Publishing History*, 7 (1980).

—— 'The English Book Trade and the Law 1695–1799', *Publishing History*, 12 (1982).

FERGUSON, MARGARET W., QUILLIGAN, MAUREEN and VICKERS, NANCY J., *Rewriting the Renaissance: The Discourses of Sexual Difference in Early Modern Europe* (Chicago and London, 1986).

FOUCAULT, MICHEL, *The Archaeology of Knowledge and the Discourse on Language*, trans. A. M. Sheridan Smith (New York, 1972).

—— 'What Is an Author?', in *Textual Strategies: Perspectives in Post-Structuralist Criticism*, ed. Josue V. Harari (Ithaca, NY, 1979).

FREEHAFER, JOHN, 'Leonard Digges, Ben Jonson, and the Beginning of Shakespeare Idolatry', *Shakespeare Quarterly*, 21 (1970).

GADAMER, HANS, *Truth and Method*, trans. Garrett Barden and John Cumming (New York, 1975).

GARBER, MARJORIE, *Shakespeare's Ghost Writers: Literature as Uncanny Causality* (New York, 1987).

GEDULD, HARRY M., *Prince of Publishers: A Study of the Work and Career of Jacob Tonson* (Bloomington, Ind., 1969).

GILDON, CHARLES, 'Remarks on the Poems of Shakespear', printed as vol. vii of Pope *WWS* (London, 1710).

GOMBRICH, E. H., *The Story of Art* 14th edn. (Englewood Cliffs, NJ, 1984, first pub. 1950).

GRADY, HUGH H., *The Modernist Shakespeare: Critical Texts in a Material World* (Oxford, 1990).

GREBANIER, BERNARD, *The Great Shakespeare Forgery* (New York, 1965).

GREG, W. W., *Some Aspects and Problems of London Publishing between 1550 and 1650* (Oxford, 1956).

—— *A Bibliography of the English Printed Drama to the Restoration* (London, 1957).

—— *Collected Papers*, ed. J. C. Maxwell (Oxford, 1966).

—— *The Editorial Problem in Shakespeare: A Survey of the Foundations of the Text*, 3rd edn. (Oxford, 1967).

—— *The Shakespeare First Folio: Its Bibliographical and Textual History* (Oxford, 1955; repr. 1969).

—— and BOSWELL, E. *Records of the Court of the Stationers' Company 1576–1602* (London, 1930).

GURR, ANDREW, *The Shakespearean Stage 1574–1642* (Cambridge, 1980).

HALE, J. R., *The Evolution of British Historiography from Bacon to Naumier* (London, 1967).

HAMILTON, CHARLES, *In Search of Shakespeare* (San Diego, Ca., 1985).

HARGRAVE, FRANCIS, *An Argument in Defence of Literary Property* in Parks, *The English Book Trade*, 20.

HERFORD, C. H., SIMPSON, PERCY, and SIMPSON, EVELYN, *Works of Benjamin Jonson*, 11 vols. (Oxford, 1929–52).

HINMAN, CHARLTON, *The Printing and Proof-Reading of the First Folio of Shakespeare*, 2 vols. (Oxford, 1963).

—— *The Norton Facsimile: First Folio of Shakespeare*, ed. Charlton Hinman (New York, 1968).

HOBDAY, C. H., 'Shakespeare's Venus and Adonis Sonnets', *Shakespeare Survey*, 26 (1973).

HOHENDAHL, PETER UWE, *The Institution of Criticism* (Ithaca, NY, 1982).

HONIGMANN, E. A. J., *The Stability of Shakespeare's Text* (London, 1965).

—— *Shakespeare: The 'Lost Years'* (Totowa, NJ, 1985).

HOSLEY, R., KNOWLES, R., and McGUGAN, R., *Shakespeare Variorum Handbook* (New York, 1971).

HOWARD-HILL, T. H., 'Spelling and the Bibliographer', *The Library*, 5th ser., 18 (1962).

HOY, CYRUS, 'The Shares of Fletcher and His Collaborators in the

Beaumont and Fletcher Canon', in *Evidence for Authorship: Essays on Problems of Attribution*, eds. David V. Erdman and Ephim G. Fogel (Ithaca, NY, 1966).

HUME, DAVID, *A Treatise of Human Nature*, ed. L. A. Selby-Bigge (Oxford, 1949).

—— *The History of England, from the Invasion of Julius Caesar to the Revolution in 1688*, 8 vols. (London, 1807).

HUNTER, DAVID, 'Copyright Protection for Engravings and Maps in Eighteenth-Century Britain', *The Library*, 6th ser., 9 (1987).

HUNTER, G. K., 'The Marking of *Sententiae* in Elizabethan Plays, Poems, and Romances', *The Library*, 5th ser., 6 (1951).

JAGGARD, WILLIAM, *Shakespeare Bibliography* (New York, 1959).

JAUSS, HANS ROBERT, 'Literary History as Challenge to Literary Theory', in *Toward an Aesthetic of Reception*, trans. Timothy Bahti (Minneapolis, 1984).

JOHNSON, SAMUEL, *Johnson on Shakespeare*, ed. Arthur Sherbo, 2 vols. (New Haven, 1968).

—— *Dictionary of the English Language* (New York, 1967).

JONES, RICHARD FOSTER, *Lewis Theobald: His Contribution to English Scholarship* (New York, 1966).

JONSON, BENJAMIN, *Q. Horatius Flaccus: His Art of Poetry Englished by Ben: Jonson, With other Workes of the Author* (London, 1640).

—— *Works* (London, 1616).

KANT, IMMANUEL, *Critique of Pure Reason*, trans. and ed. Norman Kemp Smith (New York, 1965).

KENNEY, E. J., *The Classical Text: Aspects of Editing in the Age of the Printed Book* (Berkeley, Ca., 1974).

KERNAN, ALVIN, *Printing Technology, Letters & Samuel Johnson* (Princeton, NJ, 1987).

KERRIGAN, WILLIAM and BRADEN, GORDAN, *The Idea of the Renaissance* (Baltimore and London, 1989).

LASKY, MELVIN, J., *Utopia and Revolution* (Chicago, 1976).

LEE, SIDNEY, *Shakespeare's Comedies, Histories and Tragedies: A Census of Extant Copies* (Oxford, 1902).

—— *A Catalogue of the Shakespeare Exhibit Held in the Bodleian Library to Commemorate the Death of Shakespeare* (Oxford, 1916).

LINTOTT, BERNARD, *A Collection of Poems in Two Volumes . . .* (London, 1711).

LOCKE, JOHN, *Two Treatises of Government*, 2nd edn., ed. Peter Laslett (Cambridge, 1967).

LOEWENSTEIN, JOSEPH, 'The Script in the Marketplace', *Representations* 12 (1985).

LOUNSBURY, THOMAS R., *The Text of Shakespeare* (New York, 1970).

LUBORSKY, RUTH and INGRAM, ELIZABETH, *A Guide to English Illustrated Books, 1536–1603*, (Scholar Press, forthcoming).

LYNCH, KATHLEEN M., *Jacob Tonson Kit-Cat Publisher* (Knoxville, Tenn., 1971).

LYOTARD, JEAN-FRANÇOIS, *The Postmodern Condition: A Report on Knowledge*, trans. Geoff Bennington and Brian Massumi (Minneapolis, Minn., 1988).

MACHEREY, PIERRE, *A Theory of Literary Production*, 2nd edn., trans. Geoffrey Wall (London, 1985).

MADAN, *The Original Bodleian Copy of the First Folio of Shakespeare*, eds. F. Madan, G. M. R. Turbutt, and S. Gibson, (Oxford, 1905).

MALONE, EDMOND, *Cursory Observations on the Poems Attributed to Thomas Rowley* (London, 1782).

—— *An Inquiry into the Authenticity of Certain Miscellaneous Papers and Legal Instruments, Published Dec. 2 MDCCXCV, and Attributed to Shakespeare, Queen Elizabeth, and Henry, Earl of Southampton: Illustrated by Fac-similes of the Genuine Hand-writing of that Nobleman, and of Her Majesty; A New Fac-simile of the Handwriting of Shakspeare, Never before Exhibited; and Other Authentick Documents* (London, 1795).

—— 'Some Account of the Life . . .', in *Critical and Miscellaneous Works of John Dryden* (London, 1800).

MARCUS, LEAH, *Puzzling Shakespeare: Local Reading and Its Discontents* (Berkeley, Ca., 1988).

MAROTTI, ARTHUR, ' "Love is not love": Elizabethan Sonnet Sequences and the Social Order', *English Literary History*, 49 (1982).

—— 'Shakespeare's *Sonnets* as Literary Property', in *Soliciting Interpretation: Literary Theory and Seventeenth-Century English Poets*, eds. Katherine Maus and Elizabeth Harvey(Chicago, Ill., 1990).

MAUS, KATHERINE EISMAN, *Ben Jonson and the Roman Frame of Mind* (Princeton, NJ, 1984).

MCKENZIE, D. F., 'Printer's of the Mind: Some Notes on Bibliographic Theories and Printing-House Practices', *Studies in Bibliography*, 22 (1969).

—— 'Typography and Meaning: The Case of William Congreve', in *The Book and the Book Trade in Eighteenth-Century Europe*, Proceedings of the Fifth Wolfenbutteler Symposium, eds. Giles Barber and Bernhard Fabian (Hamburg, 1981).

MCKERROW, Ronald B., 'The Treatment of Shakespeare's Text by his Earlier Editors, 1709–1768', in *Library of Shakespearean Biography and Criticism* (Freeport, NY, 1970; first publ. 1933).

—— *An Introduction to Bibliography for Literary Students* (Oxford, 1928).

MCLEOD, RANDALL, 'UNEditing Shak-speare', *Sub-Stance*, 33/4 (1982).

—— 'The Psychopathology of Everyday Art', in *The Elizabethan Theatre*, ix, ed. G. R. Hibbard (Port Credit, Waterloo, 1986).

McMILLIN, SCOTT, *The Elizabethan Theatre and The Book of Sir Thomas More* (Ithaca, NY, 1986).

MACPHERSON, C. B., *The Political Theory of Possessive Individualism: Hobbes to Locke* (Oxford, 1962).

McLUHAN, MARSHALL, *The Gutenberg Galaxy: The Making of Typographic Man* (Toronto, 1966).

MERES, FRANCIS, *Palladis Tamia*, intr. by Don Cameron Allen (New York, 1938).

MITCHELL, C. J., 'Quotation Marks, Compositorial Habits, and False Imprints', *The Library*, 6 ser., 6 (1983).

MORETTI, FRANCO, *The Prose of the World* (London, 1986).

MOXON, JOSEPH, *Mechanick Exercises on the Whole Art of Printing (1663–4)*, eds. Herbert Davis and Harry Carter (London, 1958).

MURRAY, TIMOTHY, *Theatrical Legitimation: Allegories of Genius in Seventeenth-Century England and France* (New York, 1987).

MYLNE, VIVIENNE, 'The Punctuation of Dialogue in Eighteenth-Century French and English Fiction', *The Library*, 6 (1979), 43–61.

NEVINSON, J. L., 'Shakespeare's Dress in his Portraits', *Shakespeare Quarterly*, 18 (1967).

NEWTON, RICHARD C., 'Jonson and the (Re-) Invention of the Book', in *Classic and Cavalier: Essays on Jonson and the Sons of Ben*, ed. Claude J. Summers and Ted-Larry Pebworth (Pittsburgh, Pa., 1982).

ONG, WALTER J., *Ramus, Method and The Decay of Dialogue: From the Art of Discourse to the Art of Reason* (Cambridge, Mass., 1958).

ORGEL, STEPHEN, 'Shakespeare and the Kinds of Drama', *Critical Inquiry*, 6 (1979).

—— 'Shakespeare Imagines a Theater', *Poetics Today*, 5 (1984).

—— 'The Authentic Shakespeare', *Representations*, 21 (1988).

PAINE, THOMAS, *The Rights of Man: Being an Answer to Mr. Burke's Attack on the French Revolution*, ed. Moncure Daniel Conway (New York, 1894).

PAPALI, G. F., *Jacob Tonson, Publisher: His Life and Work (1656–1736)*, (New Zealand, 1968).

PARKER, PATRICIA, *Literary Fat Ladies, Rhetoric, Gender, Property* (London and New York, 1987).

PARKS, STEPHEN, ed. *The English Book Trade 1660–1853*, 42 vols. (New York, 1974).

PARSON, IAN, 'Copyright and Society', in *Essays in the History of Publishing in Celebration of the 250th Anniversary of the House of Longman 1724–1974*, ed. Asa Briggs (London, 1974).

PATTERSON, ANNABEL, *Censorship and Interpretation: The Conditions of Writing and Reading in Early Modern England* (Madison, Wis., 1987).

PATTERSON, LYMAN RAY, *Copyright in Historical Perspective* (Nashville, Tenn., 1968).

PAULSON, RONALD, *Representations of Revolution: 1789–1820* (New Haven, 1983).

PETERSON, RICHARD S., *Imitation and Praise in the Poems of Ben Jonson* (New Haven, Conn., and London, 1981).

PFEIFFER, RUDOLF, *History of Classical Scholarship from 1300 to 1850* (Oxford, 1976).

PIPER, DAVID, '*O Sweet Mr. Shakespeare I'll have his picture*': *The Changing Image of Shakespeare's Person 1600–1800* (Washington, 1964).

—— *The Image of the Poet: British Poets and Their Portraits* (Oxford, 1982).

PLANT, MARJORIE, *The English Book Trade: An Economic History of the Making and Sale of Books* (London, 1939).

POLLARD, ALFRED W., *Shakespeare Folios and Quartos: A Study in the Bibliography of Shakespeare's Plays 1594–1685* (London, 1909).

PRIOR, JAMES, *The Life of Edmond Malone, Editor of Shakespeare* (London, 1860).

PROWN, JULIUS DAVID, *John Singleton Copley in England 1774–1815* (Cambridge, Mass., 1966).

RAYSOR, THOMAS MIDDLETON, *Shakespearean Criticism*, 2 vols. (London, 1960).

RITSON, JOSEPH, *Remarks, Critical and Illustrative on the Text and Notes of the Last Edition of Shakspeare* 1783 (New York, 1973).

ROGERS, PAT, 'Pope and His Subscribers', *Publishing History*, 2 (1978).

ROLLINS, *The Sonnets*, ed. Hyder Edward Rollins, 2 vols. (Philadelphia, Pa., and London, 1944).

—— *A New Variorum Edition: The Poems*, 2 vols. (Philadelphia, Pa., and London, 1938).

—— *A New Variorum Edition: The Sonnets*, 2 vols. (Philadelphia, Pa., and London, 1944).

ROSE, MARK, 'The Author as Proprietor: *Donaldson v. Becket* and the Genealogy of Modern Authorship', *Representations* 23 (1988).

RUSHWORTH, JOHN, *Historical Collections* . . . (London, 1721), 4 vols.

RUTTER, CAROL CHILLINGTON, *Documents of the Rose Playhouse* (Manchester and Dover, NH, 1984).

SALMON, VIVIAN, 'The Spelling and Punctuation of Shakespeare's Time', in *William Shakespeare, The Complete Works: Original-Spelling Editions*, gen. eds., Stanley Wells and Gary Taylor (Oxford, 1986).

SANDYS, JOHN EDWIN, *A History of Classical Scholarship*, 3 vols. (Cambridge, 1908).

SAUER, THOMAS G., *A. W. Schlegel's Shakespearean Criticism in England 1811–1846* (Bonn, 1981).

SAUNDERS, J. W., 'From Manuscript to Print: A Note on the circulation of poetic MSS. in the sixteenth century', *Proceedings of the Leeds Philosophical and Literary Society*, vi. 8, 1951.

SCHOENBAUM, S. *Internal Evidence and Elizabethan Dramatic Authorship: An Essay in Literary History and Method* (Evanston, Ill., 1966).

—— *Shakespeare's Lives* (Oxford and New York, 1970).

SECORD, A. W. 'I.M. of the First Folio Shakespeare and other Mabbe Problems', *Journal of English and Germanic Philology*, 47 (1948), 37–81.

SEN, SAILENDRA KUMAR, *Capell and Malone, and Modern Critical Bibliography* (Calcutta, 1960).

Seven English Poetical Miscellanies reproduced under the care of J. Payne Collier (London, 1867).

SHAKESPEARE, WILLIAM. Please see list of major eighteenth-century editions on p. x. In quoting from all of them, with the exception of Pope and Johnson–Steevens, I have used the facsimile editions published by AMS Press, New York.

—— *A Reproduction in Exact Facsimile of the Famous First Folio, 1623*: executed by R. W. Preston under the superintendence of Howard Staunton (London, 1866).

—— *Shakespeare: The Complete Works*, ed. G. B. Harrison (New York, 1952).

—— *William Shakespeare: The Complete Works*, ed. Charles Jasper Sisson (London, 1954).

—— *The Complete Works of Shakespeare*, ed. Hardin Craig (Chicago, 1951), rev. by David Bevington (1980).

—— *The Complete Signet Shakespeare*, ed. Sylvan Barnet (New York, 1972).

—— *The Riverside Shakespeare*, ed. G. Blakemore Evans (Boston, 1974).

—— *William Shakespeare: The Complete Works*, eds. Stanley Wells and Gary Taylor (Oxford, 1986).

—— *Shakespeare's Plays in Quarto*, eds. Michael J. B. Allen and Kenneth Muir (Berkeley, 1981).

SHERBO, ARTHUR, *Samuel Johnson, Editor of Shakespeare* (Urbana, Ill., 1956).

—— *The Birth of Shakespeare Studies: Commentators from Rowe (1709) to Boswell–Malone (1821)* (East Lansing, Mich., 1986).

SIMPSON, PERCY, *Shakespearean Punctuation* (Oxford, 1911).

SISSON, CHARLES J., 'Studies in the Life and Environment of Shakespeare Since 1900', Shakespeare Survey 3 (1950), p. 1.

SMITH, HALLET, *The Tension of the Lyre: Poetry in Shakespeare's Sonnets* (San Marino, Ca., 1981).

SMITH, D. NICOL, *Shakespeare in the Eighteenth Century* (Oxford, 1928).

—— ed., *Eighteenth Century Essays on Shakespeare*, 2nd edn. (Oxford, 1963; first publ. 1903).

SPIELMANN, M. H., 'Shakespeare's Portraiture', *Studies in the First Folio* (London, 1924).

—— *The Title-Page of the First Folio of Shakespeare's Plays* (London, 1924).

STEVENSON, LAURA CAROLINE, *Praise and Paradox: Merchants and Craftsmen in Elizabethan Popular Literature* (Cambridge, 1984).

STRONG, ROY, *'And When Did You Last See Your Father?' The Victorian Painter and British History* (London, 1978).

TAYLOR, GARY, *Reinventing Shakespeare: A Cultural History from the Restoration to the Present* (New York, 1989).

THEOBALD, LEWIS, *Shakespeare Restored* (London, 1726).

TROUSDALE, MARION, *Shakespeare and the Rhetoricians* (London, 1982).

TULLY, JAMES, *A Discourse on Property: John Locke and His Adversaries* (Cambridge, 1980).

URKOWITZ, STEVEN, ' "The Base Shall Top th'Legitimate": The Growth of an Editorial Tradition', in *The Division of the Kingdoms: Shakespeare's Two Versions of 'King Lear'*, ed. Gary Taylor and Michael Warren (Oxford, 1983).

VICKERS, BRIAN, ed. *Shakespeare: The Critical Heritage*, 6 vols. (London and Boston, 1974–81).

WALKER, ALICE, 'Edward Capell and his Edition of Shakespeare', in *Studies in Shakespeare*, ed. Peter Alexander (London, 1964).

WALTER, GWYN 'The Booksellers in 1750 and 1774: The Battle for Literary Property,' *The Library*, 5th ser., 29 (1974), 287–311.

WALTON, J. K. 'Edmond Malone: An Irish Shakespeare Scholar', *Hermathena*, 99 (1964).

WARBURTON, WILLIAM, *A Letter from an Author to a Member of Parliament concerning Literary Property* (London, 1747).

—— *An Enquiry into the Nature and Origin of Literary Property* (London, 1762), in Parks, *The English Book Trade*, 12.

WELLS, STANLEY and TAYLOR GARY, eds. *William Shakespeare: A Textual Companion* (Oxford, 1987).

WILLIAMS, GEORGE WALTON, 'The Publishing and Editing of Shakespeare's Plays', in Andrews, *William Shakespeare*, 3.

WILLIAMS, RAYMOND, *Culture and Society: 1780–1950* (New York, 1958).

—— *The Long Revolution* (New York, 1961).

—— *Keywords: A Vocabulary of Culture and Society* (Oxford, 1976).

WILSON, F. P., *Shakespeare and the New Bibliography*, rev. and ed. Helen Gardner (Oxford, 1970).

WILSON, J. DOVER, ' "Titus Andronicus" on the Stage in 1595', *Shakespeare Survey*, 1 (1948).

WOLPE, BERTHOLDE, ed., *A New Booke of Copies 1574* (London, 1962).

WOODMANSEE, MARTHA, 'The Genius and the Copyright: Economic

and Legal Conditions of the Emergence of the "Author" ', *Eighteenth-Century Studies*, 17 (1984).

YOUNG, EDWARD, 'Conjectures on Original Composition', in *English Critical Essays, Sixteenth, Seventeenth and Eighteenth Centuries*, ed. Edmund D. Jones (London, 1961).

INDEX